WITHDRAWN

INTRODUCTION TO LOCAL AREA NETWORKS WITH MICROCOMPUTER EXPERIMENTS

LESZEK REISS

Northeastern University

and

Optical Diagnostic Systems, Inc.

PRENTICE-HALL, INC., Englewood Cliffs, New Jersey 07632

Library of Congress Cataloging-in-Publication Data

REISS, LESZEK.
  Introduction to local area networks with microcomputer experiments.

  Bibliography.
  Includes index.
  1. Local area networks (Computer networks)
2. Computer network protocols. 3. Local area
networks (Computer networks)—Experiments.
I. Title.
TK5105.7.R44   1987   004.6′8   86-22553
ISBN 0-13-486051-9

Editorial/production supervision: Mary Bardoni
Cover design: Diane Saxe
Manufacturing buyer: Rhett Conklin

Appendix A reprinted with permission from
THE COMPLETE VLSI LAN SOLUTION,
Copyright © Intel Corporation, 1982.

Appendix B reprinted with permission from
WESTERN DIGITAL 1983 NETWORK
PRODUCTS HANDBOOK, Western Digital
Corporation, 1983.

Figures in Appendices C, D, E, G, and H are
reproduced with courtesy of Motorola, Inc.

Prentice-Hall International (UK) Limited, *London*
Prentice-Hall of Australia Pty. Limited, *Sydney*
Prentice-Hall Canada Inc., *Toronto*
Prentice-Hall Hispanoamericana, S. A., *Mexico*
Prentice-Hall of India Private Limited, *New Delhi*
Prentice-Hall of Japan, Inc., *Tokyo*
Prentice-Hall of Southeast Asia Pte. Ltd., *Singapore*
Editora Prentice-Hall do Brasil, Ltda., *Rio de Janeiro*

To Wanda and Władysław Reiss, my parents.

Contents

APPENDICES 169

Preface

With thousands of workstations, personal computers, and robots installed in business, industrial, and educational environments each year, the need to provide local data-communication links is greater than ever. Economic considerations dictate systems in which expensive resources like large data-storage units, high-performance data processors, and high-speed and high-quality printers are shared between users of workstations within an organization. Thus, the importance of local area networks (LANs) increases rapidly. LANs provide more than just physical links between computers. LAN protocols allow virtual direct communication between application tasks running on different computers in the network. The actual data-transfer mechanisms are transparent for communicating tasks.

The purpose of the book is to introduce the reader to LANs. LAN architecture and its physical and programming aspects are discussed at a level of detail appropriate for first exposure to the field. LAN design is a very complex undertaking. To simplify this task, LAN protocols are designed as a hierarchical set of function layers, with higher layers relying on operations performed by the lower layers. At the lowest layer, physical signal and interconnection problems are solved. At the highest layer, software interface to application tasks is implemented. The book concentrates on lower layers of network protocol, especially on medium-access techniques, where hardware and software have to be compatible.

Protocol programming examples are used in this book as a tool to illustrate some of the most fundamental problems that have to be solved by LAN designers. Examples can be implemented as laboratory experiments using inexpensive single-board or personal microcomputers. Examples are supplemented by additional problems designed to encourage learning by active problem solving. A single-board microcomputer, the

MC68000 based Educational Computer Board, is used in the book to illustrate laboratory implementation of programming examples. A LAN laboratory based on IBM-PC personal computers and programmable in Instant-C is also described. Any other microcomputer can be used as well, provided it is equipped with an RS232 port and convenient software development tools.

The book is aimed at computer science and engineering students and professionals who are interested in LANS. The introductory character of the book makes it suitable for readers who have no experience with computer networks and data communication. No specific knowledge in these two fields is assumed. However, the material requires good understanding of computer-programming algorithms as well as some exposure to computer architecture. All programming examples in the book are explained using Pascal-like pseudocode algorithms. Thus, a working knowledge of Pascal, C, or any structured high-level programming language will be very helpful. Input/output (I/O) operations using serial data communication ports play important roles in the LAN model used in this book. A reader should have an understanding of machine-level operations, especially I/O and interrupt processing. A sequence of two courses: a high-level language (Pascal, C, or equivalent) programming course and a computer architecture (or microprocessor systems) course would be an excellent preparation for the material covered by this book.

The book is designed as a textbook for an introductory course on LANs. It can also be used for a course on data communication. The emphasis in the course in each case should be on creative problem solving rather than on wide exposure to the data-communication field. If the students do not have any data-communication background or if a wider discussion is required, a reference book (for example, Lane or Stallings) could be used as a supplementary text. The book is written with the assumption that protocol programming examples can be implemented as laboratory experiments; however, it can also be used in a course with lectures and projects. The senior undergraduate year or an early graduate year is the best time for a course based on this textbook.

The book was written on the basis of lecture notes for a ''microcomputer applications'' course first offered in spring 1983. This is an elective course for senior engineering and computer science students at Northeastern University. I have had the pleasure of teaching the course since that time for both undergraduate and graduate students. The course evolved during these three years, and the lecture notes were the basis for this book.

This is an introductory book; it is not meant to be a comprehensive study of LAN. It is my hope, however, that your interest in the field will be sufficiently stirred up to encourage further probing. If you do become involved in LAN design or development, the background and insight gained from protocol programming examples should prove to be valuable. If your further contact with LANs is limited to being a user, the material learned from this book should provide you with sufficient understanding of LAN operations.

Chapter 1 deals with most general aspects of local networking, that is, with LAN characteristics and with fundamental concepts of computer-network architecture and multilayer network protocol. Chapter 2 presents LAN medium and topology as well as

CSMA/DC, token-bus, and token-ring medium-access schemes. LAN nodes and their architecture and network interfaces are analyzed in Chapter 3. LAN laboratory, the microcomputer-based nodes, and the LAN medium model are explained in Chapter 4. Chapter 5 contains protocol programming examples that can be implemented as experiments on the laboratory network model presented in Chapter 4. More advanced protocol problems, presented as modifications of Chapter 5 problems, are given in Chapter 6. Appendices A to H provide the reader with a collection of technical data on network interfaces and laboratory equipment. Appendix I presents assembly language programs for Chapter 5 protocol examples. Appendix J describes a laboratory network model based on IBM-PC personal computers and gives example programs written for the model in Instant-C.

Many people helped me during the preparation of this book. Northeastern University and Optical Diagnostic Systems, Inc. provided the stimulating environment and equipment necessary to verify laboratory experiments. My special thanks go to S. Hoover, D. Freeman, T. Hulbert, and E. Kamieniecki for encouragement and support. D. Goldman helped create a microprocessor lab where the LAN model was developed. My students and lab assistants, especially M. Keefe and M. Bonakdarpour, provided much needed feedback. R. Chhajed and S. Dholakia helped in editing programs for Appendix I. W. Jastrzebski provided a schematic editor and W. Czernuszenko helped with drawings for Appendix J. The reviewers and the editors of Prentice-Hall contributed substantially to the clarity and quality of the book. Finally, my wife and children supported the effort with a great sense of humor, patience, and understanding.

1

Local Networking

1.1 LAN CHARACTERISTICS

A computer network is a system of computer-based stations—also called network nodes—interconnected by data-transmission links, which allow for information exchange between the nodes. To provide error-free and maximally convenient information transfers, the network operation is regulated by a set of rules and conventions called *network protocol*. The protocol defines connectors, cables, signals, data formats, and error-checking techniques as well as algorithms for network interfaces and nodes, allowing for standard—to within a network—principles of message preparation, transfer, and analysis on different levels of detail.

Two general types of computer networks can be distinguished: centralized networks and decentralized networks. These names relate to the operation of a network rather than to physical arrangement of nodes and transmission links. In a centralized network, there is a "boss"—a network controller (or central station)—that controls data transfers between all nodes in the network. Quite often all transfers must pass through the central node even if they are only exchanges of information between two peripheral nodes. In decentralized network, all nodes have the same rights to use network links and all are governed by the same rules. There is no distinct network master, as was the case in centralized networks, and control over the access to network links is distributed among all network nodes.

Comparing centralized and decentralized networks, we notice that centralized networks are less reliable due to the fact that they cannot operate if one of the network nodes, the central node, malfunctions. A failure of any one of decentralized network nodes does not affect other nodes. On the other hand, network protocol for a central-ized network is simpler than a protocol for a decentralized network.

An example of a centralized network is given in Fig. 1.1-1. Two types of net-work nodes are distinguished here: the master node (the network controller) and slave nodes. In this model, all messages are transferred through the master node. For exam-ple, if a *kth* slave node wants to send the message to the *jth* slave node, the message will first travel from *kth* slave to the master and then from the master to *jth* slave. An algorithm for master node is given in Fig. 1.1-1 (b) and an algorithm for each slave node is given in Fig. 1.1-1 (c).

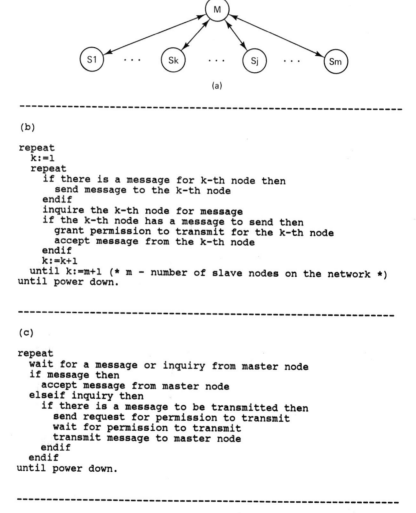

(a)

(b)

```
repeat
  k:=1
  repeat
    if there is a message for k-th node then
      send message to the k-th node
    endif
    inquire the k-th node for message
    if the k-th node has a message to send then
      grant permission to transmit for the k-th node
      accept message from the k-th node
    endif
    k:=k+1
  until k:=m+1 (* m - number of slave nodes on the network *)
until power down.
```

(c)

```
repeat
  wait for a message or inquiry from master node
  if message then
    accept message from master node
  elseif inquiry then
    if there is a message to be transmitted then
      send request for permission to transmit
      wait for permission to transmit
      transmit message to master node
    endif
  endif
until power down.
```

Figure 1.1-1 Centralized network: (a) Master and slave nodes, (b) Algorithm for master node, (c) Algorithm for slave node.

An example of a decentralized network is presented in Fig. 1.1-2. In this model, a token-passing technique is used, in which a node has the right to transmit when it possesses a *token*. A token is a special, unique message that can be transferred along the network link from one node to another. Once a node receives a token, the node assumes that it just obtained the right to use the network link. A node that has a token is obliged to pass it along to another node, thus assuring that at one time or another, every node on the network will possess the token and be able to transmit. All nodes on decentralized network are operating according to the same algorithm given for this example in Fig. 1.1-2(b).

From the point of view of geographical distribution of network nodes, two major categories of networks can be distinguished: local-area networks (LANs) and wide-area networks. In a *LAN*, network nodes are located within a short distance of each other. Typically, the distance between the two most-separated nodes within a LAN is less than a few kilometers. On the other hand, a collection of network nodes separated by large distances is called a *wide-area network*. An example of a LAN is a campus network, where all nodes are installed in buildings located on the same college campus. An airline, or hotel-reservation network may have nodes scattered throughout a country or a continent and is a typical example of a wide area network. Figure 1.1-3 illustrates local- and wide-area network concepts.

Both centralized and decentralized networks can be implemented as LANs. For example, Intel's BITBUS interconnect is a typical example of a centralized LAN, whereas Ethernet is a typical example of a decentralized LAN. Centralized LANs have been in use for relatively long time; one of the first LAN-like standards was the

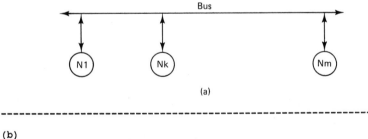

(a)

```
(b)

repeat
  wait for token or message
  if message then
    accept message
  elseif token then
    if there is a message to be sent then
      transmit message
    endif
    transmit token to the next node
  endif
until power down.
```

Figure 1.1-2   Decentralized network: (a) Network nodes and interconnection, (b) Algorithm for a network node.

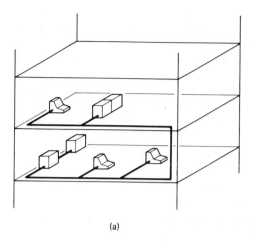

(a)

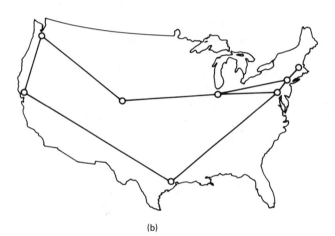

(b)

Figure 1.1-3 (a) LAN and (b) wide-area network.

IEEE-488 bus interconnection—a typical centralized network designed to support fast data communication between many computer-based stations separated by short distances. The decentralized LANs were introduced at the end of the 1970s, first examples being Datapoint's Arcnet and Xerox's Ethernet. Although Arcnet and Ethernet were pioneers, many types of LANs currently exist, and first LAN protocol standards have already been developed. The standardization does not as yet cover all aspects of local-area networking. At present, three standards are published by IEEE's LAN committee. All three standards deal with lowest layers of LAN protocol for decentralized networks and formalize different techniques of sharing communications medium between network nodes.

The 802.3 standard defines lowest layers of LAN protocol for carrier sense multiple access with collision detection (CSMA/CD) networks. The most prominent example of such a LAN is the Ethernet. Also, AT&T's Starlan network is based on the CSMA/CD principle. Token-bus networks can be based on 802.4 standard. The fastest-growing application of this standard is the manufacturing automation protocol (MAP) sponsored by General Motors. Finally, the newest standard, the 802.5, formalizes token-ring method applied by the IBM in its token-ring LAN.

In this book we are concerned only with decentralized LANs. The book concentrates on two types of LANs corresponding to IEEE standards 802.3 and 802.4. Both these standards use bus topology, and therefore models for both of them can be implemented in a laboratory using the same physical interconnection. The token-ring network is based on physical ring topology and requires more complicated interconnection hardware. Principles implemented in all three 802 standards are described briefly in Chapter 2. Detailed information of these standards can be found in IEEE publications [7, 8, 9].

LANs are used in a variety of applications. The common characteristic of these applications is a requirement for high-speed communication between many computer-based stations separated by relatively short distances. Typical data transmission rates used in LANs range from 100,000 bits per second for low-cost LANs to 100 million bits per second for most expensive LANs. The number of nodes varies from 100 to 10,000 per LAN. Other distinctive characteristics of most LANs are that all nodes on a LAN have the same access to the network medium and that each node can communicate with all other nodes.

1.2 COMMUNICATIONS ARCHITECTURE

The term *communications architecture* implies that the overall networking task is partitioned in such a way that specific subtasks are performed by distinguishable network entities—architecture elements—and information flow paths—communication links and interfaces—are established between them. The method by which messages are processed by architecture elements and transferred through information-flow paths is called a *network protocol*. The protocol is closely related to the communications architecture. Parts of the protocol are implemented in parts of the architecture. Quite often, communications architecture is referred to as protocol architecture.

Figure 1.2-1 represents a simple, generalized model of network architecture. We can distinguish m network nodes, communication link, and node/link (N/L) interfaces. Messages are created and consumed at network nodes. The purpose of a network as a whole is to ensure reliable and fast transfer of messages from their sources (nodes at which messages are created) to their destinations (nodes at which messages are consumed). Each node can create and consume messages; therefore, data paths—symbolized in Fig. 1.2-1 by arrows—are bidirectional. For example, if a message is created at node i and destined for node j, it has to travel first through the N/L interface at node i, then through the communication link, and then through the N/L interface at node j; finally it arrives at its destination—node j—where it is consumed. Of course, another message may travel from node j to node i in the opposite direction.

In Fig. 1.2-2, network communications architecture is presented in more detail. In this model, internal node operations are partitioned between applications processor

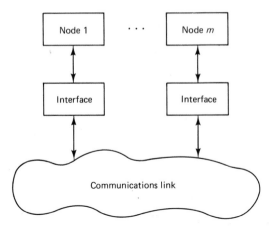

Figure 1.2-1 Communication architecture concept.

(AP) and communications processor (CP). At this point, the AP and CP are abstract and no assumption is made as to the form of their implementation. Messages are created and consumed by APs, whereas CPs are responsible for message transfers from a source AP to a destination AP. The interface between the AP and CP (A/C interface) can be regarded as a ''mailbox,'' where the AP deposits messages to be transmitted and collects messages received. Messages deposited by the AP in a source node should

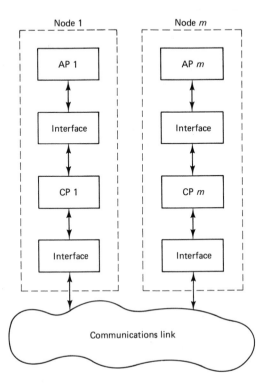

Figure 1.2-2 Three-layer architecture.

be picked up by its CP and transferred, through the C/L interface (the interface between the CP and communication link) and communication link to the CP in a destination node, which in turn should place them in its A/C interface. In the opposite direction, messages received by the CP from the C/L interface and placed in the A/C interface should be collected and consumed by the AP.

Such a partition of network operations into three parts—APs, CPs, and a communication link—brings very important benefits. Each of the parts can be defined and implemented separately, simplifying the development task. Further benefits result from the fact that network model presented in Fig. 1.2-2 follows the principle of *layered architecture*. Indeed, as illustrated in Fig. 1.2-3, we may say that the communication link is the lowest layer, upon which the middle layer (the CP) is built; finally, the highest layer (the AP) rests on the two lower layers. Nodes are interconnected through the lowest layer, the communication link. Thus, messages originating at top layer (created by the APs) first have to travel downward, through the middle layer (the CPs) to the lowest layer (the communication link). The lowest layer assures that messages are transferred between source and destination nodes. After it arrives at the C/L interface at the destination node, a message has to travel upward, through the middle to the top layer.

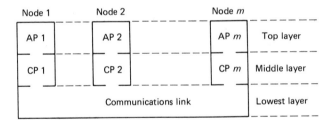

Figure 1.2-3   Communication layers.

The benefit of layered architecture results from the fact that higher layers can use services provided by lower layers and do not have to deal with details of lower layer operations. For example a top-layer AP creates a message, places it in the A/C interface, and assumes that the message will be delivered error-free to the AP in a destination node. The AP can also assume that received messages placed in the A/C interface by the middle-layer CP are error-free. In effect, from the top-layer application-processor standpoint, the network appears to be operating error-free. Of course transmission errors do happen on the network, but they are handled by middle or lowest layer and are of no concern for the top-layer APs.

Once a message is placed in the A/C interface in a source node, sooner or later it will arrive at the A/C interface in a destination node. Thus, if we consider message exchange between a pair of APs, the operations of lower layers are transparent from the top-layer point of view. We may say that virtually, the two APs exchange messages directly. The concept of virtual AP-to-AP communication is illustrated in Fig. 1.2-4. Certainly, the real information-flow path leads through all layers, downward in the source node and upward in the destination node.

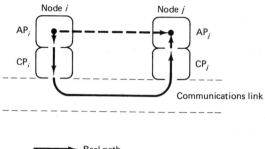

Real path

- - - ▶ Virtual path

Figure 1.2-4 Real and virtual communication paths.

1.3 OSI: ISO's REFERENCE MODEL

Development of hardware and software to allow many computers to communicate on a network is a very complex task. It requires a lot of effort even if all elements of the network are developed by a single manufacturer. Manufacturers optimize their designs to make them cost-effective and thus more competitive. As a result, products developed by different manufacturers tend to be incompatible. If we attempt to create a network using computer and communications products from several vendors, the problem of integration becomes virtually unmanageable. The need to allow computer products offered by different manufacturers to communicate with each other on a network led the International Standards Organization (ISO) to propose a network architecture model referred to as *open systems interconnection* (OSI). The goal of the ISO subcommittee developing the OSI model was to provide a framework for networking standards acceptable to all manufacturers, which would help them design unique—and thus competitive—products that could still communicate with compatible products offered by other vendors. The OSI model is general and applies both to wide area networks and LANs.

As explained in Section 1.2, the problem of complexity in computer-network communication is best handled by using a layered-architecture approach, in which all networking functions are partitioned into several groups—called *layers*—in such a way that upper layers use services provided (functions performed) by lower layers. The OSI model implements the layered architecture concept and defines a number of layers, the functions performed by each layer, and interlayer interfaces. Partition of all networking functions into layers is guided by two contradictory constraints. When more layers are used each becomes smaller and simpler. On the other hand, the use of many layers creates many interlayer interfaces, and the processing overhead necessary to handle additional interfaces may offset the benefits gained by layer simplification. The OSI model partitions networking functions into seven layers, as shown in Fig. 1.3-1.

Once the OSI reference model was adopted, standards defining each of OSI layers could be developed. For example, if a standard is established for the data-link layer, specifying its functions and upward and downward interfaces, any product that

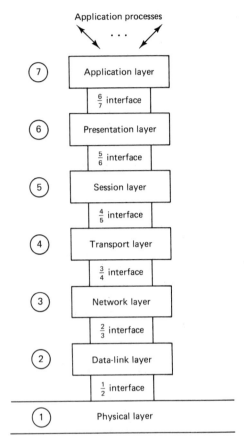

Figure 1.3-1 OSI layers.

implements the standard in any way is compatible with other products that obey the same standard. Several standardization organizations developed (or are still developing) standards for different OSI layers. The first layers to be standardized were the lowest OSI layers, the physical and data-link layers. In terms of LAN protocols, the IEEE developed the 802.3, 802.4, and 802.5 standards for data-link layers implementing CSMA/CD, token-bus and token-ring medium-access methods, respectively. OSI layers provide networking functions defined as follows:

Physical layer.   The *physical layer* provides a physical path for electric signals representing bits of transmitted information. It also defines the characteristics of these signals, such as voltage and current levels, frequencies, and timing. It specifies mechanical properties of network cables and connectors. From the point of view of upper layers, the physical layer ensures that streams of bits produced at the interface between the data-link and physical layers by transmitting node arrive at the interfaces between the physical and data-link layers in all receiving nodes in a bus-topology LAN. As Fig. 1.3-2 shows, the physical layer is the only real interconnection between network nodes.

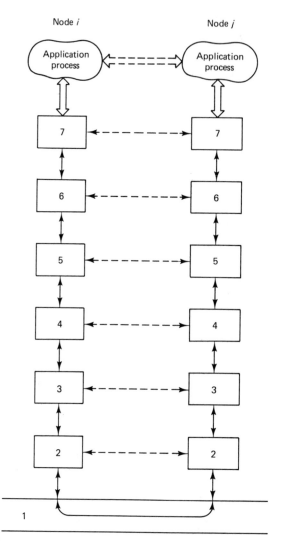

Figure 1.3-2 Real and virtual communication paths.

Data-link layer. The *data-link layer* defines rules of sharing the use of the physical layer among network nodes. On a bus-topology LAN, the medium (physical layer) is shared in time-division fashion. Information is transferred in addressed frames, one frame at a time. The format of these frames and the method by which a node decides when to transmit or accept a frame are defined. Two general types of frames are used. Data frames, which convey the upper-layer messages, are also referred to as *packets*. Other frames used by data-link layer, such as token or acknowledge frames, are called *control frames*. Error-detection and error-correction techniques are used to ensure that packets are transferred error-free from source to destination nodes. From the point of view of upper layers, data-link and physical layers provide error-free transmission of data packets.

Network layer. The OSI *network layer* is responsible for buffering and routing data packets through the network. Such routes are also referred to as *virtual circuits*. Routing is essential function in wide area networks but does not have much meaning in bus-topology LANs, since there is a direct path (route) between any pair of source and destination nodes. Thus, for LANs, network layer functions are limited to packet buffering.

Transport layer. On the transmitting side, the *transport layer* partitions long messages arriving from upper (session) layers into data packets. Partition is necessary because packets are limited in length, and a message may have to be transmitted using many packets. On the receiving side, the transport layer has to reassemble messages from collections of packets received from the medium through data-link and network layers. Packets are buffered by the network layer and, since many nodes may be transmitting messages to the same receiving node, packets from different messages most probably interleave at the time of their arrival. The transport layer has to ensure that packets from one message are reassembled in correct order and that no packets are misplaced or missing. The transport layer is a boundary, below which a data packet is a unit of information handled by the network. Above the transport layer, messages are regarded as information units.

Session layer. The *session layer* is responsible for providing a communication session between two user processes running on two separate network nodes. A session is created on the request of a user process submitted through the application and presentation layers. The request identifies both the purpose of a communications session and its partner, for example, a peer user process in the other node. A session can begin only if the partner process exists (is active) and is willing to communicate. The session layer is responsible for determining whether the session can begin as well as for session maintenance and termination.

Presentation layer. From the communications point of view, the *presentation layer* is the simplest layer. Its function is to convert user messages from the form used by the application layer to that used by all lower layers. The purpose of message conversion (encoding) is to achieve data compression, or security. At the upper interface of the presentation layer, data fields of messages have meaningful, explicit form. Below the presentation layer, data fields of messages and packets are treated as meaningless cargo, and their meaning does not influence their processing.

Application layer. The *application layer* serves as a boundary between the OSI network and application (user) processes. If a LAN operates as a distributed system, the application layer is also responsible for direct communication with elements of the distributed operating system. For example, assume that a user process running on node N requests data available in some other node on the LAN. It is up to the application layer to determine where (on which node) this data is located, formulate a request, and send it through the network, transmit and receive the requested data, and finally make it available for the requesting user process.

Effective, useful communication takes place between application processes in two or more communicating network nodes. If the full seven layers are implemented for a network, for example, if all networking functions are required, then all seven layers have to be available in each communicating node. The real interconnection between the nodes exists only at the physical layer. Therefore, messages exchanged between two application processes have to travel from application to physical layer in the source node, through the physical layer from the source node to the destination node, and from the physical layer to the application layer in the destination node. Nevertheless, as explained in Section 1.2, a *virtual* communication takes place on each layer between peer processes in communicating nodes. These real and virtual paths of communication are illustrated in Fig. 1.3-2.

In a time-sharing mode, several application processes may be running simultaneously in a given node. Each one of these processes may communicate with processes in other nodes. As a result, network layers must handle several communications occuring simultaneously, in parallel. This concept is illustrated in Fig. 1.3-3 using the example of an application layer with one mailbox assigned in the application-presentation interface for each application process. Further complications occur and have to be solved due to the fact that each of the application processes may exchange messages with more than one process in other nodes.

Two more concepts referring to OSI model need to be explained. *Encapsulation* (Fig. 1.3-4) ensures that information ia always transferred between layers in units composed of three fields: header, data field, and trailer. Header and trailer contain control information and define address, type, and error-detection code. The encapsulation technique allows each layer in OSI model to use its own control fields and treat the complete unit of the upper layer as a meaningless data field. This leads to structured and clear protocol design. In the transmit direction, header and trailer fields are added

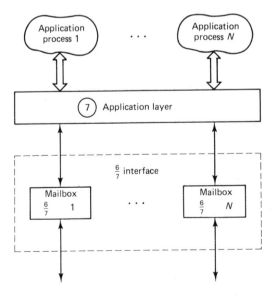

Figure 1.3-3 Multiple mailboxes.

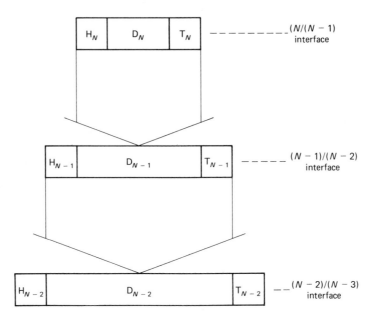

Figure 1.3-4 Encapsulation.

as the message passes from the application to the physical layer. The physical layer does not modify the information in any way, and it does not use any header or trailer on its own. In the receiving direction, control fields are used at each layer to select processing of arriving information units and are then removed. Usually, the header field contains addresses and the type of information unit, whereas the trailer field is used for error-detection purposes.

Fragmentation, illustrated in Fig. 1.3-5, allows for message partition into smaller parts, which then are processed and transmitted independently. On the receiving end, the parts have to be reassembled to recreate the original message form.

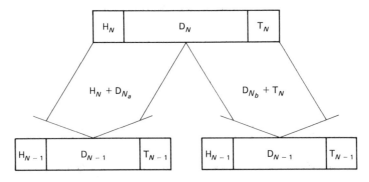

Figure 1.3-5 Fragmentation

An example of fragmentation occurs at the transport layer, when messages are partitioned into data packets in the source node and then reassembled after all packets have been received in the destination node. The fragmentation allows the use of data packets of limited size to transfer much larger messages. The use of smaller data packets simplifies design of lower protocol layers.

So far we have discussed the functions of OSI layers, but, except for the physical layer, we did not make any reference to their implementation forms. The OSI model does not formulate any requirements in this respect. As long as the functions are performed and information forms are adhered to at interlayer interfaces, it does not matter whether a layer is implemented in hardware or software. Obviously, the physical layer has to be implemented in hardware. Typically, because of high-speed requirements and heavy work load in the receive direction (all arriving frames have to be analyzed), the data-link layer is also implemented in hardware. Upper layers are usually implemented as processes either belonging to the operating system or activated by the operating system in similar way as application processes (Fig. 1.3-6).

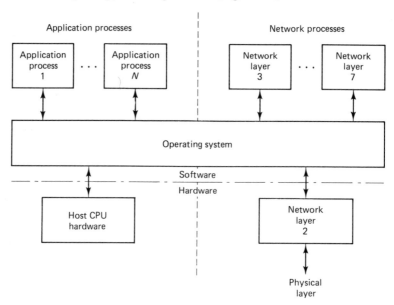

Figure 1.3-6 Upper network layers implemented as processes.

2

Medium-Access Schemes

2.1 NETWORK MEDIA AND TOPOLOGY

The term *communications medium* is used to describe the physical path between transmitting and receiving devices in a communications network. Several types of media are used in electronic communication: cables, radio waves, infrared waves, ultrasonic waves, and light waves. The most suitable media for LANs include twisted-pair and coaxial cables as well as optical-fiber links facilitating light-wave communication. Radio waves are used for wide-area networks, especially for satellite networks, and are not suitable for local networking. Infrared and ultrasonic links are used for point-to-point links and, in general, are not implemented as LAN media. A telephone network, which as a system is designed to support audio communication in the range of useful frequencies of 300 Hz to 3000 Hz and is composed of both cable and radio links, is used for wide-area networks but is too slow for LANs.

The way in which network nodes (stations) are connected using communications media is referred to as *network topology*. Topologies used for computer networks include line, star, ring, and bus interconnections. All these topologies have been implemented in LANs. Star topology is suitable for centralized LANs but not for decentralized LANs. Line and ring topologies require complicated protocols with large overheads for message buffering and retransmission. Also, star, line, and ring topologies are sensitive to node failures. Bus topology is the most popular in LAN applications and is the one used in this book.

A third important concept in addition to network media and topology is *broadcast transmission*. This term applies to a bus topology with a twisted-pair or coaxial-cable medium. In broadcast transmission, a signal injected into the medium from transmitting node propagates through the entire medium and reaches all other nodes on the network nearly simultaneously. The benefit of the broadcast transmission is that the network operation becomes simple, and no buffering or retransmission is necessary. However, this benefit is achieved at a cost. Since transmitted signals penetrate the entire medium, only one node can transmit to the medium at a time. If two or more nodes transmit simultaneously, their signals interfere with each other in the medium, and information conveyed by the signals is lost. Such a situation is called a *collision,* and the network protocols for bus-topology LANs have to solve the problem of collisions. In this book we deal with two types of bus-topology LANs: the CSMA/CD LAN, which allows collisions but assures error-free message transfers anyway, and token-bus LAN, which avoids collisions altogether.

The media used for LANs in this book are coaxial, or coax, and twisted-pair cables. Of the two, the coax cable is suitable for higher data-transfer rates. The twisted-pair cable is suitable for slower data transmission with data rates up to 1,000,000 b/s. The twisted-pair cable is more sensitive to electromagnetic noise, but it is less expensive than the coax cable. The twisted-pair cable can be used as a medium for the laboratory LAN model described in Chapter 4.

In both the twisted-pair and coax cable (Fig. 2.1-1), two conductors are used— one for the useful signal and one as reference, or a signal ground. In coax cable, the role of signal-ground conductor is always played by the external cylindrical conductor. In both cables, conductors are insulated to provide electrical separation between each other and from any external circuits.

In bus topology, all network nodes are connected to the network medium (cable) in the same way. Figure 2.1-2 represents a model of such a connection. The model is

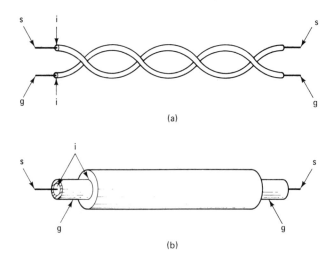

(a)

(b)

s: signal conductor
g: signal-ground conductor
i: insulation

Figure 2.1-1 Network cables: (a) Twisted pair, (b) Coaxial cable.

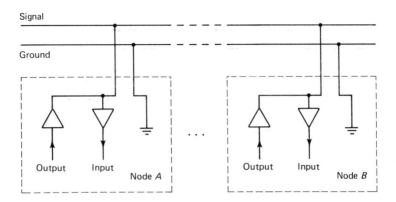

Figure 2.1-2 Node-to-cable interconnection.

generalized and applies to both twisted-pair and coax cables. Each node is equipped with signal amplifiers, marked in Fig. 2.1-2 by triangles. Neither the twisted-pair nor the coax cable is a lossless medium. The signal is attenuated while it propagates through the medium. A node that transmits has to provide a signal of sufficient energy and thus needs an output amplifier. The receiving node has to be able to recognize the attenuated signal arriving through the medium, and therefore it needs an input amplifier. Since all nodes in a LAN can be transmitting or receiving, all are equipped with both output and input amplifiers.

Because LAN nodes can be located as far as few kilometers apart, a galvanic separation is needed between the nodes. This is achieved by using radio-frequency (RF) transformers, which separate input/output (I/O) amplifiers from the medium in terms of ground potential but still allow high-frequency signals to pass through between node I/O and medium cables. Such an interconnection is illustrated in Fig. 2.1-3.

Network topologies are illustrated in Fig. 2.1-4. All but bus topologies are really collections of point-to-point links, and in most cases messages have to pass through

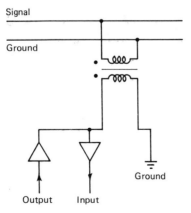

Figure 2.1-3 Galvanic separation of network nodes.

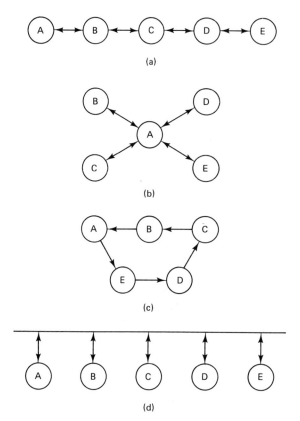

Figure 2.1-4 Network topologies: (a) Line, (b) Star, (c) Ring, (d) Bus.

several nodes and links until they finally reach their destinations. For example, in *line* topology (Fig. 2.1-4(a)), a message from node A to node E has to travel through nodes B, C, and D. If any one of them malfunctions, the message will not get through. In the *star* topology one of the nodes (node A in Fig. 2.1-4(b)) plays a central role; all message transfers require its operation. If it breaks down, the whole network stops. The *ring* topology has an interesting property: It can be implemented using solely one-directional links, as illustrated in Fig. 2.1-4(c). Since the nodes are connected in a one-way-loop fashion, any source-destination pair can exist. For example, a message from A to B can travel through E, D, and C. Again, a failure of one of the nodes breaks the ring and stops network operation. If bidirectional links are used in ring topology, then a failure of one of the network nodes results in change of topology from ring to line.

The last topology, illustrated in Fig. 2.1-4(d), is the *bus* interconnection. In this case, for any source-destination pair, the source node broadcasts the message to the network medium (bus). As shown in Fig. 2.1-5(a), all nodes on the network can receive broadcasted messages simultaneously; therefore, messages have to be addressed.

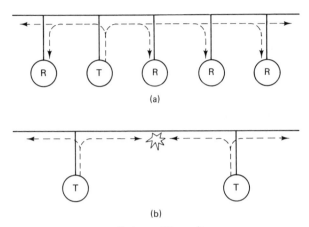

(a)

(b)

T: transmitting node
R: receiving node

Figure 2.1-5 Bus broadcast and collision:
(a) Broadcast transmission, (b) Collision.

Another property of the bus topology networks is the possibility of network collisions. A collision happens on the bus network whenever two or more network nodes
transmit to the medium simultaneously. As illustrated in Fig. 2.11-5(b), the signals representing simultaneously transmitted messages propagate through the entire medium
and interact with each other. As a result, signals arriving at receiving nodes are distorted, and message contents cannot be decoded—in other words, messages are lost.

2.2 SIGNAL ENCODING AND MEDIUM INTERFACE

Data to be transferred between LAN nodes exists in digital form. Each message is a
string of bits encoding some information. The interconnections allow one bit of information to be transferred at a time, which is called *serial data communication*. Thus, a
transfer of a message from one node to another must be achieved by sequentially
transmitting all bits of the message from source to destination node.

The source and destination nodes of a LAN are connected by a medium—usually
a twisted-pair or coax cable. Physically, data bits are transfered in a form of electrical
signals. Two major types of signaling are used: analog and digital. The term *analog* is
used for signals that can assume any value within a limited range. Nonelectrical analog
signals include temperature, pressure, and similar signals. The term *digital* is used for
signals that can only assume one of a final set of values. Nonelectrical equivalents of
digital signals are, for example, results of a dice throw. Another term used frequently
for such signals is *discrete* signals.

In analog signaling, an analog carrier signal—a sinusoidal waveform—is used to
convey encoded data. In digital signaling, a two-level, discrete signal is used. The benefit of analog signaling lies in the fact that analog signals are less susceptible to distor-

tion due to attenuation in the medium. On the other hand, data encoding and decoding are much simpler for digital-signaling methods.

Medium attenuation for analog and digital signals is illustrated in Fig. 2.2-1. In the analog-signal case (a), only the amplitude is attenuated, but the waveform is not distorted and the original signal can easily be restored by amplitude amplification in the receiving node. In the digital-signal case (b), not only the amplitude but also the shape of the waveform are distorted, and signal reconstruction is much more difficult. As a result, if a medium with high level of attenuation (e.g., long, twisted-pair cable) has to be used, then analog signaling would be the best choice. Digital signaling would be more suitable in LANs using media with a low level of attenuation.

If analog signaling is used, digital data must somehow be encoded into an analog signal before being sent. Two methods of such encoding are illustrated in Fig. 2.2-2. In the *amplitude-shift keying* method, an analog carrier signal of a fixed frequency is used. If a bit of value 1 is to be transferred, the carrier waveform is transmitted. A lack of carrier signal means that a bit of value 0 is transmitted. Another method, requiring the use of a carrier signal that can assume two frequencies is called *frequency-shift-keying*. In this case, a logical value of 1 is represented by a carrier signal of frequency $f1$ and logical value of 0 is represented by a carrier signal of frequency $f0$.

The encoding of digital data into a digital signal is straightforward (Fig. 2.2-3). Usually, the Nonreturn-to-zero (NRZ) method is used, in which logical 1 is represented by positive voltage (also referred to as high level, H) and logical 0 is represented by negative voltage (also referred to as low level, L). As a result, the signal level is always above or below the 0-V level, thus explaining the name NRZ.

As Figs. 2.2-2 and 2.2-3 show, whether analog or digital signaling is used, if two consecutive bits are identical in value (e.g., both 0 or both 1), it is difficult to tell

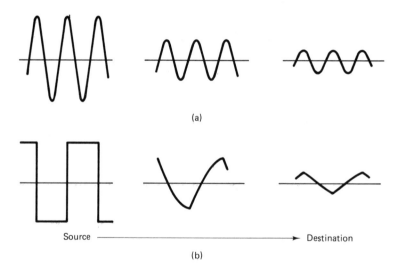

(a)

Source ⎯⎯⎯⎯⎯⎯⎯⎯⎯⎯⎯⎯⎯⎯⎯⎯➤ Destination

(b)

Figure 2.2-1 Medium attenuation for (a) analog and (b) digital signals.

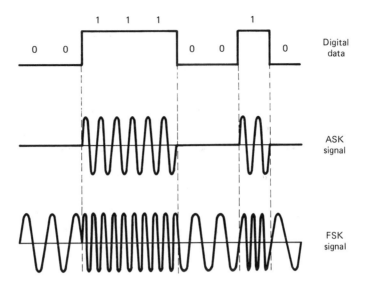

Figure 2.2-2   Analog-signal encoding for digital data.

when the first one ends and the second begins. To solve this problem, the signal transmitter (source node) and receiver (destination node) have to be *synchronized*, that is, they have to have the same perception of time. For example, as illustrated in Fig. 2.2-4(a), a transmitter may provide a clock signal for the receiver in addition to a data signal. In this case, the receiver samples the data signal at the moments of clock pulses, and data can be received correctly. Transmission of narrow clock pulses, as shown in Fig. 2.2-4(b), is difficult because of medium attenuation in digital signaling or encoding-decoding problems in analog signaling. To avoid this problem, another form of clock signal—shown in Fig. 2.2-4(c)—can be used. In this case, the clock signal is a *square* waveform, and sampling moments are indicated by transitions from 1 to 0.

The use of an additional clock signal line is very efficient in solving the synchronization problem, but it requires an additional line connecting the transmitter and receiver. To avoid the use of a clock line while keeping the transmitter and receiver syn-

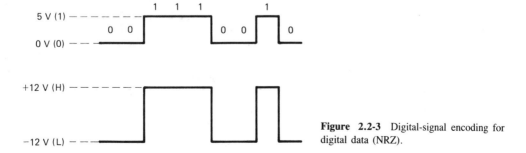

Figure 2.2-3   Digital-signal encoding for digital data (NRZ).

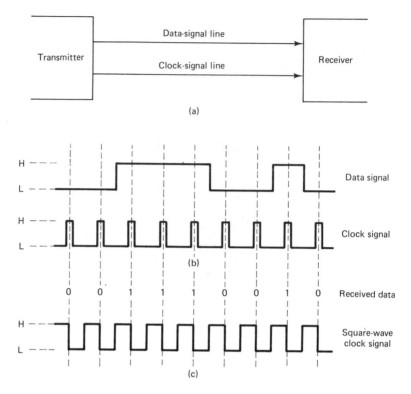

Figure 2.2-4 Synchronous transmission.

chronized, two methods of data transmission are used, *asynchronous* and *self-clocked*. Asynchronous transmission is used for lower data rates, whereas high-data-rate transmission is more efficient using the self-clocked method.

In asynchronous transmission (Fig. 2.2-5), the stream of bits to be transmitted is partitioned into fixed-size units, usually bytes. Both transmitter and receiver are equipped with internal clock generators operating at approximately the same frequency. However, clocks cannot be made to operate at exactly identical frequencies forever, so they have to be resynchronized periodically. In asynchronous transmission, the receiver's clock is synchronized with the transmitter's clock at the beginning of each byte transmission. The method is based on the assumption that the difference between two clocks is small enough not to cause any errors during a 1-byte transmission. The synchronization of the receiver's clock is achieved by preceding each byte transmission with an additional bit—a *start bit*—and by following each byte transmission with another additional bit—a *stop bit*. The start bit is always a 0 bit and the stop bit is always a 1 bit. If no data is sent, the data line is kept in the 1 state, which is referred to as the *idle state*. Therefore, the beginning of each byte transmission is always marked by a 1-to-0 transition, which indicates the beginning of the start bit. This 1-to-0 transition is used to resynchronize the receiver's clock.

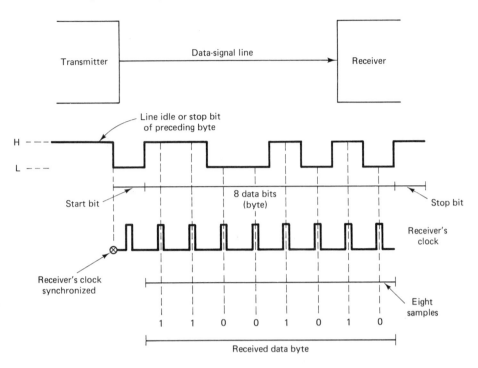

Figure 2.2-5   Asynchronous transmission.

The self-clocked transmission uses *Manchester encoding* of a digital signal (Fig. 2.2-6). In this case, the receiver's clock is resynchronized on every bit transmission and bit streams of any length can be sent. The self-clocking of the data signal is achieved by assuring an H-to-L or L-to-H transition in the middle of every bit time. These transitions are used to resynchronize receiver's clock. Data bits are encoded in the following way. A 0 bit is represented by L followed by H (thus, there is an L-to-H transition if 0 is transmitted). A 1 bit is represented by H followed by L (thus, there is an H-to-L transition if a 1 is transmitted). If no information is sent, there are no transitions on the data line at all, and transmitter's and receiver's clocks are completely out of synchronism. In the Manchester-encoded signal, transitions happen not only in the middle of bit times but also between bits (when two consecutive bits are of identical value). Thus, the receiver's clock has to be initially synchronized after each idle-line period. This is achieved by sending a special, fixed sequence of bits, *preamble* (or *alert sequence*) bits, which ensure initial synchronization. For example, a preamble consisting of 8 bits; 11111110, can be used. In this case, the first 7 bits are used for initial clock synchronization and the last, differently valued bit informs the receiver about the end of preamble, i.e., that all following bits will be data bits.

All internal computer operations are performed using strictly digital signals. Typically, transistor-transistor logic (TTL) signal levels are used with a voltage level between 2.4 V and 5 V, representing a logical value 1, and a voltage level between 0

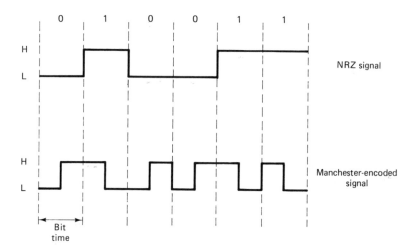

Figure 2.2-6 Manchester encoding—self-clocked transmission.

and 0.8 volts representing logical value 0. On the other hand, to transmit or receive data to and from a medium, some form of signal encoding must be used. This function is performed by the *medium interface*. Specific operations performed by the medium-interface unit depend on the signaling and synchronization methods used. In general, we may say that medium interface provides bidirectional signal *conditioning*. In the transmit direction, streams of transmitted data bits are converted by a medium interface to electric signals appropriate for medium use. In the receive direction, a signal arriving from the medium is decoded, and the resulting stream of received data bits is produced. As shown in Fig. 2.2-7, there is one more element between the medium

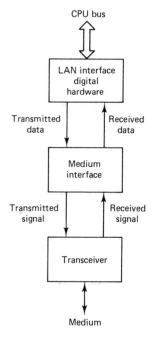

Figure 2.2-7 Medium interface.

interface and the medium itself, the *transceiver*. The transceiver's role is to connect two unidirectional signal lines into one bidirectional line, which then can be tapped directly to the LAN cable bus.

An example of a medium interface using analog signaling and Manchester code for synchronization is shown in Fig. 2.2-8. On the digital hardware (network-interface unit) side, pure digital signaling with TTL signal levels and an additional clock-signal line for each data line is used. This form of signaling between digital hardware (network interface) and medium interface is used for both very large scale of integration (VLSI) network interfaces discussed in Chapter 3.

An example of a medium interface for asynchronous communication using digital signaling is shown in Fig. 2.2-9. This form of medium interface is used in the laboratory LAN model described in Chapter 4.

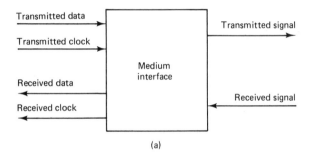

(a)

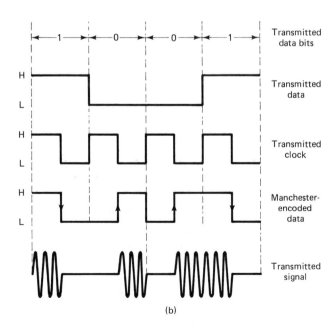

(b)

Figure 2.2-8 Medium interface using Manchester code and analog signaling with amplitude-shift keying (ASK): (a) Input and output lines, (b) Encoding of transmitted data.

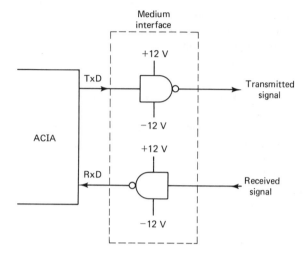

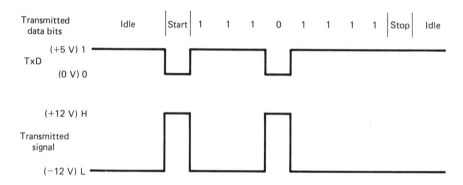

Figure 2.2-9 RS = 232C line buffers and NRZ signal encoding.

2.3 CSMA/CD MEDIUM-ACCESS SCHEME

The CSMA/CD technique is a contentious scheme, in which network nodes compete for the right to use the medium. A winner can transmit one packet and then has to release the medium for other nodes. If a node is already using the medium, all other nodes must defer their transmissions until the medium becomes idle. The activity on the network is detected (carrier sense), and a lack of activity means that the medium is idle and is available. Several nodes may then start transmitting to the medium. If only one node starts transmitting, then the medium becomes busy, and all other nodes that were late to start will have to wait until the medium becomes idle again. If several nodes start transmission more or less simultaneously, a collision occurs. In this case all transmitters have to abort their transmissions and back off for some time before trying again. The back-off time is random to avoid repetitive collisions.

Figure 2.3-1 represents a state diagram illustrating operation of a data-link layer implementing the CSMA/CD scheme. Most of the time, the layer is in the *listen* state. In this state, all frames arriving from the physical layer (the medium) are analyzed. If a frame's header contains a destination address matching the node's address, the data-link layer changes to the *accept* state, in which the frame is accepted.

When the frame acceptance is completed, the upper (network) layer is signaled and the data-link layer returns to the *listen* state. It is possible that a collision happens during frame acceptance. In such a case, the frame reception is aborted and the data-link layer returns to the *listen* state.

A frame may be transmitted to the medium only as a result of a request made by the network layer. When such a request is made and the node is not in the process of frame acceptance, the state of the data-link layer is changed to *wait*. In this state, the node waits for the medium to become idle (free). When the medium becomes free, the packet transmission begins. If transmission is completed successfully without collision, the state is changed back to *listen*. If a collision happens during frame transmission, the transmission is aborted and has to be repeated from the beginning. The state is changed to *back-off*. In this state, the node waits for a period of time and then the state is changed back to *wait*.

The back-off time is computed anew on every collision. A variety of methods are used to determine the back-off time. The main goal is to prevent a deadlock, in which a pair of colliding nodes never stops colliding. For example, such deadlocks would occur if the back-off time were constant and identical for all nodes on the network. After a collision, the two nodes would back off for the same time; then they would both find

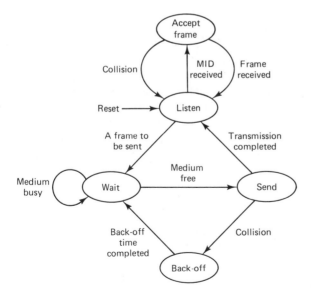

Figure 2.3-1 CSMA/CD algorithm.

the medium free and simultaneously start transmitting again. As a result, the next collision would occur, and this process would never end. One method of preventing deadlocks is to make the back-off time proportional to node's address (ID). It is an efficient
method but gives a certain type of priority to nodes with lower IDs. After a collision,
the node with the lowest ID ends its back-off time first and acquires the medium. Other
nodes involved in the collision find the medium busy when they exit from their *back-
off* states. Another method makes the back-off time random. It does not have the implied priority property, but consecutive collisions may still happen. It is impossible in
this case to guarantee a fixed time limit for packet transfers, because repetitive collisions are allowed and their number is random.

2.4 TOKEN-BUS MEDIUM-ACCESS SCHEME

The token-bus medium-access scheme is a noncontentious method in which the right to
use the network medium is passed from node to node in an organized way. The right to
use is passed by transferring a unique frame called the *token* along a *logical ring*
formed on the network using IDs. Each node is identified by its ID. In the token-bus
scheme, each node is also informed about the ID of the node that is next in the logical
ring (NID). Normally, the successor has higher-valued ID. Figure 2.4-1 illustrates the
concept of logical ring.

 In addition to token passing, the token-bus scheme has to solve the problem of
token loss and ring reconfiguration. Token loss may occur when one of the nodes in the
logical ring breaks down. At some point in time, the token is passed to the failed node,
but the node does not pass the token along, and other nodes never get the token again.
Ring reconfiguration has to be performed whenever a new node is to be added to the
logical ring or one of the nodes is to be removed from it.

 During normal operation, for example, when neither token recovery nor ring
reconfiguration are performed, each node operates according to state diagram presented in Fig. 2.4-2. Most of the time, the data-link layer is in the *listen* state. If the
header of an incoming frame contains the node's ID as its destination address, the state
is changed to *accept,* and the frame is accepted. If the accepted frame happens to be a
data-packet frame, its reception is reported to the network layer, and the DL layer returns to the *listen* state. However, if the accepted frame proves to be the token frame, it
means that the node has just acquired the right to use the medium for its transmitting
needs. If, at this time, a data packet is waiting to be transmitted, the state is changed to

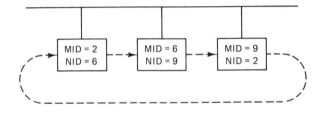

Figure 2.4-1 Logical ring.

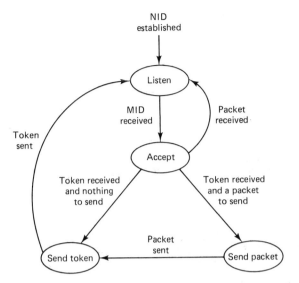

Figure **2.4-2** Token-bus protocol—normal operation.

send packet, and packet transmission begins. When the packet transmission is completed, the state is changed to *send token,* and token-frame transmission begins. The state of the data-link layer is changed directly from *accept* to *send token* if, at the moment when the token frame is received, the node does not have any data packet to transmit. After sending the token frame, the state is changed back to *listen.*

A state diagram representing operations of the data-link layer during ring reconfiguration and token recovery is given in Fig. 2.4-3. Three states, *jam, sleep,* and *poll,* are used during successful ring reconfiguration. The ring cannot be configured if there is only one operational node. In this case, the reconfiguration attempt by the ''lonely'' node fails, and it remains in the *wait for jamming* state until another node is added to the network. Only two states; *sleep* and *poll,* are used during token recovery. In both reconfiguration and token-recovery cases, once the NID is established, the state of the data-link layer is changed to *normal operation.* Details of this state are given in Fig. 2.4-2 and are discussed in the previous paragraph. Note that while entering the *normal operation* state, the data-link layer is actually entering the *listen* state of Fig. 2.4-2. Also note that the token may be perceived as lost, causing the state to change to *sleep,* only when the data-link layer is in the *listen* state. In all other states of Fig. 2.4-2, the node is in possession of the token and thus cannot lose it.

When a node wants to join the network, it enters the *jam* state, in which a jamming sequence is unconditionally transmitted to the network medium. The purpose of jamming the medium is to cause token loss, thus forcing all nodes participating in passing the token along the existing logical ring to begin a token-recovery procedure. After jamming, all nodes on the network, including the new one, enter the *sleep* state. A node can be awakened when its sleep time expires or when it receives the token. The sleep time is different for each node, and it is proportional to the node's ID. Since all nodes enter the *sleep* state nearly simultaneously, the node with lowest ID wakes up first.

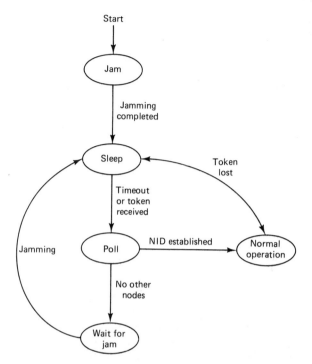

Figure 2.4-3 Token-bus protocol—network reconfiguration and token recovery.

After waking up, a node enters the *poll* state, in which it sends token frames to potential successors in the logical ring, beginning with the NID higher by one than its own ID (called "my" ID, or (MID). The polling algorithm is given in Fig. 2.4-4. After sending the token to a node addressed by current value of NID, the polling node waits some time for response. If there is no node on the network with such an ID, there is no response, and the polling node increments the NID by 1 and sends the token again. If a node with this ID exists on the network, it must be in the *sleep* state. But receiving the token frame wakes it up and it starts polling the network on its own. This start of polling by the next node is perceived as a response by the previous polling node, and it assumes that NID has been established and enters the *normal operation* state. Thus the polling activity migrates from one existing node to another towards higher IDs.

```
NID := MID + 1

repeat

    send token to NID

    wait for response

    NID := NID + 1

    if NID > MAXID then NID := MINID

until response received or NID = MID
```

Figure 2.4-4 Polling algorithm.

The logical ring becomes closed when the node with highest ID establishes its NID, which has to be the ID of the node that woke up first (the lowest ID present on the network). At this time, the node with lowest ID is already in *normal operation* state. Thus, when it receives the polling token, this node does not start polling but sends the token to the node with previously established NID. In this way, the polling process terminates and ring reconfiguration or token recovery is completed.

2.5 TOKEN-RING MEDIUM-ACCESS SCHEME

The major difference between the token-ring medium-access scheme and the previous two methods is in the physical topology of the medium. Both CSMA/CD and the token bus use physical bus interconnections, whereas the token-ring scheme is built on the physical ring topology.

Signals transmitted by a node of a network based on physical bus topology propagate across an entire medium (broadcast). In the physical-ring topology, signals propagate over unidirectional point-to-point paths between network nodes (Fig. 2.5-1). The nodes and unidirectional links are connected in series to form the physical ring. In the bus topology, the nodes operate only as transmitters or receivers. If a node is removed

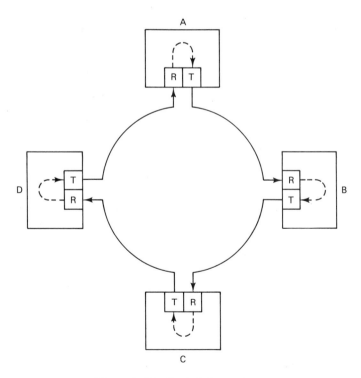

Figure 2.5-1 Physical-ring topology.

from a bus-based network—for example, as a result of a failure—it does not affect the signal propagation for other nodes. In the ring topology, nodes play an active role in signal propagation. In order to reach a destination node, signals originating at the transmit port of a source node have to be retransmitted by all nodes located along the ring between the source and destination nodes. Note that, as indicated in Fig. 2.5-1, each node transfers network signals internally from the receive to the transmit port. While doing so, the nodes can analyze incoming signals as well as modify them.

The benefit of such a solution is that signals are reinforced during retransmission and, therefore, the total length of the physical ring is not limited by signal attenuation in the medium. However, a failure of a single node or cable segment in the physical-ring network results in a break in the signal path, and the whole network ceases to operate. To avoid this reliability problem, a mixed star-ring topology is used for token-ring networks (Fig. 2.5-2). This solution requires the use of wiring concentrators, which can be easily (possibly automatically) reconfigured to bypass faulty nodes. As shown in Fig. 2.5-2, a simple change of internal configuration of the wiring concentrator results in isolating node C while preserving the ring interconnection of the remaining nodes.

As is the case in the token-bus scheme, the token-ring medium-access scheme implements a unique sequence of bits as a token message. However, the tokens in the

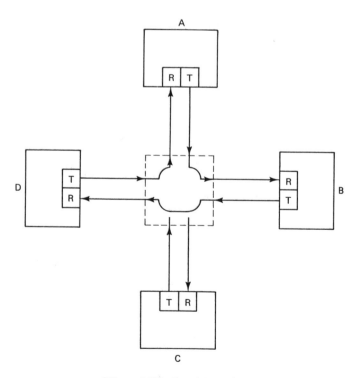

Figure 2.5-2 Star-ring topology.

token-ring scheme are not addressed. Instead, a token can have free or busy forms. As long as none of the nodes on the ring has a data packet to send, a free-token message circulates along the ring. Note that at a given instant, only one token is present in the entire ring (Fig. 2.5-3(a)). A node that has a data packet to send has to wait until it receives a free token. At this moment, the node changes the token to busy, transmits it farther along the ring, and appends the data packet to the busy token. The busy token, followed by the data packet, is then retransmitted around the whole ring (Fig. 2.5-3(b)). Only the node that changed the token to busy can change it back to free. The data packet contains a destination address field in its header. The destination node copies the packet as it passes through the node. For example, if a data packet originated at

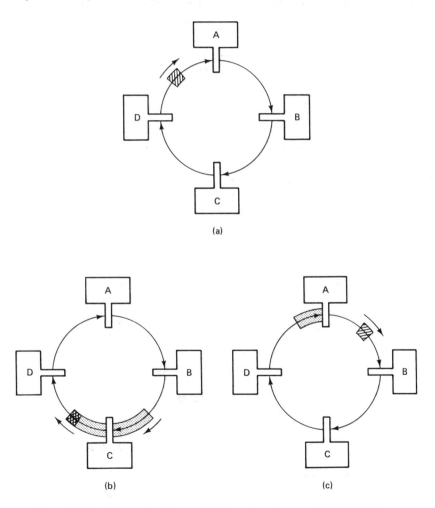

Figure 2.5-3 Token and packet transfers in a token-ring network: (a) Circulating free token, (b) Busy token followed by data packet, (c) Free-token regeneration and data-packet removal.

node A and was sent to node C, the busy token (followed by the data packet) would be retransmitted by nodes B, C, and D. However, at node C, a copy of the data packet would be made. In other words, all nodes on the ring—except for the packet source node—retransmit the packet, whereas only one of them—the destination node—accepts it. When the busy token, followed by data packet, returns to the source node, the token is changed back to free and the data packet is removed from the ring. The data packet is removed by simply not retransmitting it any more (Fig. 2.5-3(c)). Once the free token starts circulating along the ring again, any node can change it to busy and start data-packet transmission. The basic algorithm describing the operation of the token-ring network nodes is given in Fig. 2.5-4.

```
repeat
   repeat
      retransmit received data
   until free token received
   if a data packet is waiting to be sent then
      send busy token
      send data packet
      wait until busy token received
      send free token   (*)
      receive (but not retransmit) data until packet received   (*)
   else
      retransmit free token
   endif
until reset.
```

(*) These two activities happen simultaneously, at transmit and
    receive ports correspondingly.

Figure 2.5-4   Basic algorithm for a token-ring network node.

The protocol for the token-ring network has to solve the problems of token loss due to transmission errors and node or medium faults. These functions are performed by a *network-monitor* node. For example, lack of any transmission on the ring indicates loss of token. If token loss is detected, the network monitor will initiate a ring-reconfiguration procedure. Detailed discussion of the token-ring medium-access scheme can be found in [9].

3

Local Network Nodes and Interfaces

In this chapter we discuss most typical architectures of local network nodes and exemplary VLSI chips used as network interfaces in LAN nodes. The types of network nodes include workstations, file servers, print servers, and internetwork communication servers, the so-called gateways. Intel 82586 LAN coprocessor and Western Digital 2840 LAN controller are used as VLSI LAN interface examples. Both LAN node and VLSI LAN interface chip architectures are discussed from the general point of view necessary to understand their operation and architectural properties.

3.1 LAN NODES

Figure 3.1-1 represents a model of a bus-topology LAN equipped with various nodes (LAN stations). It has *N workstation* nodes and three specialized nodes—also referred to as *function servers*. The workstation nodes are computers optimized to support human work, and each workstation is used as a work place for one user. Quite often, workstations are also referred to as *user servers*. The services provided by specialized nodes are shared by all workstation users on the network. The file-server node provides large mass-memory capacity for file storage and retrieval. The print-server node provides high-speed hard-copy output capability. The gateway node interfaces an entire LAN with another LAN or with a wide-area network.

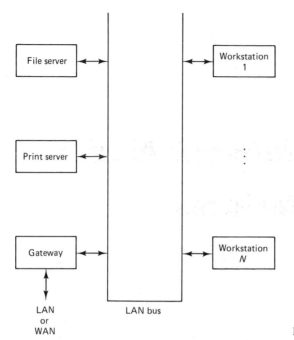

Figure 3.1-1 Bus-topology LAN.

3.2 WORKSTATION ARCHITECTURE

The workstation node is used in large quantity on a given LAN and supports user-oriented functions. To an extent, a workstation node can be defined as a highly sophisticated terminal. Depending on the LAN application, workstations may be tailored to support data entry, word processing, banking, scientific, or computer-aided design (CAD) functions. Typically, all workstations on a LAN are identical or at least similar. However, if the application needs require that different types of workstations be used on the same LAN, it is quite possible as long as their LAN interfaces conform to the same LAN protocol. Workstations are equipped with their own local processing power, small mass storage capability, and human interface optimized for the kind of work performed by workstation user. For example, workstations used for CAD purposes have to be equipped with advanced interactive graphics capabilities.

   Local processing power allows user programs to be run directly in the workstation, thus minimizing system-response time and providing more convenient and more sophisticated services for the workstation user. Floppy-disk memory provides the user with small mass-storage capacity, allows for local entry of user programs and data, and also allows the user to store results of his or her work on personal, locally accessible diskettes. The interactive graphics terminal may provide advanced, high-resolution color display with interactive input in the form of a light pen or a mouse as well as a conventional or specialized keyboard. The fact that workstations are connected to the LAN or, better yet, are parts of the LAN allows for file transfers between workstations; also, workstation has access to common LAN resources such as print and file servers and the gateway.

An architectural model of a CAD workstation is given in Fig. 3.2-1. Architectural models of workstations for different applications are similar, differing only in user interface—that is, for a word-processing workstation, an optimized alphanumerical terminal can replace the graphics terminal.

The processing power is provided by a microprocessor (CPU, or central processing unit), which runs operating system and applications programs. Workstation firmware is located in the read-only memory (ROM), a nonvolatile memory. Operating system, LAN communications software, and applications programs are loaded from disk to random-access memory (RAM). All information transfers within the workstation occur through the CPU bus shared by the CPU with three I/O controllers: a graphics terminal controller, a disk-drive controller, and a LAN controller.

All controllers may access RAM memory using direct memory access (DMA) read or write operations. Normally, the CPU operates as bus master—for example, it asserts address and control lines on the bus to fetch and execute program instructions. To perform a DMA operation, an I/O controller must first obtain CPU's permission to use the bus (for example, to become a temporary bus master). Bus use is requested by an I/O controller through the bus request (BR) line. A controller may start using the

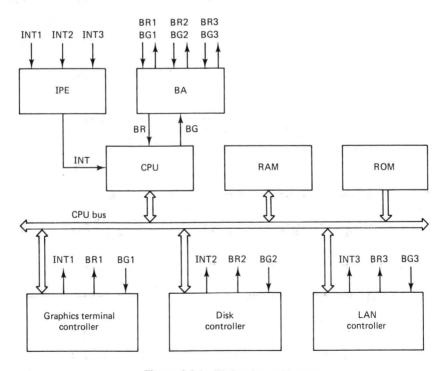

Figure 3.2-1 Workstation architecture.

bus for DMA transfers when it obtains CPU's permission through the bus grant (BG) line.

There can be only one bus master at a time, so the CPU is supported by bus arbiter (BA), which solves the problem of more than one controller simultaneously requesting the bus from the CPU. If more than one BRi line is asserted and the CPU grants the bus by asserting the BG line, the BA allows only one of I/O controllers to assume bus mastership by asserting only one of the BGi lines. The choice of a controller to be given the bus use is performed by the BA according to a fixed *arbitration algorithm* (also referred to as *bus-arbitration protocol*).

CPU's attention is drawn by I/O controllers through the interrupt (INTi) lines. Again, there may be more than one controller trying to obtain CPU's attention at a given time. This problem is solved by interrupt-priority encoder (IPE), which informs the CPU about only one interrupt at a time. The choice of interrupt to be forwarded to the CPU is performed according to the priorities assigned to I/O controllers. A controller with highest priority obtains the CPU's attention first, and interrupts of lower priorities are pending (awaiting service) until the CPU completes servicing of higher-priority interrupts.

The term *CPU's attention* means that as a result of an interrupt, the CPU will quit a currently executed program (possibly a user-application program) and start executing a routine that services the accepted interrupt. For example, an interrupt may be generated by the LAN controller when a new frame is received from the network. As a result, a currently executed program is suspended and a routine—part of LAN protocol software—is executed, which accepts, analyzes, and perhaps reacts to the contents of the just-received frame. After the interrupt is served, for example, when the execution of the interrupt service routine is completed, the CPU resumes the suspended user-application program.

3.3 LAN INTERFACE DESIGN CRITERIA

As shown in Fig. 3.3-1, the LAN interface operates between the CPU bus and medium-interface unit. All LAN interface inputs and outputs have the form of pure digital signals with standard TTL levels. The LAN interface functions include the following:

- All data-link (DL) layer operations, for example, node-level addressing, error detection, and medium-access control. In the token-bus protocol, medium-access control consists of token passing, network reconfiguration, and token recovery. In the CSMA/CD protocol, LAN interface performs all collision-related operations, for example, computation of the back-off time and transmission retry.

- Input and output of frames represented by bit streams from and to the medium, through the medium interface, at a fixed data rate. This function is particularly

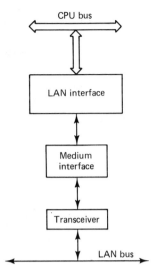

Figure 3.3-1 LAN interface in a LAN node.

demanding in the receive direction. Bits arrive from the medium, through the medium interface, at a high, fixed data rate and cannot be slowed down. Frames represented by these bit streams have to be analyzed and accepted or rejected very rapidly.

Finally, data frames (in both directions) as well as control and status information have to be exchanged between the LAN interface and CPU programs. LAN interface implements the (DL) layer, and higher protocol layers are implemented in a form of CPU programs. Thus this frame and control and status exchange amounts to an exchange of information between DL and higher—in particular, network—layers. CPU programs operate on data located in main memory; therefore, frames and control and status information have to be between LAN interface and CPU programs through a shared area in the main memory. Main memory can be accessed by the LAN interface only through the CPU bus. As a result, the LAN interface has to share the CPU bus with the CPU and possibly other elements of node's architecture—for example, the disk-drive controller or the dynamic memory-refresh unit—that also have to use it.

The goals to be achieved by LAN interface designer can be formulated as follows:

- Assure all DL layer operations for a given medium-access protocol and data rate.
- Minimize the use of CPU bus time necessary for frame and control and status information exchange.
- Minimize system cost by developing a standard LAN interface unit that can be used in any LAN implementing a given DL layer standard.

These goals lead to the following design requirements:

- The LAN interface should be designed as a hardware unit, preferably in VLSI technology, independent of the CPU and capable of high-speed operation.
- The interface should be capable of DMA operations to perform information exchange with shared memory through the CPU bus without the CPU's intervention and with high efficiency.

3.4 VLSI LAN COPROCESSOR—INTEL 82586

The Intel 82586 VLSI integrated circuit was designed to support DL layer functions for CSMA/CD LANs. The design is based on IEEE-802 standard requirements and is suitable for Ethernet and other 802 LANs. It is called a *LAN coprocessor* because it can operate on the same bus as the host CPU (main processor) and can execute instructions from main memory shared with the host CPU. The coprocessor uses DMA to read or write instructions and frames from or to main memory, and these operations are transparent to the host CPU. In effect, the coprocessor and host processor operate on the bus in parallel. The coprocessor instruction set is different from that used by the host CPU. User programs or operating system routines that implement higher layers of LAN protocol can exchange frames with the 82586 coprocessor through shared areas in main memory.

The LAN coprocessor performs all operations required by CSMA/CD channel-access scheme automatically, independent of the CPU. CPU attention is required only to handle error-free frames. In the transmit direction, the coprocessor waits until a medium becomes free before starting to output a frame. It also generates the preamble and error-checking sequences and performs automatic back-off and transmission retry in case of collisions. Back-off time is computed using a random exponential cut-off algorithm. All this is done without CPU intervention, and the CPU is informed only about successful completion of frame transmission. In the receive direction, the coprocessor monitors all incoming frames. Only the frames with addresses matching ID numbers stored in coprocessor during its initialization are accepted. Bad frames—for example, frames with errors or frames that collided—are rejected. The CPU is informed only about reception of error-free frames.

The coprocessor also supports extensive diagnostic algorithms that are not used during normal operation but are very helpful in case of network malfunction or during network installation and start-up. The diagnostics performed by the coprocessor allow for self-testing—for example, testing of coprocessor operation—as well as testing of network-medium interface and the medium itself.

Fig. 3.4-1 represents a model of a network node equipped with an i82586 LAN coprocessor. The only direct communication between host CPU and coprocessor is performed via channel-attention (CA) and interrupt-request (IRQ) lines. The CPU can neither read from nor write to the coprocessor. A program running on the CPU can prepare in-

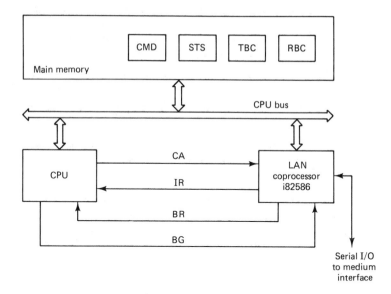

Figure 3.4-1 Network node with LAN coprocessor.

structions and frames to be transmitted for the coprocessor by placing them in the shared memory area. The coprocessor can also prepare status information and received frames for CPU programs by placing them in the shared memory area. If the CPU requires the coprocessor's attention—for example, after placing new instructions for it in shared memory—the CPU asserts the CA line. This activates the coprocessor, which reads shared memory to obtain new instructions. When the coprocessor completes the operation prescribed by its instructions, it informs the CPU about it by asserting the IRQ line. The coprocessor also asserts the IRQ line if it demands CPU's attention as a result of its own network-related operations, such as after a new frame arrives from the network.

The DMA operations require that the coprocessor become the bus master. During normal operation, the CPU operates as the bus master, and only one device can be the bus master at a given instant of time. When the coprocessor wants to access the shared memory, it asserts the BR line. The CPU allows the coprocessor to use the bus by asserting the BG line. As long as the coprocessor uses the bus, the CPU cannot access the memory; however a program executing on the CPU is not aware of this fact. Simply, its execution time is slightly prolonged. All information transfers between coprocessor and memory are achieved using the DMA method.

The shared memory area consists of four parts: command field, status field, transmit buffer chain, and receive buffer chain. Instructions for the coprocessor are placed in the command field by CPU programs. The coprocessor places information about its status, to be used by CPU programs, in the status field. Frames prepared by CPU programs (upper network layers) for transmission to the network are placed in the transmit buffer chain. Frames arriving from network are placed in the receive buffer chain by the LAN coprocessor.

The command field is used by CPU programs to pass two types of information to the coprocessor: initialization data and executable instructions. Instructions for the coprocessor are called *commands* to distinguish them from the instructions executed by the CPU. First, when the system starts up (power on), the coprocessor has to be initialized. At this time, initialization data has to be present in a part of the command field referred to as the *initialization root*. The initialization information consists of data specifying system configuration and pointers defining initial addresses for all other fields in shared memory. At power up, the coprocessor automatically reads the initialization root first; thus the initialization root has to begin at a fixed address in memory.

Instructions for the coprocessor, that is, the commands, are prepared by CPU programs whenever the coprocessor's action is required. The instruction set for the coprocessor is limited—there are only eight commands executable by the i82586. For example, when a CPU program wants to send a frame to the network, a *transmit* command has to be prepared in the command field of shared memory. Then, the coprocessor's attention is drawn by asserting the CA line. As a result, the coprocessor reads the command from the command field and executes it. The transmit command contains, as its operand, the pointer locating the frame to be transmitted in the transmit buffer chain. One transmit command is necessary to make the coprocessor transmit one frame. Another important command, the *address setup* command, allows CPU programs to establish a network address for the coprocessor. This command should be executed after coprocessor initialization by the initialization root information but before any frame transmission or reception. The network address is also referred to as its MID.

The status field in shared memory is used by the coprocessor to inform CPU programs about the coprocessor's status and reasons why an interrupt was generated. After every interrupt, the CPU can read the status field to determine the interrupt cause. The status information is prepared by the coprocessor before asserting the IRQ line. The coprocessor can generate interrupt and provide status information because of three reasons: completion of a command, an error, or a frame arrival from a network.

Transmit and receive buffers are both organized as buffer chains, for example, as sets of variable number of fixed-size buffers, each associated with a buffer descriptor pointing to the memory address where next buffer in a chain is located. The use of buffer chains allows for better memory utilization. Frames used in LANs vary in size; for example, Ethernet frame lengths range from 60 to 1600 bytes. If each buffer were assigned for one frame and were large enough to accommodate the longest frames, then very often only a fraction of memory allocated for buffers would be used. In buffer chains, each buffer has the size of a minimum-length frame. If a frame is longer, it simply occupies more buffers. Every frame begins at the beginning of a buffer in memory, but, since frame length is not necessarily a multiple of buffer length, the last buffer of the chain occupied by a given frame may be only partially used. The chained buffer concept is illustrated in Fig. 3.4-2.

Transmit buffer chains are prepared by the CPU programs and contain frames to be transmitted to the network, one chain per frame. Since the coprocessor transmits

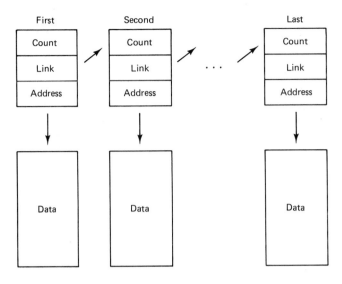

Figure 3.4-2 Chained buffers.

one frame per one transmit command, the operand field of the transmit command points to the descriptor of the first buffer in this frame's chain.

Receive buffer chains are filled by the coprocessor with frames arriving from the network. Each frame has its own frame descriptor, which points to the descriptor of the first buffer in chain. Frame descriptors are prepared by the coprocessor and analyzed by the CPU program after the coprocessor asserts the IRQ line.

Internal architecture of the LAN coprocessor is shown in Fig. 3.4-3. Three major sections can be distinguished: the CPU-bus interface, the transmit section, and the receive section. The transmit section consists of a transmit-control unit (TCU), a transmit first-in-first-out (TFIFO) register, and a serial-output interface (SOI). The receive section consists of a receive control unit (RCU), receive first-in-first-out (RFIFO) register, and serial-input interface (SII). The transmit and receive sections implement DL layer of the CSMA/CD channel access protocol and operate independently from the CPU and each other. Functions performed by the transmit and receive sections include preamble and error-detection code generation and detection, collision handling, and frame source and destination addressing.

Transmit section is responsible for execution of transmit commands, that is, for transmitting frames from transmit buffer chains in shared memory to network medium. In the CSMA/CD protocol, frame transmission may begin only if the network medium is found to be free (carrier sense function). If a collision occurs during frame output, transmission is aborted, and, after the back-off time, the transmit section attempts to transmit the same frame again. Only after successful transmission, that is, without collision during frame output, will the transmit section request the CPU-bus interface to assert the IRQ line.

The TFIFO register is used as intermediary storage to provide necessary buffering between shared memory and SOI. Once a frame transmission begins, all bits of

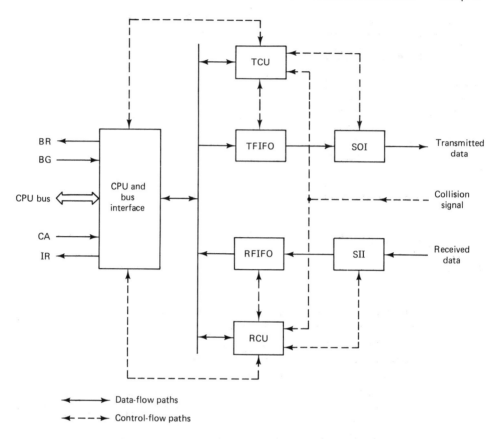

Data-flow paths

Control-flow paths

Figure 3.4-3   Internal architecture of the LAN coprocessor.

the frame have to be sent to the network medium, one after another, without any delay between consecutive bits. The TFIFO buffer is 16 bytes long, and the coprocessor moves a frame from shared memory to TFIFO in bursts—for example, 8 bytes at a time, using a DMA read operation. The output of frame bytes from the TFIFO register to the network medium through the serial-output interface is smooth, bit after bit, and synchronous with coprocessor's clock, which determines the data-transfer rate (for example, 10 MHz for Ethernet). If all bytes from TFIFO are output before the next DMA read burst, the frame output flow will be distorted. In Ethernet, the lack of a signal in the medium marks the end of a frame; thus, such a distorted frame could not be received properly by a receiving node. It is an error situation, referred to as a DMA underrun, and it is reported to CPU programs through status field and interrupt. The DMA underrun may happen if the bus use is not granted to the coprocessor fast enough. The delay between bus request, signaled by the coprocessor on the BR line (see Fig. 3.4-1) and bus grant (signaled by the CPU or, in more complicated systems, by a bus-arbitration unit), is referred to as *bus latency*.

The receive section is responsible for frame reception. Out of the frames arriving from network medium through the serial-input interface, only the frames with DID (destination address) field matching the MID (network address), stored in the coprocessor during initialization, should be accepted. If a collision happens during frame reception, the frame is rejected and the buffer chain used to store this frame as it was being received is cleared. A frame is also rejected if it was received with errors. When a frame is successfully received, with no collisions or errors, the receive section prepares status information and requests the CPU-bus interface to assert the IRQ line.

The receive FIFO register is used as intermediary storage between serial input interface and a buffer chain in shared memory. Once the RCU decides that an arriving frame should be accepted, incoming bits of the frame are composed in bytes and placed in the RFIFO. From there, they are moved to a receive buffer chain in shared memory in DMA write bursts. The RFIFO is also 16 bytes long, and the DMA write bursts may have the same length as DMA read bursts (that is, 8 bytes). If data from RFIFO is not moved to shared memory in time, the RFIFO may be overwritten by consecutive bytes incoming from the medium through a serial-input interface. Such a condition, which causes the received frame to be distorted, is referred to as *DMA overrun* and is reported to CPU programs as an error through the status field and interrupt. If a frame reception is completed without errors, the RCU requests the CPU-bus interface to assert the IRQ line.

3.5 VLSI LAN CONTROLLER—WESTERN DIGITAL WD2840

The WD2840 VLSI integrated circuit was designed by Western Digital to support DL functions for token-bus LANs. The design is suitable for Arcnet and other LANs using a token-bus medium-access scheme. As opposed to Intel's i82586, the WD2840 is referred to not as a LAN coprocessor but as a LAN controller. The reason is that the WD2840 was not designed to execute commands (instructions) fetched from shared memory, that is, it does not operate as a processor on the host CPU's bus. The orders from programs running on the host CPU to the LAN controller are passed by writing order codes to control registers located inside the WD2840 and accessible by CPU programs at fixed addresses. As was the case with the i82586, the WD2840 can operate as a bus master on the host CPU's bus for DMA read or write transfers.

Programs running on the host CPU, that is, routines implementing higher layers of LAN protocol, can exchange frames with the LAN controller through shared areas in main memory. The LAN controller performs all operations required by the token-bus medium-access scheme automatically and independently from the CPU. CPU attention is required only to handle error-free data frames. The controller is able to perform a network-reconfiguration algorithm when joining a token-bus LAN, that is, network jamming, polling, and establishment of the NID. It is also able to detect a token-loss situation and perform the token-recovery algorithm. All this is done without CPU intervention, and the CPU is informed only about ultimate failure or success.

During normal operation, when LAN nodes pass the token along logical ring established during the last network reconfiguration, the controller monitors all frames arriving from the network medium. Only the error-free frames with destination addresses matching MIDs stored in the controller during its initialization are accepted. The CPU is informed only about acceptance of error-free data frames. The token and acknowledge frames are handled by the controller and do not require the CPU's attention.

If an accepted frame happens to be the token frame, the controller assumes that it just obtained the right to transmit to the network medium. If, at this moment, a data frame is waiting in shared memory to be transmitted to the network, the controller starts the transmission process. If the transmission is a successful one, that is, if an acknowledge frame is received from the destination node, the CPU is informed about the transmission completion. Whether a data frame was sent or not, the controller sends the token frame to the network medium using the NID established during last network reconfiguration as a token-frame destination address.

As was the case with the i82586, the LAN controller supports extensive diagnostic algorithms that can be used during network installation or debugging. Diagnostic tests available in WD2840 include self-testing and network-testing algorithms.

Figure 3.5-1 represents a model of a network node equipped with WD2840 LAN controller. The CPU can either write to or read from the controller's internal registers. The controller can draw the CPU's attention—for example, after frame reception—via the IRQ line. A program running on the CPU can prepare data frames to be transmitted by the controller by placing them in the shared memory area. CPU programs can affect the controller's operation. For example, they can request frame transmission by writing order codes to the controller's internal control registers. The controller can prepare re-

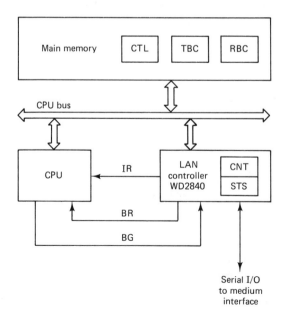

Figure 3.5-1 Network node with LAN controller.

ceived frames for CPU programs by placing them in shared memory. Status information reflecting the controller's operation is made available for CPU programs partially in the internal status registers of the controller and partially in the shared memory.

All the controller's accesses to shared memory are performed as DMA read or write operations. The DMA access is controlled by the BR and BG lines in the same way as by the i82586 LAN coprocessor (Section 3.4).

Shared memory area consists of three parts: status field, transmit buffer chain, and receive buffer chain. The LAN controller places information about its status, which is to be used by CPU programs, in the status field. Frames prepared by CPU programs for transmission are placed in the transmit buffer chain. Frames arriving from the network, except for token and acknowledge frames, are placed by the LAN controller in the receive buffer chain. Token-frame and acknowledge-frame transmission or reception is handled completely by the controller, and therefore these frames never appear in either transmit or receive buffer chains.

Initialization of the LAN controller is performed by CPU programs at the node start-up by writing initialization information to the controller's internal control registers. The initialization information includes the MID, protocol parameters, and so on. CPU programs may also request specific controller's action, for example, diagnostic tests or frame transmission, by writing to control registers. Status information is prepared by the LAN controller partially in its internal status registers and partially in its status field in shared memory. Status field in memory is used to hold *event counters*, that is, each memory location in the status field is assigned to a specific event, such as an error in a frame received or a token loss. CPU's attention is requested every time the status field is updated.

Transmit and receive buffer chains are similar in structure and use to those used by the i82586 LAN coprocessor and are explained in Section 3.4. The major difference is that buffer descriptors are pointed to by internal registers of the LAN controllers and not by frame descriptors in memory as is the case for LAN coprocessor. Therefore, in the transmit direction, a CPU program prepared a frame by putting it in a transmit buffer chain and then loads the controller's internal register with the pointer pointing to a buffer descriptor of the first buffer in the chain. Similarly, another register is used to point to the buffer descriptor of the first buffer in the receive buffer chain available for the controller to store an accepted data frame. Both internal pointer registers are loaded by CPU programs and are used by the controller to access buffer chains.

A model of the internal architecture of the LAN controller is shown in Fig. 3.5-2. Functionally, four major sections can be distinguished: a CPU-bus interface, a transmit section, a receive section, and the control-status registers. Transmit and receive sections are more interrelated here than was the case of CSMA/CD LAN coprocessor. This closer relationship is due to the fact that transmit operations in the token-bus LAN controller can be activated only by the receive section when the token frame is received. As long as the receive section does not recognize the token frame among frames arriving from the network medium, the transmit section remains idle. On the other hand, once the transmit section starts outputting a frame to the network, the receive section becomes idle until it is activated by the transmit sections at the end of the transmission.

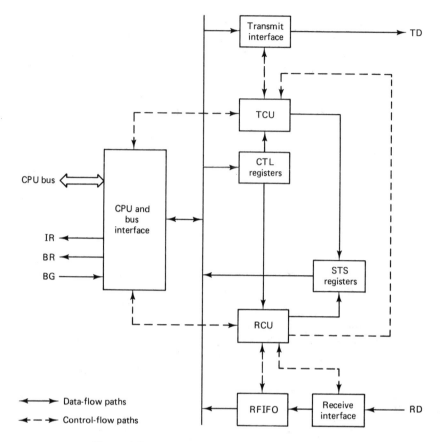

Figure 3.5-2 Internal architecture of the LAN controller.

4

Laboratory Environment

4.1 LOCAL NETWORK LABORATORY

To facilitate experimenting with local network protocols, the laboratory should be equipped with microcomputer-based network nodes with a bus-topology interconnection between them. The nodes should be equipped with alphanumerical video terminals, which are necessary for program editing and debugging as well as for implementing an application layer (creating and consuming messages).

On the network-bus side, all nodes should have identical data-communication interface ports. The simplest and least-expensive solution is the use of standard asynchronous RS232 ports with simple cable adapters to allow bidirectional data transfers over a single-line data bus. Asynchronous communication limits data-transmission rates for the laboratory network but is completely sufficient for the laboratory experiment purposes.

To provide physical interconnection, a twisted-pair cable can be used with appropriate connectors. A single twisted-pair bus is completely sufficient for all experiments with token-passing protocols, but such a bus would require complicated circuitry to allow collision detection by the hardware. To eliminate this problem, we use a multiwire flat cable (or multiple twisted pairs) with one line for the data bus, one line for the electric ground, and one additional line per each node on the network to support collision detection. This solution is explained in detail in Section 4.3.

Since most of the protocol is implemented in microcomputer's software, the network nodes should be equipped with software-development tools. Many students are expected to develop their protocols simultaneously; therefore, all software-development tools should be available in each of the network nodes. Software-development tools needed, as a minimum, are an editor, an assembler, and an assembly-level debugger.

Also the laboratory network should be equipped with the means to store and retrieve student programs. Each node can have an audio cassette interface for this purpose, but experience shows that this is not very convenient. The best medium for program storage or retrieval for this laboratory is the floppy disk. Not all the nodes have to have storage capacity, because programs can be sent over the network cable from any node to a node that is equipped with disk drive or vice versa (see Fig. 4.1-1). To provide the students with hard-copy program listings for off-line analysis, at least one of the network nodes should be equipped with a printer.

The algorithm design and implementation for laboratory network protocols relies on an interrupt system, which has to support the following sources of interrupts: terminal port, network port, timer, and collision detector. Therefore, network nodes should be based on a CPU that is able to handle at least four different hardware interrupts.

No operating system is necessary to execute programs for laboratory experiments. However, if personal computers are used as network nodes, their operating sys-

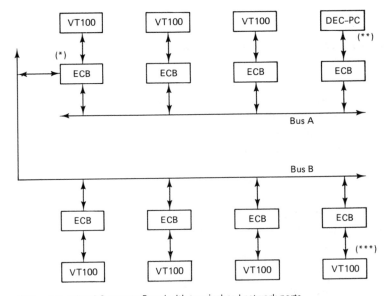

ECB   Educational Computer Board with terminal and network ports.
VT100   CRT terminal — DEC VT100 or equivalent.
(*)   Gateway — ECB with terminal and two network ports.
(**)   File-server node — ECB plus DEC Rainbow PC with two diskette drives.
(***)   Print-server node — ECB plus terminal equiped with printer for hard-copy output.

Figure 4.1-1 Laboratory network with two bus segments and specialized server nodes.

tems will be used during program development and debugging. Also, some parts of operating systems, specifically interrupt handlers, may have to be taken into account when developing experiment programs.

The laboratory environment used in this book is based on Educational Computer Board (ECB) single-board microcomputers (see Appendix E); however, similar networks can easily be built using any single-board microcomputers or personal computers as long as they are equipped with RS232 communication ports, programmable timers, and alphanumerical terminals. An example configuration of a laboratory network with four nodes is shown in Fig. 4.1-2.

The ECB microcomputers are equipped with 32Kb RAM memory for user programs, and 16Kb ROM memory containing line assembler-disassembler, editor, and debugger firmware. A good description of the architecture and programming of the ECB can be found in [14]. Should another type of microcomputer be used for laboratory network, the availability of an editor, an assembler, and a debugger in each node is essential.

The laboratory network can be upgraded by adding more network nodes and providing program storage, retrieval, and printout facilities. A configuration with eight nodes, two bus segments, a diskette drive, and a printer is shown in Fig. 4.1-1.

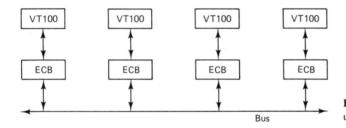

Figure 4.1-2 Laboratory network configuration.

4.2 LAN NODES

All nodes of our laboratory network are based on the ECB microcomputers (Appendix E) with modified RS232 ports to support bidirectional network communication. As shown in Fig. 4.1-1, two network segments can be used. It is possible to assign one of them—for example, segment A—to a collision-type network and the other one, segment B, to a token-passing network. Network collisions have to be detected by special hardware, which has to be installed on segment A nodes but not segment B nodes. Also, the gateway node, which can operate on both segments, has to have two network ports—one with the collision detector and one without it. Of course, segment A and its nodes can be used to implement a token-passing network as well. Collision detectors should not be used in such a case.

4.2.1 A Node for a Token-Passing Network

The organization of a node for a token-passing network (without a collision detector) is shown in Fig. 4.2-1. In addition to the 68000 CPU and main memory (ROM/RAM), the node is equipped with a programmable timer and two programmable data-communication interfaces: ACIA-1 and ACIA-2, where ACIA stands for asynchronous communication interface adapter (see Section 4.3 and Appendix G). The ACIA-1, with RS232 signal adapters, supports the video terminal port. The ACIA-2, with RS232 signal adapters and bidirectional cable adapter, supports the network port. The timer and both ports can generate CPU interrupts through the *interrupt priority encoder* (IPE). Three interrupts, each on a different priority level, are used in this node: interrupt-priority level 2 is assigned to the timer, and interrupt priority levels 5 and 6 are assigned for terminal and network ports, respectively. The 68000 CPU supports seven interrupt priority levels, with level 7 having the highest priority and level 1, the lowest. A detailed description of programming techniques and hardware design of the timer and both communication ports is given in Section 4.3 and Appendices G and H.

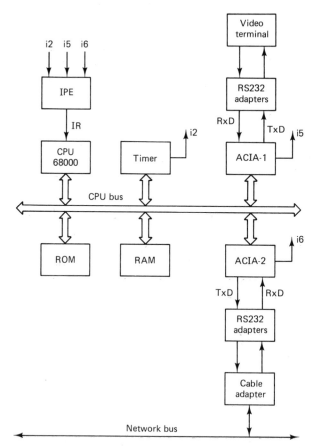

Figure 4.2-1 Organization of a node for token-passing network.

4.2.2 A Node for a Collision Network

The organization of a node for a collision-type network is shown in Fig. 4.2-2. In addition to functional blocks existing in a token-network node, as shown in Fig. 4.2-1, the collision-network node is equipped with a collision detector (CD), and its network port connects to a multiline network bus. Only one of these lines, the data line, is used for the purpose of bidirectional data transfers. All other lines are used for collision detection. A CD can generate an interrupt whenever a collision situation occurs on the network bus. This interrupt is assigned priority level 3. All collision-detection lines use

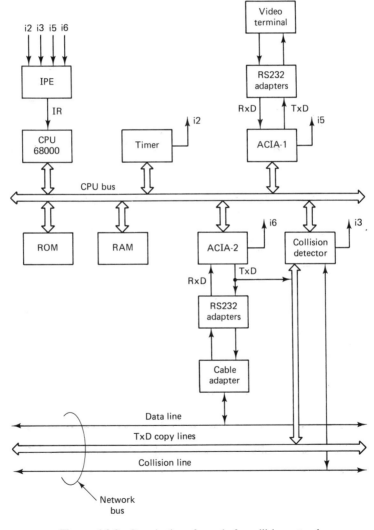

Figure 4.2-2 Organization of a node for collision network.

TTL signal levels, whereas the data line uses the RS232 signal levels. A TTL level copy of data-signal transmitted by ACIA-2 (the TxD signal) is available on a network bus—one transmit-copy line per network node. The collision line is used to broadcast the collision signal throughout the network. Even if only one of the nodes detects collision, all nodes are informed about it. The programming considerations and hardware design for collision detectors are given in Section 4.3 and Appendix H, respectively. The remaining parts of the collision-network node and their programming are identical to those used for the token-network node.

4.2.3 The Gateway Node

The purpose of a gateway node is to allow for interconnection, via software, between the token-network segment and the collision-network segment. Therefore, the gateway node has to be equipped with two network ports, as shown in Fig. 4.2-3. In addition to ACIA-1 and ACIA-2, the gateway node is equipped with a third data-communications interface, the ACIA-3. The ACIA-2 is assigned to the collision-network port and the ACIA-3 is assigned to the token-network port. The interrupt generated by ACIA-3 is assigned priority level 4. Except for the difference in interrupt priority level for the token network, the organization and operation of both token- and collision-network ports in the gateway node are identical to those for token- and collision-network nodes (Sections 4.2.1 and 4.2.2), respectively.

4.2.4 The Print-server Node

The organization of a print-server node is identical to either a token-network node or a collision-network node. Actually, any node on any network segment can be used as a print-server node. The only difference between a regular network node and the printer node is, as shown in Fig. 4.2-4, the use of a special video terminal equipped with an additional printer port. If a printer is connected to this additional port, all data that is being displayed on the video terminal screen can be simultaneously printed by the printer. This way, hard copies of program listings or network messages can be obtained. If VT101 terminals are used, the additional printer port is also an RS232 port, and any RS232 printer can be used.

4.2.5 The File-server Node

The file-server node consists of two computers: the ECB, in either token- or collision-network organization, and a personal computer with diskette drives, which can be used either as a terminal or for the purpose of program (file) storage or retrieval; see Fig. 4.2-5. Note that if a personal computer were equipped with a printer, then both file- and print-serving functions could be combined in one node. Using operating-system

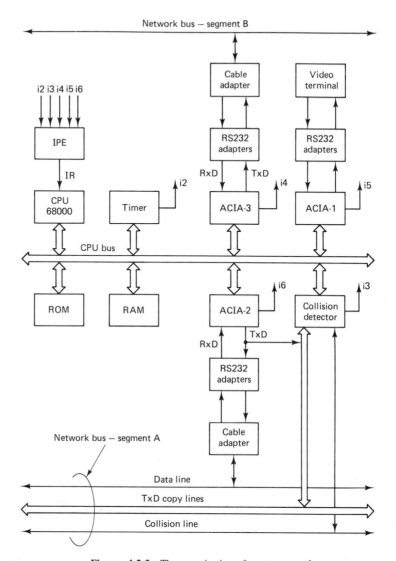

Figure 4.2-3 The organization of a gateway node.

commands and communications software, the personal computer can be switched into the terminal-emulation mode or can be used to store or retrieve data blocks dumped from or to ECB's memory through the terminal port. DEC Rainbow personal computer is used in a node represented in Fig. 4.2-5; however, any personal computer can be used for the file-server function as long as it has an RS232 port, terminal-emulation mode, and data-communication software that can handle files transferred in the S-code format.

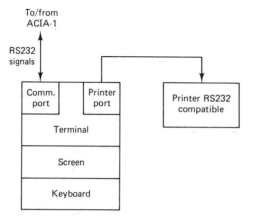

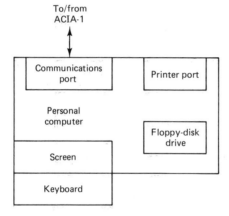

Figure 4.2-4 The video terminal with attached printer.

Figure 4.2-5 File-server node.

4.3 LAN NODE INTERFACES AND PROGRAMMING

In this section, we discuss the interfaces of LANs from the point of view of their
programming characteristics. Also, we define the assembly-code sequences necessary
to initialize and serve these interfaces for proper operation. All discussion refers to the
laboratory nodes implemented using ECB microcomputers; however, most of the concepts apply to the nodes using other microcomputers as well.

4.3.1 The Terminal Interface

The terminal interface is illustrated in Fig. 4.3-1. Its basic element is the MC6850
ACIA integrated circuit (see Appendix G). In ECBs, the terminal interface is named
Port 1, and thus the ACIA in this port is also labeled ACIA-1. The purpose of the

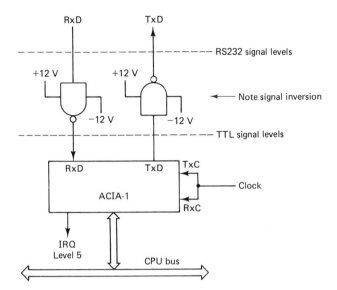

Figure 4.3-1 Terminal interface.

ACIA is to perform parallel to serial data conversion, error checking, and buffering for both data transmission and reception. In addition to the ACIA, the port is equipped with RS232 signal-level adapters, which convert signal levels between TTL logic levels (0 V, 5 V) used by the ACIA and RS232 signal levels (+ 12 V, − 12 V) required on the RS232 interface. In addition to transmit-data (TxD) and receive-data (RxD) signals and their adapters, the terminal port supports other RS232 signals, such as data-carrier-detect (DCD) and request-to-send (RTS) signals. These signals are completely handled by ECB's hardware and thus not discussed here.

Data-transfer rates for the ACIA are determined by the clock signal and an internal, programmable clock divider, which are identical for both data-transfer directions: the transmit clock (TxC) and the receive clock (RxC). On the CPU side, the ACIA-1 interfaces with the CPU bus and can generate an interrupt, which, after priority encoding, represents CPU autovectored interrupt with priority level 5.

The ACIAs have four software-accessible 8-bit registers: a transmit-data register, a receive-data register, a control register, and a status register. For the ACIA-1, the control and status registers are both addressed by $10040, whereas the transmit- and receive-data registers are both addressed by $10042. If a write operation is performed to address $10040 or $10042, then a byte is written to the control- or transmit-data register, respectively. If a read operation is performed from address $10040 or $10042, then a byte is read from status or receive-data register, respectively.

The ACIAs can operate without interrupts, with receive interrupts only, with transmit interrupts only, or with both receive and transmit interrupts. The selection of an operation mode is performed by writing an appropriate code to the control register. When a byte is written to the control register, several aspects of the operation mode are defined simultaneously. In addition to the selection of an interrupt option, data format, parity control, and data rate (clock division ratio) are defined by different bits of a byte written to the control register (Appendix G).

The assembly-code instruction necessary to initialize the ACIA-1 to operate without interrupts follows. This is the normal initialization of Port 1, also performed by the TUTOR firmware whenever the ECB is reset. It initializes the ACIA-1 to operate without interrupts, without parity bit, with 8 data bits plus 1 stop-bit byte frame, and with a 2400 bps data-transfer rate (see Appendix G). The 2400 bps data rate and 8 data bits plus 1 stop-bit byte frame will be used in all laboratory experiments and for all data-communication ports unless stated otherwise.

ACIA-1 control register : = control byte   MOVE.B #$15,$10040
Control byte = $15 means

- Clock divide = 16 (results in 2400 bps),
- Byte format: 8 bits, no parity, 1 stop bit,
- Transmit interrupt disabled
- Receive interrupt disabled

To initialize the ACIA to operate with transmit interrupts enabled and receive interrupts disabled, we have to execute the initialization instruction with control byte equal to $35, where control byte = $35 means

- Clock divide = 16 (results in 2400 bps),
- Byte format: 8 bits, no parity, 1 stop bit,
- Transmit interrupt ennabled
- Receive interrupt disabled

After this initialization, the ACIA generates an interrupt whenever the transmit-data register becomes empty. If the register is empty when this instruction is executed, the ACIA generates an interrupt immediately after the MOVE.B #$35,$10040 instruction. The interrupt request is sustained until a byte is written by the CPU to the transmit-data register.

If initialization is performed with the control byte equal to $95, the ACIA will start operating with transmit interrupts disabled and receive interrupts enabled.

Control byte = $95 means

- Clock divide = 16 (results in 2400 bps)
- Byte format: 8 bits, no parity, 1 stop bit
- Transmit interrupt disabled
- Receive interrupt enabled

After such initialization, the ACIA-1 generates an interrupt whenever the receive-data register becomes full. The interrupt is sustained until a byte is read by the CPU from the receive-data register.

It is possible to enable both transmit and receive interrupts of the ACIA using $B5 as control byte; however, only one interrupt line is available for the ACIA and an interrupt service routine would have to analyze the ACIA's status register to decide which interrupt generating situation really happened. In our experiments, operating modes in which both transmit and receive interrupts are enabled simultaneously are not used.

4.3.2 The Network Interface—Token-Network Node

The network interface for a token-network node is presented in Fig. 4.3-2. The ECB communications port used for network interface is named Port 2, and thus the ACIA-2 is the basic element of network interface. All the discussion of the ACIA operating modes and programming from Section 4.3.1 applies to the ACIA-2 as well, with only difference being that, for ACIA-2, the control and status registers are addressed by $10041 and transmit-data and receive-data registers are addressed by $10043. The only—but important—functional difference between the terminal and the network port appears on the RS232 signal-level side, where TxD and RxD lines are logically connected. As a result, whatever is being transmitted by the ACIA-2 is also automatically received. The TxD and RxD lines have to be logically connected to ensure the bidirectional data line for the network bus. Therefore, in addition to initializations pre-

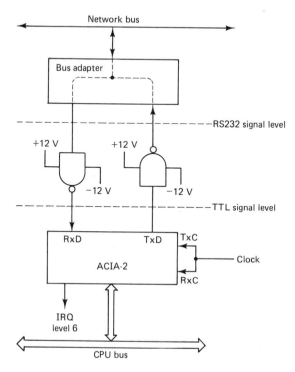

Figure 4.3-2 Network interface for token network node.

sented in Section 4.3.1, more control bytes have to be written to the ACIA-2 control register to ensure correct operation of the network interface.

The unidirectional TxD and RxD signal lines on the RS232 original level are connected to the bidirectional network bus via a bus adapter. An example circuit for the bus adapter, appropriate for the ECB network ports, is shown in Fig. 4.3-3.

When the ACIA-2 is initialized with transmit interrupts enabled, the initialization is the same as for the ACIA-1. However, when ACIA-2 is initialized with receive interrupts enabled, it has to be reset first to clear any pending interrupts. The resetting of the ACIA is done by writing a control byte equal to $03 to the control register immediately before writing a control byte $95.

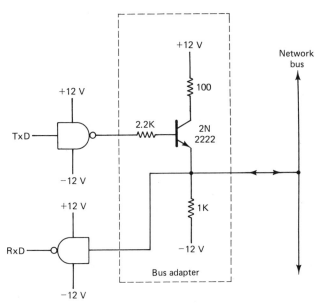

Figure 4.3-3 Network port bus adapter.

Another very important situation occurs when switching from transmit-interrupts-enabled to receive-interrupts-enabled mode during node operation. In addition to transmit-data and receive-data registers, the ACIA's are equipped with transmit-shift and receive-shift registers (see Appendix G). Thus the ACIAs can buffer 4 bytes at a time—2 bytes to be transmitted and 2 bytes recently received. If a node transmits a string of bytes—for example a data packet—to the network, at the time when the last byte of string is written to the transmit-data register, all four buffer registers are full. The transmit registers contain last 2 bytes of the packet, and therefore the ACIA should not be reset until the bytes are serially output to the network. The receive registers contain meaningless bytes received unintentionally during transmission. Furthermore, 2 more bytes will arrive—the last 2 that will be transmitted. If the receive interrupts are enabled immediately after the last byte of a transmitted packet is written to a transmit-data register, four unnecessary receive interrupts are generated.

To avoid this problem, the following sequence should be executed before switching to the receive-interrupts-enabled mode:

```
WAIT1    BTST.B    #0,$10041
         BEQ       WAIT1
         MOVE.B    $10043,Rn
WAIT2    BTST.B    #0,$10041
         BEQ       WAIT2
         MOVE.B    $10043,Rn
WAIT3    BTST.B    #0,$10041
         BEQ       WAIT3
         MOVE.B    $10043,Rn
```

This sequence clears receive registers of ''trash'' data, and by the time this sequence ends, both receive and transmit registers are empty. If receive interrupts are enabled at this moment, the first interrupt is generated only after the first meaningful byte is received from the network.

4.3.3 Network Interface for Collision-Network Node

The network interface for collision-network nodes is shown in Fig. 4.3-4. In addition to ACIA-2 and associated signal-level and bus adapters, it is equipped with a collision detector. Programming of the ACIA-2 for this interface is identical to the token-network node. Therefore, we concentrate here only on the operation and programming of the collision detector.

The collision detector is a combinational logic with no memory as shown in Fig. 4.3-5. It has one input for every node on the network and only one output: C. The output of the collision detector is in state 0 (low) whenever a collision situation occurs on the network. A collision situation happens whenever two or more nodes are transmitting to the network simultaneously. In asynchronous communication, the idle state of the data line as well as a bit equal to 1 are marked by 1 (high). Therefore, the only possibility is to declare a collision whenever two or more nodes are transmitting a 0 (low) to the network at the same time. Thus the output of the collision detector is low whenever two or more of its inputs are low. The C signal is wire ORed on the collision line. Therefore, if any node detects a collision, the collision line will be low in all nodes. The collision line is connected to the handshaking signal 3 (H3) input of the

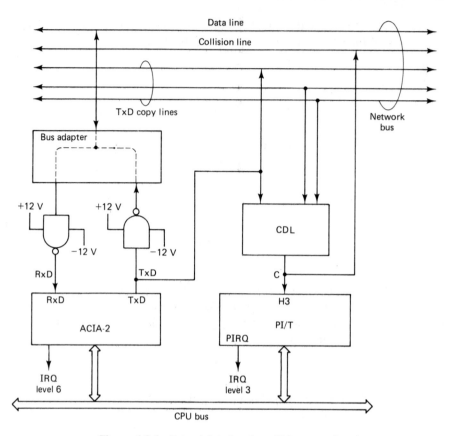

Figure 4.3-4 Network interface for collision network nodes.

parallel interface and timer (PI/T) integrated circuit (Appendix H). If the PI/T is initialized properly, the transition of the H3 line from 1 to 0 will result in an interrupt, which is connected to the CPU as a nonautovectored interrupt with priority level 3.

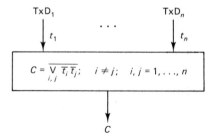

Figure 4.3-5 Collision-detection logic.

The initialization sequence enabling the collision interrupts is as follows:

PIVR := $42	- Define PIRQ vector number
$108 := collision vector	- Vector number = $42 → vector address = $108
PGCR := $20	- Mode 00, H3 enabled, H3 active low
PSRR := $18	- PIRQ and PIACK pins active,
PSR := $04	- Clear H3S bit, that is, clear pending interrupt
PBCR := $82	- PortB submode 1x, H3 service request enable, that is, enable-collision interrupt

where

PIVR	Port interrupt vector register	Addressed by $1000B
PGCR	Port general control register	Addressed by $10001
PSRR	Port service request register	Addressed by $10003
PSR	Port status register	Addressed by $1001B
PBCR	Port B control register	Addressed by $1000F

The assembly-language equivalent of this initialization sequence is as follows:

```
MOVE.B      #$42,$1000B
MOVE.L      #vector,$108
MOVE.B      #$20,$10001
MOVE.B      #$18,$10003
MOVE.B      #$04,$1001B
MOVE.B      #$82,$1000F
```

Whenever a collision interrupt request happens, it should be cleared by executing the following instruction:

```
MOVE.B      #$04,$1001B      Clear H3S bit.
```

The method for connecting the collision detectors and TTL level TxD signals to the multiwire network bus is shown in Fig. 4.3-6. Assuming that there are N nodes on the collision-network segment, N wires will be used for TTL level TxD signals. Each node has to have its own wire. The most regular interconnection shown in Fig. 4.3-6 assumes th... all collision detectors are connected to N wires in parallel and at each ith node the TxD line is connected to the ith wire.

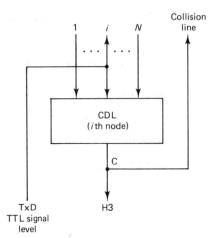

Figure 4.3-6 Collision network cable interconnections.

4.3.4 Programmable Timer

The programmable timer does not perform any data-communication interface role; however, it has to be initialized and served in a way similar to communication interfaces. The timer is shown in Fig. 4.3-7. Its operation is synchronous with CPU clock. The timer can be programmed and tested, and it can generate level 2 nonautovectored interrupt. The timer is ECBs is a part of the PI/T device (Appendix H). The ECBs timer has three 8-bit preload registers, which are used as one 24-bit counting register during the timer's operation. Timer interrupt is generated when its count reaches 0. To start

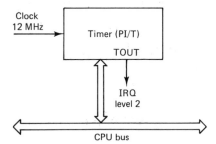

Figure 4.3-7 ECB's programmable timer.

the timer and enable its interrupt, the following sequence of instructions has to be executed:

MOVE.B #$40, $10023	Load timer-interrupt vector number
MOVE.L #vector, $100	Vector number = $40 → vector address = $100
MOVE.B #N1, $10027	Load timer preload register, most sign. byte

MOVE.B #N2, $10029   Load timer preload register, middle byte

MOVE.B #N3, $1002B   Load timer preload register, least sign.
                            byte

MOVE.B #$A1, $10021   Select operation mode and start timer

Whenever a timer interrupt request happens, it should be cleared by executing the following instruction:

MOVE.B #$A0, $10021   Stop timer

As long as this instruction is not executed, the timer continuously requests interrupt service.

5

Laboratory

Experiments

The experiments are designed to utilize the material presented in this book; however, no additional experience in local networking is necessary. The presentation style and level of detail assume reader's ability to analyze structured algorithms represented in Pascal-like pseudocode and an understanding of interrupt mechanisms and programmable interface ports.

Local networking concepts as well as the specifics of the laboratory network are introduced step by step, starting with simple experiments and progressing toward more complicated ones. The first experiments introduce elementary methods of microcomputer programming for data communication and fundamental concepts of local networking, such as addressed frames, bus broadcast, bidirectional data transfers, and multilayer design. The last two experiments represent complete, though limited, implementations of two types of local networks: one based on CSMA/CD channel access scheme, and the other based on token-bus scheme. Networking and node programming concepts as well as subroutines introduced in simpler experiments are incorporated in later experiments. For example, interlayer interface and the application layer, which are defined in experiments 3 and 4, are used without change in experiments 5 to 10. Thus step by step, the modules of network protocol software are developed and finally integrated in the last two experiments.

Experiments 1 and 2 introduce elementary data communication and programming concepts such as network- and terminal-port programming, port status and interrupts, data-byte frame formats and data-transmission rate. Multiple-byte frames and front- and end-frame delimiters are also introduced. The first two experiments deal with fundamentals of data communication using RS232 asynchronous serial ports and related programming techniques and experiment 3 introduces fundamental networking concepts of multilayer protocol design, interlayer interface, and bidirectional data transfers. Experiment 4, the last general experiment, explains frame addressing.

Experiments 5, 7, and 9 deal with a protocol based on a CSMA/CD channel-access scheme. CSMA technique is explained in experiment 5 and collision detection is introduced in experiment 7. Both concepts are integrated in experiment 9 to create full CSMA/CD network. Experiments 6, 8, and 10 explain the operation of a token-bus network. Token-passing technique is introduced in experiment 6, while token recovery and logical-ring reconfiguration are illustrated in experiment 8. Finally, the concepts and modules developed in experiments 6 and 8 are used in experiment 10 to develop a complete token-bus network.

Not all of OSI protocol layers are illustrated in the laboratory experiments (Fig. 5-1). To limit their complexity to a size manageable within a one-term course, the LAN protocols consist of three layers: the physical layer, the network layer (NL), and the application layer (AL). The physical layer certainly has to be used because it is the only real interconnection between network nodes. Without it, there could be no network. To make experiments meaningful, an AL has to be implemented to illustrate the creation and consumption of messages, the very reason why computer networks are used.

The NL in the experiment protocols deals primarily with channel-access schemes belonging to data-link layer according to OSI recommendation. The term DL layer is thus appropriate. However, the part of the protocol called the NL in the experiments interfaces with the physical layer on one side and the AL on the other. It is the only part

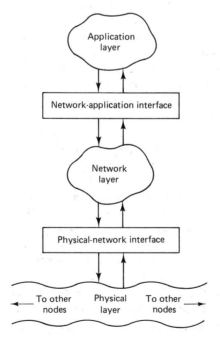

Figure 5-1 Laboratory network-node layers and interlayer interfaces.

that solves all networking problems. Therefore, the name *network layer* seems more appropriate.

   With three layers, there are two interlayer interfaces. All messages in the experiments are of the text type, variable in size but limited to one-line (80-character) strings. Also, only one packet per message is used, so that the problems of message partition or reconfiguration are not illustrated. As a result, the interface between the AL and NL consists of two one-packet (one-message) buffers—one for each data-transfer direction—buffer pointers, and associated control-status flags.

   Data communication over the network bus is supported in the laboratory nodes by the ACIAs. These devices are capable of byte buffering, formatting, and error detection. Therefore, to an extent, they perform functions assigned by the OSI recommendation model to the data-link layer. The boundary at which the physical layer begins is the external side (input and output) of the ACIAs. This definition is chosen because other microcomputers that use different (not ACIA) devices but still support the RS232 standard could be used as well. Such an approach would require an additional layer defining the functions performed by ACIAs.

   For clarity, in all experiments, we assume that ACIAs belong to the physical layer and the physical-network interlayer interface consists of ACIAs data and control-status registers.

5.1. LAB 1—ASYNCHRONOUS BYTE TRANSFERS

5.1.1. Purpose

The first experiment concentrates on elementary issues related to the use of terminal and network ports and asynchonous data transmission. Both status-polling and interrupt techniques are used to process terminal and network I/O. From the data-communication point of view, Lab 1 implements one-directional, point-to-point data transfers with the data frame limited to 1 byte. Also, no frame addressing is implemented.

   In summary, the main topics illustrated by Lab 1 are as follows:

Programming concepts

- Polled I/O, port status, and control registers
- Interrupts, vectors, and priority levels

Communication concepts

- Simplex-data transfer
- Data transmitter and receiver
- Data-transmission rate

- Implications of bus topology
- Broadcast of transmitted data

After this experiment you should be able to use both terminal and network ports in further programs.

5.1.2. Equipment

Lab 1 requires at least three network nodes, each equipped with a terminal and each allowing for changes in the data-transmission rate at both network and terminal ports. The nodes used in Lab 1 have to be connected by the local network bus at network ports. The same equipment is necessary for all the following laboratory experiments. Therefore, this section is not repeated in the descriptions of Labs 2–10. The only variation to this rule is that collision-related experiments require the use of LAN nodes equipped with collision detectors, whereas token-related experiments can be performed on nodes either equipped with collision detectors or not.

5.1.3. Node Operation

Two types of network nodes are used in Lab 1: transmitter and receiver. The transmitter node should directly and unconditionally transmit all characters entered from its keyboard. The receiver node should accept every character appearing on the network bus and display it on its screen. If we consider a transmitter-receiver pair of nodes, the overall operation should be as follows: Each character entered at the transmitter's keyboard should appear, after a transmission delay, at the receiver's screen.

Additionally, characters entered at the transmitter's keyboard should be also displayed (echoed) on the transmitter's screen to make it possible for transmitter's operator to view the text being entered. Since all bytes entered are to be transmitted immediately, there is no possibility to erase or replace a character once a key on the keyboard is pressed.

If one transmitter and two or more receivers are operating at the same time, all characters sent to the network bus appear simultaneously on the screens of both receivers. If two or more transmitters operate at the same time, there is a possibility of collisions, for example, two transmitters outputting byte frames to the bus at the same moment. If this happens, electrical signals on the bus interact, and, as a result, the receiver(s) receive distorted information. This case is illustrated in Fig. 2.1-5.

5.1.4. Algorithm Design

The algorithms for the transmitter and receiver nodes are designed separately, using the concept of a state machine. Algorithm details are expressed using pseudocode notation. As a final implementation, assembly-language programs that run on ECBs are given in Appendix I. First, the algorithm for transmitter node is discussed; then, using the same design approach, the algorithm for the receiver node is explained.

Algorithm for transmitter node: The state diagram and state transition table are created first. There are three recognizable states in transmitter's operation (Fig. 5.1-1): idle, input, and send. In the idle state, the transmitter waits for a character to be input (a key on the keyboard pressed) and performs no other functions. When an operator presses the key on the keyboard, the transmitter inputs the ASCII code representing the pressed key from terminal port. This operation is performed in the input state. Once the ASCII code (a byte) has been inputted, the transmitter immediately sends this code to network bus. The transmitter outputs a byte by writing it to the network port. This operation is accomplished in the send state. After the byte has been written to the network port, the transmitter returns to the idle state to wait for the next byte from keyboard.

Reasons for state transitions are summarized in Fig. 5.1-2.

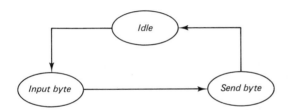

Figure 5.1-1   State diagram for the transmitter node.

FIGURE 5.1-2.   STATE-TRANSITION TABLE (TRANSMITTER).

Current state	Next state	Reason for state change
Idle	*Input*	Terminal port interrupt, new byte
Input	*Send*	Byte inputted from terminal, s keyboard
Send	*Idle*	Byte sent to network

Algorithm for the receiver node: The algorithm for the receiver node is designed using the same approach as in the case of transmitter. First, the three states of the receiver node are related in the state diagram (see Fig. 5.1-3). In the idle state, the receiver waits for a new byte to arrive from the network bus (at the network port) and performs no other function. When a byte arrives, it is received (read from network port) and immediately displayed on the receiver terminal's screen.

State transitions for the receiver node are defined in the state-transition table in Fig. 5.1-4.

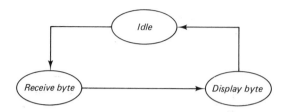

Figure 5.1-3 State diagram for the receiver node.

FIGURE 5.1-4 STATE-TRANSITON TABLE (RECEIVER).

Current state	Next state	Reason for state change
Idle	*Receive*	Network port interrupt, new byte
Receive	*Display*	Byte inputted from network port
Display	*Idle*	Byte written to terminal port

5.1.5. Algorithm Implementation

The state machine for transmitter node as defined by the state diagram (Fig. 5.1-1) and state-transition table (Fig. 5.1-2) is implemented in software. Both interrupt and status-polling techniques are used for port I/O. The algorithm for transmitter's software consists of a main segment and subroutines, one of them invoked by the terminal-port interrupt.

The Main segment of the algorithm is given in Fig. 5.1-5. The program is assumed to run as a user program, that is, the CPU is in the user state while executing the Main segment. Since interrupt and subroutines are used, there is a need to initialize the stack pointer before interrupts are enabled and before any subroutine is invoked. In this experiment no subroutine is called from the Main segment; the only subroutine calls occur from the Terminal interrupt-service routine (Tisr), which is invoked by the terminal-port interrupt. Therefore, in this experiment, only the supervisor stack is used. All further experiments require the use of both supervisor and user stacks.

The Main segment initializes the stack pointer first. Then, it initializes the vector for terminal-port interrupt. This vector points to the Tisr. The location of the vector in system's memory is defined by the priority level assigned to the terminal port because the communications ports (ACIAs) cannot generate their own vector numbers, and therefore the CPU has to use autovectoring.

Next, the Main has to program the terminal and network ports, that is, select data-transmission rates, byte frames, and enable or disable port interrupts. Terminal-port receive interrupts are enabled and all interrupts at the network port are disabled. The terminal port generates an interrupt every time it receives a byte from terminal's keyboard. Byte frames have to be selected for both terminal and network ports. The byte frame for the terminal port has to be compatible with the one used by the terminal itself. As for the network port, byte frames used by both transmitter and receiver have

```
Main

var
  byte : character
begin
  initialize stack pointers  (* for both user and supervisor stacks *)
  initialize vector for Tport interrupt
  initialize Tport           (* data rate, byte frame, enable      *)
                             (* receive interrupts                 *)
  initialize Nport           (* data rate, byte frame, disable     *)
                             (* interrupts                         *)
  enter user state and enable CPU interrupts
  repeat
    idle                     (* "do nothing" loop                  *)
  until reset
end.
```

Figure 5.1-5 Main segment of transmitter's algorithm.

to be identical. Otherwise, the receiver would be unable to accept frames sent to the network bus by the transmitter. For the purpose of Lab 1, we experiment with different byte frames; however, only the 8-bit, no-parity frames will be used in all remaining experiments.

After initializing the stack pointer, the interrupt vector, and the ports, the Main segment enables CPU interrupts, changes CPU state to the user state, and enters the idle loop.

The terminal-port interrupt-service routine (Tisr), which is invoked every time a key is pressed on terminal's keyboard, is described in Fig. 5.1-6. The CPU enters Tisr as a result of a terminal-port interrupt, which is generated by the ACIA whenever it receives a byte from terminal. First, the input from terminal port has to be performed. The interrupt request is cleared by the ACIA when a read byte from terminal-port operation is performed by the CPU. The ACIAs have the capability to detect several types of data transfer errors (see Appendix G). Therefore, the Tisr checks the status register of the terminal port, and a received byte is accepted only if there are no errors. If there are any errors detected, the byte is discarded. Even in this case, the byte has to be read from the terminal port to clear the port-interrupt request.

Note that whenever interrupt invoked routines are used, the CPU registers must be protected from any undesirable modification by the routine. This is achieved by saving them on stack (save context statement in pseudocode algorithms). At the end of the routine, the CPU registers are restored from the stack (restore context). It is extremely important to protect the registers if algorithms are implemented in a high level

```
Tisr                       (* invoked by Tport interrupt       *)

save context               (* save CPU registers on stack      *)
input byte from Tport      (* byte := Tport                    *)
if status OK then          (* otherwise disregard the byte     *)
  Send_byte
  Display_byte
endif
restore context            (* restore CPU registers from stack *)
return.                    (* return from exception            *)
```

Figure 5.1-6 Terminal interrupt-service routine.

language where the programmer has no control over the use of CPU registers. In assembly language, only the registers actually modified within a routine must be protected (see Appendix I).

If the byte is accepted (status OK), the Tisr routine calls two subroutines. First, Send_byte is called to output the just-input byte to the network port. Then, the Display_byte is called to echo the character to the terminal's screen. After that, the Tisr returns; that is the CPU continues in the idle loop.

The purpose of the Send_byte routine (Fig. 5.1-7) is to output one byte of data to the network port. To avoid a possibility of writing the next byte to the network port before a previous one is transmitted, the routine first tests the status register to determine whether the network port ACIA is ready to accept the next byte for output. If not, the CPU remains in Send_byte routine, polling the ACIA's status register until the network port becomes ready for output. When this happens, the CPU writes a byte to the network port and returns from the subroutine without waiting for the end of the transmission.

```
Send_byte

wait until Nport ready for output
Nport := byte
return.
```

Figure 5.1-7 Algorithm for the Send _ byte routine.

The Display_byte routine (Fig. 5.1-8) operates analogously to the Send_byte, the only difference being that the terminal port instead of the network port is used. Please recall that terminal-port interrupts are used in this experiment, but only the receive interrupts are enabled for the terminal port ACIA. Therefore, all outputs to the terminal port have to use the status-polling technique as is the case for network port in the Send_byte routine.

Algorithms for the Main segment and routines for the receiver node are given in Figs. 5.1-8, 5.1-9, and 5.1-10. The Main segment (Fig. 5.1-9) is very similar to that for the transmitter node; however, this time the network port has receive interrupts enabled, whereas all interrupts are disabled for the terminal port. The network port-interrupt vector has to be initialized to point to the network-port interrupt-service routine (Nisr, Fig. 5.1-10).

The network-port interrupt-service routine (Nisr) inputs a byte from the network port and, if no errors are found, the Display_byte routine—identical to the one used in the transmitter algorithm (Fig. 5.1-8)—is used to display the received byte on the screen.

The assembly-language programs for transmitter and receiver nodes are given in Appendix I. The programs are written for laboratory network nodes based on ECB microcomputers, as described in Chapter 4.

```
Display_byte

wait until Tport ready for output
Tport := byte
return.
```

Figure 5.1-8 Algorithm for the Display_byte routine.

```
Main

var
  byte,Tport,Nport
begin
  initialize stack pointers  (* both for supervisor and user stacks *)
  initialize vector for Nport interrupt
  initialize Tport           (* data rate, byte frame, disable port *)
                             (* interrupts                          *)
  initialize Nport           (* data rate, byte frame, enable       *)
                             (* receive interrupts                  *)
  enter user state and enable CPU interrupts
  repeat
    idle                     (* "do nothing" loop                   *)
  until reset
end.
```

Figure 5.1-9   Main segment of the algorithm for receiver node.

```
Nisr                    (* invoked by Nport interrupt      *)

save context            (* save CPU regeisters on stack    *)
input byte from Nport
if status OK then       (* otherwise, disregard the byte   *)
  Display_byte
endif
restore context         (* restore CPU registers from stack *)
return.
```

Figure 5.1-10   Network-port interrupt routine.

5.1.6 Demonstrations

1. Type and send a one-line text from transmitter node to the receiver node.
   - Use different byte frames for the transmitter and receiver.
   - Use a different data-transmission rate for the transmitter and receiver.
   - Use 9600 bps for terminal ports and 50 bps for network ports.
   - Use 50 bps for terminal ports and 9600 bps for network ports.
   - Type and send a multiline text.

2. Use three nodes on the network and demonstrate properties of bus topology (broadcast, contention, and collision).
   - Use one transmitter and two receivers (broadcast).
   - Use two transmitters and one receiver (contention).
   - Using a 50-bps network, try to create collisions (two transmitters, one receiver).

5.1.7 Problems

1. In this experiment, all characters entered at transmitter's keyboard are unconditionally transmitted to the network bus. The receiver accepts all bytes from the bus and displays characters represented by received bytes on its screen. As a result, if more than one line of text is to be sent, both carriage return (CR) and line feed (LF) charac-

ters have to be typed at the transmitter between strings of characters representing the transmitted text. If only the CR were typed, the characters following it would appear on the receiver's (and on the transmitter's) screen on the same line as the characters of the previous line. This forces the human operator to remember about the LF character. Rewrite your program to make it automatically append the LF character after every CR character. Do you have to change programs for both transmitter and receiver?

2. It is possible that errors occur during data transmission over the network bus. Modify your program to detect errors and do the following.

   (a) Reject characters received with errors.

   (b) Display * character in place of characters received with errors.

   (c) Depending on the type of error, display 'wrong byte format' or 'parity error' text.

3. Is it possible, by analyzing transmission errors at the receiving node, to determine whether a collision occurred?

5.2 LAB 2—DATA-FRAME TRANSFERS

5.2.1. Purpose

The major topic of this experiment relates to the multiple-byte frame transfers between transmitter and receiver nodes. As in Lab 1, only one-directional data transfers are considered. Data frames are formatted and buffered both at the transmitter node and at the receiver node. Both terminal and network ports are served exclusively by interrupt-driven routines.

Topics illustrated by Lab 2 are as follows:

Programming concepts

- Interrupt-invoked device drivers
- I/O buffering

Communications concepts

- Multiple-byte data frame transfers
- Frame delimiters
- Frame buffering
- Frame formatting

This experiment should clarify programming techniques referring to interrupt-invoked port drivers and frame formatting and buffering.

5.2.2. *Operation*

The multiple-byte frame (referred to as *frame*) is first inputted from the transmitter's keyboard. The CR signifies the end of frame input. At this moment, the transmitter starts sending the frame, byte after byte, to the network bus. The receiver accepts the frame as a string of bytes arriving from the network bus. When the terminating character is received, the frame is displayed as a string of characters on the receiver's screen.

To allow the receiver to recognize both the beginning and the end of data frame, all frames are composed by transmitter according to the frame format:

PRE , . . . data . . . , EOT

Preamble (PRE) is a front delimiter and end of transmission (EOT) is an end delimiter. The PRE byte used is an all-zero byte, that is, all bits are zeros. This type of front delimiter is used because of the properties of the collision detector, as described in Chapter 4. The PRE byte should never be included in the data field of any frame. The arrival of the PRE byte is always regarded by the receiver as a beginning of a new frame transfer.

The EOT delimiter always marks the end of a data frame. Therefore, it also should never be included in the data field. The binary code used for the EOT byte equals the ASCII code for the EOT, that is, $04.

In this experiment, as in all following experiments, data messages will be in the form of strings of characters. For each message, one data frame will be used. The character strings are limited in size to one line, that is, to 80 characters. During message input, the CR key will be used to terminate the message. To provide for clarity of messages on terminal screens both during frame input and display, the last two characters of the data field will always be the ASCII codes for CR and LF. Therefore, the frame conveying a data message will always have the format:

PRE , character string , CR , LF , EOT

Again, CR and LF should not be used in the character string.

If one transmitter and two receivers are operating on the network, both receivers simultaneously receive data frames sent to the network bus by the transmitter. However, if there are two transmitters, message input at transmitter nodes can occur simultaneously without any interaction. As long as the transmissions occur at different times, the two transmitters do not disturb each other. Should message inputs end at the same moment in both transmitters, they start sending their frames to the network bus at the same time and both frames are distorted (see Fig. 2.1-5). In this lab both cases are demonstrated.

5.2.3. Algorithm Design

Algorithms for transmitter and receiver nodes are again designed separately. First, the transmitter's algorithm is considered. As was the case in Lab 1, the transmitter has three states: *ready, input frame,* and *send frame* (Fig. 5.2-1). In the *ready* state, the transmitter node waits for first character to arrive from the keyboard (the first key pressed). The difference between the *ready* state here and the idle state in Lab 1 is that a character from the keyboard is regarded as the first one only if it arrives when transmitter node is in the *ready* state. All characters from the keyboard arriving while the node is in the *input frame* state are considered to be next characters in the frame. All characters arriving in the *send frame* state are neglected.

The arrival of a character from the keyboard while the node is in the *ready* state signifies the beginning of the frame input. The transmitter state is changed to the *input frame* state. In this state all characters arriving from the keyboard are accepted and saved in the frame buffer. Also, each arriving character is compared with ASCII code representing the CR key. The arrival of the CR character marks the end of frame input. To satisfy the requirements of the frame format, LF and EOT characters are appended to the frame buffer after the CR character. Next, the transmitter's state is changed to the *send frame* state and data-frame output to the network begins.

In the *send frame* state, the transmitter outputs consecutive bytes from the frame buffer to the network port until all of them are outputted. During this time, no new characters arriving from the keyboard should be written to the frame buffer because this would distort the original frame, which is still being used. Therefore, all characters arriving from the keyboard in the *send frame* state are neglected. When all bytes of the frame have been outputted, transmitter's state is changed to *ready*. Reasons for state changes are summarized in state-transition table given in Fig. 5.2-2.

To design the algorithm for the receiver node, we use the same approach as we used for the transmitter node. First, the state diagram for the receiver node is constructed, as in Fig. 5.2-3. The receiver can assume one of three states: *ready, receive frame,* and *display frame.* The reasons for state changes are defined in Fig. 5.2-4.

When the receiver node is started, it assumes the *ready* state, in which it awaits the first byte of a data frame from the network. The byte expected is the PRE byte. Should any other byte arrive from the network while the receiver remains in the *ready*

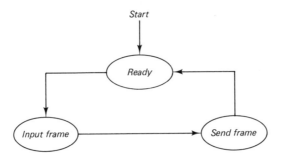

Figure 5.2-1 Transmitter's state diagram.

FIGURE 5.2-2 STATE-TRANSITION TABLE (TRANSMITTER).

Current state	Next state	Reason for state change
Ready	*Input frame*	Terminal port interrupt, new byte from keyboard (first byte of frame)
Input frame	*Send frame*	Last byte of frame (CR) inputted from terminal's keyboard
Send frame	Ready	Last byte of frame sent to newtork

state, such a byte will be ignored. When the PRE byte is received, the receiver's state changes to the *receive frame* state.

In the *receive frame* state, the receiver accepts every byte arriving from the network until the EOT byte is received. All accepted bytes are saved in the frame buffer (except for the PRE and EOT bytes), and at the moment when the EOT is received, the data contained in the frame buffer is ready to be displayed on the receiver's screen. Therefore, as soon as the EOT is received, the receiver node changes its state to the *display frame* state.

In the *display frame* state, consecutive bytes from the frame buffer are written to the terminal port and displayed on terminal's screen. After the last byte from the frame buffer has been outputted to the terminal port, the receiver's state changes to *ready*, and a new data frame is awaited.

Note that while a frame is being displayed, nothing should be written to the frame buffer. Otherwise, its original contents would be modified and previous data lost. Therefore, for as long as it takes to display a frame, the receiver is unable to accept any new bytes from the network. Specifically, while a previous frame is being displayed, a new frame transmission may be initiated by some transmitter on the network. As a result, the first bytes of this frame may be neglected by the receiver. Then, it may happen that the receiver returns to the *ready* state while a transmitter is still continuing the frame transmission. Now, the receiver is ready, but the frame is not

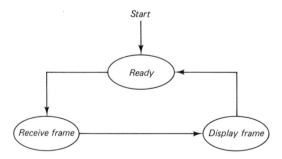

Figure 5.2-3 State diagram for the receiver node.

FIGURE 5.2-4   STATE-TRANSITION TABLE (RECEIVER).

Current state	Next state	Reason for state change
Ready	*Receive frame*	Network port interrupt, first byte of frame (PRE) received
Receive frame	*Display frame*	Complete frame accepted, last byte of frame (EOT) received
Display frame	*Ready*	Complete frame displayed, last byte (LF) written to terminal port

accepted because the PRE byte has already been transmitted by the transmitter and neglected by the receiver. Recall that in the *ready* state, all bytes arriving from the network, except for the PRE byte, are neglected.

5.2.4. Algorithm Implementation

To implement the state machine defined in Figs. 5.2-1 and 5.2-2, we will design a program consisting principally of Main segment and two interrupt invoked routines (Fig. 5.2-5). The Tisr is invoked by the terminal-port (Tport) interrupt whenever a new key is pressed on the terminal keyboard (this results in a new byte arrival at Tport). The Nisr is invoked by the network-port (Nport) interrupt whenever the Nport's transmit data register becomes empty. Since the transmit-only operation of a node is considered here, the Tport ACIA has only its receive interrupts enabled. For as long as there is no frame to be transferred, all interrupts of the Nport ACIA remain disabled. Transmit interrupts of the Nport's ACIA are enabled when a frame input from the keyboard is completed and disabled after the last byte of frame has been written to Nport for transmission.

The program-flow diagram in Fig. 5.2-5 is very similar in its form to the state diagram of Fig. 5.2-1. It is important to realize the conceptual difference between the two diagrams. The transmitter node remains in the *input frame* state for a long time (as long as it takes to key in the text of frame). The program (or the CPU) will remain in the Tisr routine for the very short time necessary to process 1 byte arriving from terminal's keyboard.

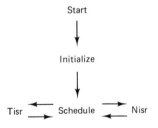

Figure 5.2-5 Program-flow diagram for the transmitter node.

The other important part of the transmitter's software is the data structure (Fig. 5.2-6) used for frame buffering and program control. The frame buffer is constructed as an array in RAM memory defined by its origin (absolute address of the first byte). The access to the frame buffer is controlled by two pointers, one pointing to the next location and a second pointing to the end of the buffer. The location of the frame buffer in memory does not change, and therefore the origin of frame buffer has constant value. The size of a data frame can vary (within a one-line limit) and, as a result, the value of the pointer pointing to the end of buffer changes from frame to frame.

In addition to the buffer pointers, two flags (located in RAM memory as logical variables) are used to control access to the frame buffer. The send frame (SF) flag is used to inform the Main program (scheduler loop) that a frame input has been completed. The *busy sending* (BYS) flag is used to inform the scheduler that a frame from the frame buffer is in the process of being transmitted to the network. If we consider the buffer-ownership concept, the frame buffer is owned by the Tisr routine when both SF and BYS flags are zeros. As long as this is true, the Tisr can write to the buffer. At the end of frame input (CR), the Tisr routine sets the SF flag to 1, which essentially is the request to send the frame to the network. The buffer is now owned by the scheduler. When the scheduler detects that SF is set, it clears the SF frame, sets the BYS flag, and enables transmit interrupts at the network port. This transfers buffer ownership to the Nisr routine and invokes the Nisr for the first time. (Since no bytes have been written to the Nport recently, the Nport ACIA has an empty transmit-data register and immediately generates an interrupt.) The ownership is transferred back to the Tisr routine by the Nisr routine when the last byte of frame is written to Nport. The *busy inputting* (BYI) and BYS flags can be regarded as state-encoding information, as shown in Fig. 5.2-7.

The details of the operation of the transmitter node are presented using a pseudocode description of the algorithm. First, the Main segment of the algorithm is given in Fig. 5.2-8. After initializing the CPU's stack pointers, the Main segment initializes buffer-controlling data. The SF and BYS flags are cleared. The first byte of the frame always contains the PRE. The PRE is loaded into the first byte of the buffer during initialization and is never changed during the operation of the transmitter node.

At the time of transmitter-node start-up, when the initialization is performed, the buffer is empty, and the expected buffer-related operation is data input. Data is inputted to the buffer from terminal's keyboard. The ASCII code of the first key pressed should be placed in the second, not the first, location in the buffer because the first location is occupied by the PRE byte. Therefore, the *bufnxt* pointer is initialized to point to the second byte of the buffer.

buforg →	PRE	bufnxt
	•	
	•	bufend
	•	
	CR	SF
	LF	
	EOT	BYS

Figure 5.2-6 Data structure for the transmitter-node software.

FIGURE 5.2-7 STATE ENCODING
FOR THE TRANSMITTER NODE.

State	BYI	BYS
Ready	0	0
Input frame	1	0
Send frame	0	1

Next, terminal and network ports are initialized. We initialize both of them to operate with the same data rate and same byte frames. The terminal port is initialized to operate with receive interrupts enabled. For the network port, all interrupts initially are disabled. Network port is used only for transmission in this experiment; however, transmit interrupts are enabled for the Nport only after a frame has been inputted from keyboard into the frame buffer.

Even though only terminal-port interrupts are initially enabled, interrupt vectors for both terminal and network ports have to be defined during the initialization. Recall that an interrupt vector is nothing but the value of the absolute address of the beginning of the interrupt service routine.

After these initializations, the CPU's interrupts are enabled, the CPU's state is changed to the *user* state, and the scheduling loop of the main segment begins. The purpose of the scheduling loop is to keep testing the status of the frame buffer and, if

```
Main

const
  CR,NL,PRE,EOT : character
  buforg : integer
var
  SF,BYS : logical
  bufnxt, bufend : pointer
  byte : character
begin
  initialize stack pointers
  SF:=0                   (* clear 'send frame' flag                *)
  BYS:=0                  (* clear 'busy sending' flag              *)
  buforg^:=PRE            (* load 'preamble byte' into the buffer   *)
  bufnxt:=buforg+1        (* initialize buffer pointer              *)
  initialize vector for Nport interrupt
  initialize vector for Tport interrupt
  initialize Nport    (* data rate, byte frame, disable interrupts *)
  initialize Tport    (* data rate, byte frame, enable receive     *)
                      (* interrupts                                *)
  enable interrupts   (* and enter user state                      *)
  repeat              (* schedule                                  *)
    if SF=1 then      (* if new frame input completed              *)
      Start_send_frame (* initialize frame transmission            *)
      SF:=0           (* clear the 'send frame' flag               *)
    endif
  until reset
end.
```

Figure 5.2-8 Main segment of the transmitter's algorithm.

necessary, to initialize the frame transmission. The frame transmission is initialized by the Start_send_frame routine defined in Fig. 5.2-9. This routine should be invoked only after the frame input from the terminal has been completed, that is, after the SF flag is found to be set. Also, it should be invoked only once after each frame input. Therefore, once the frame transmission has been initialized, the SF flag is cleared.

```
Start_send_frame

bufnxt:=buforg
BYS:=1
enable transmit interrupts at Nport
return.
```
                                                                Figure 5.2-9   Start_send_frame routine.

The algorithm for the Start_send_frame routine is given in Fig. 5.2-9. First, the BYS flag is set to inform other routines, specifically the terminal input routine, that the data from the frame buffer is being transmitted to the network port. Next, the transmit interrupts of the network port are enabled. Since the transmit data register of the Nport ACIA is empty at this time, the Nport immediately generates an interrupt and the transmission process begins.

The Tisr (Fig. 5.2-10) handles data input from terminal's keyboard into the frame buffer. The receive interrupts of the terminal port always remain enabled in this experiment. Therefore, the Tisr routine is always invoked when a key is pressed on the terminal's keyboard. This routine should write a byte into the frame buffer only when it owns the buffer, that is, when no frame has been written to the buffer yet or when the previously inputted frame has been already transmitted to the network. Also, each byte that is written into the buffer should be echoed to the terminal's screen so that the person inputting the text can view it. When the CR key is pressed while writing into the frame buffer, the Tisr routine should complete the frame by appending the LF and EOT bytes to the frame buffer and request frame transmission by setting the SF flag to 1.

```
Tisr                    (* invoked by Tport interrupt            *)

save context            (* save CPU's registers on stack         *)
input byte from Tport   (* new byte from keyboard                *)
if status OK then       (* otherwise ignore byte                 *)
   if BYS=0 and SF=0 then    (* otherwise buffer owned by nisr,  *)
                        (* ignore byte                           *)
      bufnxt^:=byte     (* store byte in next location in buffer *)
      bfnxt:=bfnxt+1    (* increment buffer pointer              *)
      Echo_byte         (* display byte on terminal's screen     *)
      if byte=CR then   (* if end of frame input                 *)
         byte:=LF
         Echo_byte      (* append and display the LF             *)
         bufnxt^:=byte
         bufnxt^:=EOT   (* append the EOT to the frame buffer     *)
         bufend:=bufnxt (* prepare buffer pointers for the       *)
         bufnxt:=buforg (* frame transmission                    *)
         SF:=1          (* set the 'send frame' flag             *)
      endif
   endif
endif
restore context         (* restore CPU's registers               *)
return.
```

Figure 5.2-10   Algorithm for the terminal interrupt-service routine.

The first operation performed by the Tisr routine, save context, saves the CPU's registers on stack. This way the contents of the registers that will be used by the Tisr routine can be preserved and restored again at the end of the Tisr routine. Then a byte is inputted from the terminal port. Note that even if the frame buffer is full and the new byte cannot be accepted, this read operation always has to be performed in order to clear pending interrupt. Recall from Section 4.3.1 that if an ACIA interrupt is generated because of new byte arrival, it has to be cleared by reading the newly arrived byte from ACIA's receive data register.

The status of the ACIA is checked to detect any possible errors. If a byte arrives with any kind of error, it is ignored. If there are no errors, the status of the frame buffer is checked. If both SF and BYS flags are clear, the byte is written into the frame buffer. Otherwise, the buffer contains the previously inputted frame, and the received byte is ignored.

If a byte is accepted, it is stored in the frame buffer using the bufnxt pointer. Then, the pointer is incremented by 1 to point to next location available in the buffer. The byte is then echoed to the terminal's screen by the Echo_byte subroutine.

After the byte has been saved in the buffer and echoed to the screen, it is compared with ASCII code for the CR character. If it is found to be equal to the CR code, the ASCII code for the LF character is appended to the buffer and echoed to the screen. The CR marks the end of frame input; therefore, the ASCII code for EOT is appended to the frame buffer. At that point, the value of the bufnxt pointer points to the end of buffer. It is copied into the bufend pointer, and then the bufnxt is loaded with the constant value of buforg, that is with the address of the first location in the frame buffer. This way, the buffer pointers are prepared for use by the Nisr routine that will transmit all bytes from the frame buffer to the network. Finally, the SF flag is set to 1 to inform the scheduling loop that the frame input has been completed.

The last operation performed by the Tisr routine, restore context, restores the CPU's registers used by the Tisr routine to their original values. This operation is always performed at the end of Tisr routine.

The Echo_byte routine (Fig. 5.2-11) is invoked from the Tisr routine to display a byte on terminal's screen. The transmit interrupts of the terminal port are disabled. Therefore, the Echo_byte routine first waits in a loop until Tport becomes ready for output and then writes the byte to Tport.

Data frames are transmitted with the use of the Nisr (Fig. 5.2-12). This routine is always invoked by the transmit interrupt of the Nport's ACIA, that is, whenever the transmit-data register of the ACIA becomes empty. As with all interrupt-invoked routines, the first operation saves CPU's registers on a stack. The registers are restored at the end of the Nisr routine.

```
Echo_byte

wait until Tport ready for output      (* test ACIA's status *)
Tport:=byte                            (* output byte to screen *)
return.
```

Figure 5.2-11 Echo_byte routine.

```
Nisr                     (* invoked by Nport interrupt          *)

save context             (* save CPU's registers on stack       *)
if bufnxt=bufend then    (* if frame output completed           *)
  BYS:=0                 (* clear 'busy sending' flag            *)
  disable interrupts at Nport
  bufnxt:=buforg+1       (* prepare bufnxt pointer for tisr routine *)
else
  Nport:=bufnxt^         (* output next byte from buffer to Nport *)
  bufnxt:=bufnxt+1       (* increment buffer pointer             *)
endif
restore context          (* restore CPU's registers from stack   *)
return.
```

Figure 5.2-12   Network-port interrupt-service routine.

If the frame-buffer pointers bufnxt and bufend are found to be equal, it means that all bytes of the frame have been already outputted to the network port. In this case, the BYS flag is cleared, the transmit interrupts of the Nport's ACIA are disabled, and the buffer pointer bufnxt is reinitialized to the value expected by the Tisr routine, that is, to 1 more than the constant value of buforg.

If buffer pointers are not equal yet, the next byte from the frame buffer is written to the Nport, and the buffer pointer bufnxt is incremented by 1. Note that the transmit interrupts of the Nport ACIA remain enabled so that next Nport interrupt occurs as soon as the transmit-data register in the Nport ACIA becomes empty.

The state machine defined for the receiver node in Figs. 5.2-3 and 5.2-4 is implemented in software using a main segment and two interrupt-invoked routines (Fig. 5.2-13). The main segment consists of the initialization sequence and scheduling loop. The Nisr is invoked by network-port interrupt whenever a new byte arrives from network bus, that is, when the receive-data register of the network port ACIA becomes full. The receive interrupts of the network port ACIA are enabled all the time. When invoked, the Nisr inputs 1 byte from the network port and, depending on the current state of the receiver node, saves the byte in the frame buffer or neglects it.

The Tisr is invoked by the terminal port when the transmit-data register of Tport's ACIA becomes empty. When invoked, the Tisr outputs 1 byte from the frame buffer to the terminal port. In the receiver node, the terminal port is used only for data output. Most of the time, all interrupts of the Tport ACIA are disabled. After a frame has been received, the transmit interrupts of the Tport ACIA are enabled by the scheduler. The transmit interrupts of the Tport ACIA are disabled by the Tisr after the last byte from the frame buffer has been outputted to the Tport.

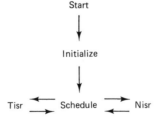

Figure 5.2-13   Program-flow diagram for the receiver node.

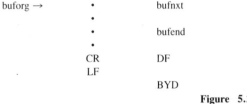

Figure 5.2-14 Data structure for the receiver-node software.

Data used by the receiver's program is illustrated in Fig. 5.2-14. The frame buffer is used to store data bytes accepted from frames transmitted on the network. To control buffer access, two pointers, bufnxt and bufend, are used. As was the case in the transmitter node, the frame buffer is placed in RAM memory in a fixed place and is defined by its origin, the constant-address value buforg. Note that the frame buffer in the receiver node does not contain the PRE and EOT bytes. These bytes, the front and end delimiters, are used for transmitter-receiver synchronization on the network. They are not a part of useful data. They are placed in the transmitter's frame buffer to facilitate frame output to the network port. They are received by the receiver node but do not have to be saved in receiver's buffer. After serving their purpose on the network, they are useless. Only the data field of a received frame should be sent to terminal's screen.

The transmitter creates required frame format by appending the PRE and EOT bytes to the data field. The receiver retrieves the data field by stripping the PRE and EOT bytes from the received frame.

The *display frame* (DF) and *busy displaying* (BYD) flags are used to control buffer ownership. The DF flag is used to inform the scheduling loop in the main program that a frame has been received. The BYD flag is used to inform the scheduling loop that a frame from the frame buffer is in the process of being sent to the terminal's screen, in other words, is in the process of being displayed. As long as both the DF and BYD flags are clear, the Nisr owns the buffer and can write into it. When the Nisr completes the frame reception, it sets the DF flag, and buffer ownership is passed to the scheduler. After finding that the DF flag is set (frame display is requested), the scheduler transfers the buffer ownership to the Tisr by clearing the DF flag and setting the BYS flag. Next, the scheduler enables transmit interrupts of the terminal port ACIA. This results in the Tisr being invoked for the first time. The buffer ownership is transferred back to the Nisr after the Tisr outputs the last byte from the frame buffer to the terminal port.

The *busy receiving* (BYR) flag has quite a different meaning. It is used to distinguish two different states of the receiver: (1) BYR = 0, in which the PRE byte is awaited and (2) BYR = 1, in which every byte arriving from the network is accepted and placed in the frame buffer. The BYR flag is set by the Nisr when it receives the PRE byte while owning (DF = 0 and BYD = 0) the frame buffer. The Nisr clears the BYR flag after receiving the EOT byte. Note that at the same time, the Nisr sets the DF flag to request display of the just-received frame. The relationship between the receiver states and BYR and BYD flag values is shown in Fig. 5.2-15.

FIGURE 5.2-15 STATE ENCODING
FOR THE RECEIVER NODE.

State	BYR	BYD
Ready	0	0
Receive frame	1	0
Display frame	0	1

A discussion of the pseudocode algorithms for receiver's program follows. Fig. 5.2-16 presents the algorithm for the Main segment.

First, CPU stack pointers are initialized. This is necessary to allow the use of subroutines and interrupt-service routines in the program. Then, all flags are cleared, and the frame buffer pointer is initialized. Note that in the receiver node, the buffer pointer is initialized to point to the buffer origin (compare to the buffer-pointer initialization for the transmitter). The byte expected by the receiver from the network is the PRE byte, but it will not be placed in the frame buffer. Therefore, the byte that is first placed in the frame buffer is a data byte.

Next, the vectors for network- and terminal-port interrupts are initialized, and then the terminal and network ports are initialized. Both are initialized to operate with the same data rate and byte frames as the terminal and network ports of the transmitter node. Note that the network ports of both transmitter and receiver nodes have to use

```
Main

const
  CR,NL,PRE,EOT : character
  BUFORG : integer
var
  DF,BYD,BYR : logical
  BUFNXT,BUFEND : pointer
begin
  initialize stack pointers
  DF:=0                       (* clear 'display frame flag        *)
  BYD:=0                      (* clear 'busy displaying flag      *)
  BYR:=0                      (* clear 'busy receiving' flag      *)
  bufnxt:=buforg              (* initialize buffer pointer        *)
  initialize vector for Nport interrupt
  initialize vector for Tport interrupt
  initialize Nport            (* data rate, byte frame, enable receive  *)
                              (* interrupts                       *)
  initialize Tport            (* data rate, byte frame, disable   *)
                              (* interrupts                       *)
  enable interrupts           (* enter user state                 *)
  repeat                      (* schedule                         *)
    if DF=1 then              (* if new frame received from network  *)
      Start_display_frame        (* initialize frame displaying   *)
      DF := 0                 (* clear the 'display frame' flag   *)
    endif
  until reset
end.
```

Figure 5.2-16   Main segment of the receiver's algorithm.

identical data rates and byte frames. The terminal ports may use different data rates and byte frames (as long as ASCII code is supported). The receive interrupts of the network port are enabled during the initialization and remain enabled all the time. Transmit interrupts of the network port will never be enabled for the receiver node. All interrupts are initially disabled for the terminal port. They are enabled temporarily for frame displays.

After initialization, the CPU interrupts are enabled and the CPU state is changed to the *user* state. Next, the program enters the scheduling loop. The scheduling loop keeps testing the status of the frame buffer (the DF flag), and, if necessary, invokes the Start_display_frame routine to initialize frame displaying. The Start_display_frame subroutine is called when the DF flag is found to be equal to 1. On return from this routine, the DF flag is cleared. Thus, frame displaying is initialized only once for each frame received from the network.

The Start_display_frame routine (Fig. 5.2-17) reinitializes the buffer pointer to its original value, thus preparing it for the first use by the Tisr. Then the BYD flag is set to inform the Nisr that data from the frame buffer is still being displayed and no write operation to the frame buffer is allowed. Finally, transmit interrupts of the terminal-port ACIA are enabled, and this immediately invokes the Tisr for the first time (as a result, the first byte from the frame buffer is displayed). Thus the frame display process begins.

The algorithm for the Nisr is given in Fig. 5.2-18. First and last operations peformed by this routine (as for all interrupt-invoked routines) are "save context" and "restore context," respectively.

After the CPU registers have been saved on stack, the Nisr inputs a byte from the network port. Recall that receive interrupts of the network port in the receiver node always remain enabled. Therefore, the Nisr is invoked to process every byte received by Nport ACIA. Even if a byte is to be neglected because of a transmission error or because the buffer is full with a previously received frame, it has to be read (inputted) from the ACIA's receive-data register to clear a pending interrupt request.

Next, the status of the network port ACIA is tested to determine if the byte was received error-free. If there is any error, the byte is neglected. If the byte is received without errors, the receiver's state and the just-received byte are analyzed to determine whether the byte should be placed in the frame buffer and whether the receiver's state should be modified.

An error-free byte arriving from the network can be accepted only when the Nisr owns the frame buffer, for example, when the DF and BYD flags are both clear. If this is the case, the BYR flag and byte value are tested to determine if this is the first byte of

```
Start_display_frame

bufnxt:=buforg                          (* reinitialize frame buffer pointer *)
BYD:=1                                   (* set the 'busy displaying' flag     *)
enable transmit interrupts at Tport
return.
```

Figure 5.2-17 Start_display_frame routine.

```
Nisr                             (* invoked by Nport interrupt        *)

save context
input bute from Nport            (* to clear pending interrupt        *)
if status OK then                (* otherwise ignore byte             *)
  if BYD=0 and DF=0 then         (* otherwise buffer owned by tisr;   *)
                                 (* ignore byte                       *)
      if BYR=0 and byte=PRE then   (* if start of packet              *)
        BYR:=1                   (* change state to "receive"         *)
      elseif BYR=1 then          (* if already receiving              *)
        if byte=EOT then         (* if last byte of frame             *)
          DF:=1                  (* request frame display             *)
          bufend:=bufnxt         (* establish end of buffer pointer   *)
          bufnxt:=buforg         (* reinitialize buffer pointer       *)
        else
          bufnxt^:=byte          (* store byte in next location       *)
                                 (* available in buffer               *)
          bfnxt:=bfnxt+1         (* increment buffer pointer          *)
        endif
      endif
    endif
  endif
restore context
return.
```

Figure 5.2-18   Network interrupt-service routine—receiver node.

a frame. If the receiver is not receiving yet (BYR = 0) and the received byte is the PRE byte, the state of the receiver is changed to *receive frame* (see Figs. 5.2-4 and 5.2-11) by setting the BYR flag. From this time on every received byte (until the EOT is detected) is placed in the frame buffer.

If the BYR flag is set—in other words if the frame reception is in process—every received byte is compared with the ASCII code for the EOT delimiter. If the byte is found to be equal to EOT, it marks the end of the frame, and the DF flag is set to request the frame to be displayed. Also, the buffer pointers are prepared for the Tisr.

If the received and accepted byte is not equal to the EOT, it is simply written to next location pointed to by the value of frame pointer bufnxt. After the write operation, the pointer is incremented by 1 to point to next available location.

The purpose of the Tisr (Fig. 5.2-19) in the receiver node is to output data frames from the frame buffer to the terminal screen. This routine is always invoked whenever Tport-transmit interrupts are enabled and the transmit-data register of the Tport ACIA becomes empty. When Tport-transmit interrupts are enabled by the Start_frame_display routine, this register is empty, and an interrupt is immediately generated. Later, interrupts are generated after a byte is displayed.

If the frame pointers bufnxt and bufend are found to be equal after all bytes of the frame have been outputted to the Tport, the BYD flag is cleared, Tport interrupts are disabled, and the buffer pointer is reinitialized for the Nisr. Otherwise, the next byte from the frame buffer, as pointed by the current value of the frame pointer bufnxt, is written to the terminal port, and then the pointer is incremented by 1. Transmit interrupts remain enabled so the Tisr is invoked again.

The assembly-language programs for transmitter and receiver nodes are shown in Appendix I. Programs are written for laboratory network nodes based on the ECB microcomputers.

```
Tisr                              (* invoked by Tport interrupt       *)

save context
if bufnxt=bufend then             (* if all bytes from buffer displayed *)
   BYD:=0                         (* clear "busy displaying" flag      *)
   disable interrupts at Tport
   bufnxt:=buforg                 (* reinitialize buffer pointer       *)
else
   Tport:=bufnxt^                 (* display next byte from buffer     *)
   bufnxt:=bufnxt+1               (* increment buffer pointer          *)
endif
restore context
return.
```

Figure 5.2-19 Terminal-port interrupt-service routine—receiver node.

5.2.5 Demonstrations

1. Enter and send a few one-line frames from the transmitter to the receiver node.
2. Use two receiver nodes and demonstrate a frame broadcast.
3. Change the PRE byte and demonstrate the effects of frame format mismatch.
4. Use two transmitters and one receiver and send frames from the transmitters simultaneously. Explain the data that is displayed on the receiver's screen.
5. Set different data rates for terminals at transmitter and receiver nodes. Use a third data rate for network ports. Show frame transfers.
6. Use two pairs of transmitter and receiver nodes. Set a data rate of 2400 bps for one pair and 1200 bps for another pair. Which nodes can communicate? Can they communicate on the same cable? Can they communicate simultaneously?

5.2.6 Problems

1. Modify the receiver's algorithm so that empty frames (i.e., consisting of CR and LF characters only) in the data field are rejected.
2. Can the receiver's algorithm be modified so that it can reject frames distorted due to collisions?
3. Modify the algorithm to allow for messages longer than one line of text.
   (a) Insert an LF character after every CR and terminate message entry by the CTRL_Z character.
   (b) Send the frame without LF inserted and insert it only during display.
4. Can the number of logical variables (flags) used in the algorithm be reduced? Is it worth it? Reduction of the number of variables is not worthwhile if it leads to a more complicated algorithm. It is better to use more variables and have simpler, clearer algorithm.
5. Assume that the network uses a higher data rate than the terminal. It is possible in such a case that a new frame arrives at the receiver node while the previous one is still being displayed. (Note that such a case is also possible if equal data rates are used for network and terminal ports.) Modify the algorithm for the receiver node to allow for multi-frame first-in first-out (FIFO) buffering.

5.3 LAB 3—BIDIRECTIONAL FRAME TRANSFERS

5.3.1 Purpose

This experiment serves as a practical example illustrating a design approach based on the multilayer communications architecture concept, as discussed in Chapter 1.3. Labs 1 and 2 introduced elementary data-communication concepts as applicable to the local network and thus formed a basis for more complicated experiments on network protocols. The multilayer design approach introduced here will be used as the backbone for all further experiments.

In summary, this experiment concentrates on the following topics:

• Multilayer design approach
• Bidirectional frame transfers
• Elimination of the parasite echo from the bidirectional data-bus line

5.3.2 The Multilayer Design Concept and Operation

The basic design concept is illustrated in Fig. 5.3-1(a). The messages (the meaningful, useful information) originate at terminals and are utilized at terminals as well. Of course, the messages that originate at a terminal of one network node are intended to be utilized on the terminal of another network node. When a text is typed on the terminal's keyboard, a message is created. When this text appears on the screen of a node that has received it, the message is consumed. Since all network nodes should be able both to create and consume messages, the network protocol as well as the network data path— the cable—have to be bidirectional.

As illustrated in Fig. 5.3-1(a), in addition to multilayer design, this experiment introduces bidirectional data transfers. All nodes in this experiment have identical software and every node is able to create and transmit messages as well as receive and consume messages.

Figure 5.3-1(b) illustrates the multilayer design of network protocol for this experiment. This protocol is implemented on the ECBs, which perform the role of protocol processors. Only two layers are distinguished here, the application layer and the network layer. The application layer handles creation and consumption of messages, whereas the network layer handles message transmission and reception. In the model, a layer represents an algorithm. In all experiments, the layers—excluding the physical layer—are implemented in software. Therefore, a layer in Fig. 5.3-1(b) also may be said to represent a group of routines. Clear understanding of this relationship between layers and routines is very essential.

The purpose of the application layer is to accept messages arriving from the terminal's keyboard and to submit them to the Network layer for transmission. Also, in the opposite direction of data flow, the Application layer has to accept messages

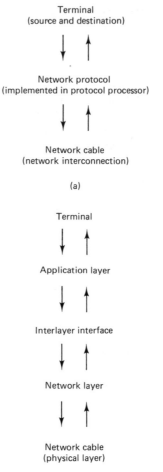

Figure 5.3-1 Layered model of node's architecture (hardware and software): (a) Network node model, (b) Internal design of the network protocol processor.

submitted by the network layer (messages that were received by network layer from network cable) and display them on the terminal's screen.

The overall purpose of the network layer is quite similar to that of the application layer. It has to accept messages arriving from network cable and submit them to the application layer for consumption. In the opposite direction, it has to accept messages arriving from the application layer and transmit them to the network cable.

The exchange of messages between the application and network layers is supported by an interlayer interface. Since both layers in this experiment are implemented in software, the interface has a form of data—flags and buffers in ECBs memory—that is accessed—tested and/or modified—by both layers. The interlayer-interface data for this experiment is defined in Fig. 5.3-2. Actually, similar interface data is used in Lab 2 as well.

For example, briefly consider a flow of one message from its creation to its consumption. The network protocol at a node at which the message is created accepts it

Interlayer interface

```
TBUF - transmit buffer; multiple byte, variable size buffer
TBF  - transmit buffer full, flag
SP   - send frame, flag
tbnxt, tbend - pointers

RBUF - receive buffer; multiple byte, variable size buffer
RBF  - receive buffer full, flag
DP   - display frame, flag
rbnxt, rbend - pointers
```

Figure 5.3-2 Interlayer-interface data.

from terminal's keyboard and places it in the transmit buffer TBUF. Then, when the message is complete, the application layer sets the send packet (SP) flag to inform the network layer that a message from TBUF should be transmitted to the network. When the network layer detects the SP flag being set, it transmits the message from TBUF to the network cable. While the message is being transmitted, the network layer in the receiving node accepts it from the cable and places it in the receive buffer (RBUF). When reception is complete, it sets the display packet (DP) flag to inform the application layer that a new message has arrived from the network and should be displayed. When the application layer detects the DP flag being set, it displays the message from RBUF on the terminal's screen. Thus the message is consumed and its voyage through protocol layers, interlayer interfaces, and network cable is finally completed. The flow of messages through terminal and network ports and through transmit and receive buffers is illustrated in Fig. 5.3-3.

All messages used in this experiment have the format used in Lab 2, for example,

PRE , . . . data . . . , CR, LF, EOT

Thus, messages are not addressed, and if one node transmitts a message, all other nodes present on the network receive—and display—this message. The problem of directing a message to one receiving node only—the destination node—is solved in Experiment 4.

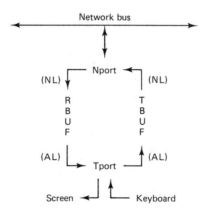

Figure 5.3-3 Information flow through frame buffers and I/O ports.

5.3.3. Algorithm Design

In Experiments 1 and 2, the algorithms were designed separately for the receiver and transmitter nodes. Here, all nodes will be both receivers and transmitters. However, separate algorithms will be designed for the network and application layers. Both layers can be regarded as state machines. Corresponding state diagrams are given in Fig. 5.3-4.

Consider the AL first. In the *ready* state, the AL does not do anything. When a key is pressed on the terminal keyboard while AL is in the *ready* state, it is assumed that a message creation (input) begins, and AL changes state to *input*. If the DP flag of the interlayer interface is found to be set while AL is in the *ready* state, it is understood that the network layer received a message and it should be displayed. Therefore, the AL's state is changed to *output* (display) in such a case. While the AL is in the *input* state, all bytes arriving from the keyboard are placed into the TBUF buffer until a CR key is pressed. This marks the end of message input, and AL sets the SP flag and then returns to *ready* state. The AL remains in the *output* state for as long as it takes to display a message from the RBUF and then immediately returns to the *ready* state.

Note that the state diagram explicitly demonstrates that there is no possibility for direct transitions between *input* and *output* states. Such direct transitions are not allowed to happen because when a message is being created, it is typed on terminal's keyboard, but, at the same time, its text should appear on the screen so that the person entering the message can see it. If we allowed the AL to change state from Input to Output before the message input has been completed, we would have the texts of both messages—the one being inputted and the one being displayed—intermixed on the screen. The same problem could occur if the AL were allowed to change state from Output to Input before the message display is completed.

The state diagram of the NL is very similar to that of the AL. Again, it appears that the NL does not do anything while in the *ready* state. However, the NL accepts and analyzes every byte arriving from the network cable. If a byte accepted is the PRE byte—the first byte of every frame—the NL assumes that a message is being sent over the network cable and switches to the *receive* state. If the SP flag is found to be set

State diagram

Application layer   Start

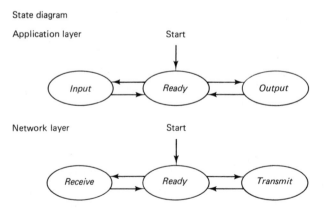

Network layer   Start

Figure 5.3-4 Application and network layers as state machines.

while the NL is in the *ready* state, it is understood that the AL has completed a new message in the TBUF buffer and this message should be transmitted. Therefore, the NL changes to the *transmit* state. While the NL is in the *receive* state, every byte arriving from network cable is accepted and placed in the RBUF buffer until the EOT byte—the last byte of every frame—is received. This marks the end of frame, and the NL sets the DP flag and returns to the *ready* state. The NL remains in the *transmit* state for as long as it takes to transmit a message frame from the TBUF buffer to the network cable. Immediately after that, the NL returns to the *ready* state.

Again, direct transitions between *receive* and *transmit* states are not permitted. If the NL switched from *receive* to *transmit* before EOT was received, there would be at least two nodes transmitting to the cable at the same time, and both messages would be distorted. If the NL switched from *transmit* to *receive* before completing frame transmission—for example, before sending the EOT—then the receiving node(s) would never be able to complete frame reception.

The states of the application and network layers are encoded using four flags (logical variables): BYI, BYD, BYR, and BYS. The relationship between layer states and flag values is given in Fig. 5.3-5.

It is interesting to try to decide whether these flags should be regarded as a part of interlayer interface or not. As state-encoding information, they properly belong to corresponding layers, for example, the BYI and BYD are owned by the application layer, whereas the BYR and BYS are owned by the network layer. However, as it can be seen in Figs. 5.3-6 and 5.3-7, flags belonging to AL have to be used by the NL, and vice versa. This is due to the fact that the AL should not write to the TBUF until the NL completes transmission of a previous message. Thus the BYS flag, if set, also seems to represent the meaning "TBUF full" to the AL. In truth, the situation when AL should not write into the TBUF occurs in two cases: the first, as described above and the second, when the SP is set. The SP is set by the AL at the end of the message input. Then,

FIGURE 5.3-5 STATE ENCODING USING LOGICAL VARIABLES (FLAGS).

State—flag values arrangement Newtork layer		
State	BYR	BYS
Ready	0	0
Receive	1	0
Transmit	0	1
Application layer		
State	BYI	BYD
Ready	0	0
Input	1	0
Output	0	1

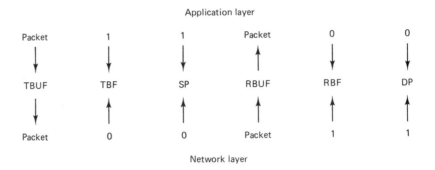

Figure 5.3-6 Data flow through interlayer interface.

for a short time, SP is set but BYS is not. Still, the TBUF is full and the AL should not write to it so that previous messages are not destroyed.

To simplify matters, two special flags, the *transmit buffer full* (TBF) and the *receive buffer full* (RBF), which belong to the interlayer interface (see Figs. 5.3-2 and 5.3-6) are used. The TBF flag, when set, informs the AL layer that TBUF buffer still contains a previous message and it should not be written to. The TBF flag is set, together with the SP flag at the moment when AL completes message input. It is cleared, together with BYS flag, at the moment when the NL completes frame transmission. Similarly, the RBF flag, when set, informs the NL that RBF buffer still contains a previously received message and should not be written to. The RBF is set, together with DP flag, at the moment when NL completes the frame reception and cleared, together with BYD flag, at the moment when AL completes the message display.

To complete the discussion of the interlayer interface, consider the meaning of the SP and DP flags again. The SP flag is used by the application layer to request message transmission by the network layer, whereas the DP flag is used by the Network layer to request a message display by the application layer. One can argue that an SP's change from zero to one conveys identical information as the zero-to-one change of the TBF flag. It is true, but the SP flag has a dynamic nature, whereas the TBF

FIGURE 5.3-7 DEFINITION OF THE AL STATE MACHINE.

Application layer			
Current state	Next state	Condition	Action
Ready	*Input*	First byte from keyboard and TBF = 0	BYI := 1
Ready	*Output*	DP = 1	DP := 0, BYD := 1
Input	*Ready*	CR inputted from keyboard	BYI := 0, SP := 1, TBF := 1
Output	*Ready*	Last character displayed	BYD := 0, RBF := 0

represents more static information. Clearly, a message written to the TBUF by the AL should be sent only once. On the other hand, nothing new should be written to the TBUF for as long as the NL needs to accept AL's request and then transmit the message from TBUF to network cable. Similar reasoning can be applied to the DP and RBF flags. The need for clear distinction between DP/SP and RBF/TBF flags will become apparent while analyzing protocol application—specifically, an algorithm for the Scheduler routine. Fig. 5.3-6 illustrates information flow between layers and interlayer interface.

State machines implementing application and network layers are defined in detail by state-transition tables in Figs. 5.3-7 and 5.3-8. It is very important to realize when the state changes can occur. The conditions are tested at different situations and, specifically, are not in synchronism with any specific clock. This problem should be analyzed and clarified in the description of software implementation of Lab 3 node algorithms.

FIGURE 5.3-8 DEFINITION OF THE NL STATE MACHINE.

Network layer			
Current state	Next state	Condition	Action
Ready	*Receive*	PRE received and RBF = 0	BYR := 1
Ready	*Transmit*	SP = 1	SP := 0, BYS := 1
Receive	*Ready*	EOT received	BYR := 0, DP := 1, RBF := 1
Transmit	*Ready*	EOT sent	BYS := 0, TBF := 0

5.3.4 Algorithm Implementation

Software implementing these algorithms for the Lab 3 network node consists of the main segment and two groups of routines, one for each layer (Fig. 5.3-9). The purpose of the main segment is to initialize ports and layer data (flags and pointers) and then perform the scheduling function (a miniature model of an operating system). Routines that belong to the AL group are always invoked by the terminal port interrupt. The NL

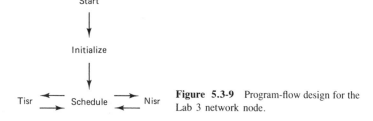

Figure 5.3-9 Program-flow design for the Lab 3 network node.

```
routines

main segment            application layer        network layer

Main                    Tisr                     Nisr
Clear_flags             Input                    Receive
Initialize              Echo_byte                Transmit
Schedule                Output                   Enable_receive
Start_send
Start_display
```

Figure 5.3-10 Lab 3 node routines.

routines are always invoked by the network-port interrupt. The grouping of routines is demonstrated in Fig. 5.3-10.

The pseudocode algorithm for the Main routine is given in Fig. 5.3-11. The routine is composed of two parts: the initialization sequence and the scheduling loop. CPU stack pointers have to be initialized in the main segment before any subroutine is called. Then, the Clear_flags and Initialize routines are called to initialize data and interfaces for application and network layers. As the last step of initialization sequence, the hardware interrupts are enabled and the CPU is switched to user mode. From this time on, the schedule routine is called in a loop until the system is reset.

The Clear_flags routine is shown in Fig. 5.3-12. The purpose of this routine is to clear (present to 0) all logical variables (flags) used by application and network layers. Logical variables can be partitioned into four groups: service request flags (SP and DP), buffer-status flags (TBF and RBF), AL state-encoding flags (BYI and BYD), and NL state encoding flags (BYR and BYS).

Figure 5.3-13 presents the Initialize routine. The buffer pointers are initialized for both TBUF and RBUF buffers. The first byte of TBUF always contains the PRE byte, which is loaded into this position during the initialization. At the time of

```
Main

const
  PRE,CR,NL,EOT : character
  rborg,tborg : integer

var
  SP,DP,TBF,RBF,BYS,BYR,BYD,BYI : logical
  RBUF,TBUF : array
  rbnxt,rbend,tbnxt,tbend : pointer
  byte : character

begin

  initialize stack pointers  (* for both supervisor and user stacks *)
  Clear_flags                (* clear all logical variables          *)
  Initialize                 (* initialize buffer pointers and ports*)
  enable CPU interrupts and enter user mode
  repeat
    Schedule
  until reset
end.
```

Figure 5.3-11 Algorithm for the Lab 3_main routine.

```
Clear_flags

SP:=0; DP:=0
TBF:=0; RBF:=0
BYD:=0; BYI:=0
BYS:=0; BYR:=0
return.
```
Figure 5.3-12 Clear_flags routine.

```
Initialize

rbnxt:=rborg          (* initialize rbnxt pointer *)
tbnxt:=tborg+1        (* initialize tbnxt pointer *)
tborg^:=PRE           (* load "preamble byte" into first byte of TBUF *)
initialize interrupt vectors for Tport and Nport
initilaize byte frame, data rate for Tport and Nport
enable receive interrupts for Tport and Nport
return.
```
Figure 5.3-13 Initialize routine.

initialization, both buffers are empty. It is expected that first operation performed on TBUF buffer is data input by the AL. Therefore the TBUF pointer (tbnxt) is initialized to tborg + 1, for example, to point to the second byte of TBUF. The first operation to be performed on the RBUF buffer is data input by the network layer. There is no need to put the received PRE byte into the RBUF buffer. Therefore, the RBUF pointer (rbnxt) is initialized to point to the first byte of RBUF.

Recall that the scheduling loop of the Main segment (Fig. 5.3-14) can be regarded as a miniature operating system. Indeed, if we analyze its operation with the notion that the AL and NL can be regarded as processes, then these processes can be activated by the scheduling loop.

Specifically, the SP and DP flags can be regarded as process-activating-request information, whereas flags BYD, BYI, BYS, and BYR can be regarded as process-state information. A process can be activiated when it is ready and its activation is requested by some other process. The NL "process" is ready when both BYR and BYS flags are clear. Its activation is requested by the AL "process" when it sets the SP flag. The Schedule routine can recognize the AL's request and activate the NL. If at the time of request (SP changing from 0 to 1) the NL is already active (either BYS or BYR flag is set), then the request will be held pending.

In addition to layer (process) activation by the Schedule routine due to SP or DP flags, these processes can be activated directly by port interrupts. Interrupt handlers

```
Schedule

if SP=1 and BYS=0 then                  (* if new frame input completed *)
                                        (* and NL ready                 *)
   Start_send
elseif DP=1 and BYD=0 and BYI =0 then   (* if new frame received and    *)
                                        (* AL ready                     *)
   Start_display
endif
return.
```

Figure 5.3-14 Schedule routine.

normally belong to the operating system, and, arguably, the Nisr and Tisr routines could be removed from AL and NL groups (see Fig. 5.3-9) and added to the main segment group.

The NL is activated by the Start_send routine (Fig. 5.3-15) to send a frame from the RBUF buffer to the network. The BYS flag is set to 1 to mark the change of NL's state and the SP flag is cleared to ensure that the Schedule routine starts a frame transmission only once. Finally, the transmit interrupts are enabled at the network port and the transmitting begins. The Start_display routine (Fig. 5.3-16) activates the AL to display a frame from the RBUF buffer. The operation of this routine is analogous to that of the Start_send routine. The BYD and DP flags replace the BYS and SP flags, and the terminal port is used instead of the network port.

All AL operations are invoked by the terminal-port interrupts, which are served by the Tisr routine given in Fig. 5.3-17. The CPU registers are first saved on stack to prevent any modifications. The registers are restored at the end of the Tisr routine. Depending on the state of the AL at the moment when the Tisr is invoked, either the Input or the Output routine is called. The Input routine (Fig. 5.3-18) inputs one byte at a time from the terminal port to the TBUF buffer. The bytes arriving from the terminal port are accepted, provided that they are error-free and the TBUF buffer is not yet full. Accepted bytes are echoed to the terminal's screen by the Echo_byte routine (Fig. 5.3-19). The inputting terminates and message transmission is requested when the CR character is entered from the terminal's keyboard. The Output routine (Fig. 5.3-20) outputs one byte at a time from the RBUF buffer to the terminal's screen. The outputting terminates when all bytes have been displayed. At this moment, transmit interrupts of the terminal port are disabled and its receive interrupts are enabled to allow for input operations.

The NL operations are invoked by the network-port interrupts which are served by the Nisr routine (Fig. 5.3-21). Either the Receive or the Transmit routine is called from the Nisr, depending on the current state of the NL. The Receive routine (Fig.

```
Start_send

BYS:=1     (* set "busy sending" flag, i.e. change NL's state to "transmit" *)
SP:=0      (* clear "send frame" flag, i.e. clear the AL's request         *)
enable transmit and disable receive interrupts for Nport
return (*rts*)
```

Figure 5.3-15 Algorithm for the Start_send routine.

```
Start_display

BYD:=1     (* set "busy displaying" flag, i.e. change AL's state to "output" *)
DP:=0      (* clear "display frame" flag, i.e. clear the NL's request        *)
enable transmit and disable receive interrupts for Tport
return (*rts*)
```

Figure 5.3-16 Algorithm for the Start_display routine.

```
Tisr                          (* invoked by Tport interrupt *)

save context
if BYD=1 then      (* if AL is in the "output" state *)
  Output
else               (* assume that Al is in the "input" state *)
  Input
endif
restore context
return (*rte*)
```

Figure 5.3-17 Terminal-port interrupt-service routine.

```
Input
input byte from Tport    (* always read to clear interrupt *)
if Tport status OK then  (* otherwise ignore byte           *)
  if TBF=0 then          (* if TBUF empty                    *)
    if BYI=0 then        (* if first byte from keyboard      *)
      BYI:=1             (* change AL's state to "input"     *)
    endif
    Echo_byte            (* send byte to screen              *)
    tbnxt^:=byte         (* save byte in TBUF                *)
    tbnxt:=tbnxt+1       (* increment tbnxt pointer          *)
    if byte = CR then    (* if last byte of message          *)
      byte:=NL
      Echo_byte          (* send NL to screen                *)
      tbnxt^:= byte      (* save NL in TBUF                  *)
      tbnxt:=tbnxt+1
      tbnxt^:=EOT        (* save EOT in TBUF                 *)
      tbnxt:=tbnxt+1
      SP:=1              (* request message transmission     *)
       TBF:=1            (* TBUF became full                    *)
      BYI:=0             (* change AL's state to "ready"     *)
      tbend:=tbnxt       (* prepare TBUF pointers for        *)
      tbnxt:=tborg       (* the NL routines                  *)
    endif
  endif
endif
return (* rts *)
```

Figure 5.3-18 Application layer, the Input routine.

```
Echo_byte

wait until Tport ready for output
Tport:=byte
return.
```
Figure   5.3-19 Application   layer,   the
Echo_byte routine.

```
Output
if rbnxt=rbend then    (* if all bytes from RBUF already displayed *)
  BYD:=0               (* end displaying                             *)
  RBF:=0               (* RBUF became empty                          *)
  rbnxt:=rborg         (* reinitialize rbnxt pointer                 *)
  disable transmit and enable receive interrupts for Tport
else
  Tport:=tbnxt^        (* write next byte from RBUF to Tport         *)
  tbnxt:=tbnxt+1       (* increment tbnxt pointer                    *)
endif
return (*rts*)
```

Figure 5.3-20 Application layer, the Output routine.

```
Nisr                  (* invoked by Nport interrupt *)

save context
if BYS=1 then         (* if NL is in the "transmit" state        *)
  Transmit
else                  (* assume that NL is in the "receive" state *)
  Receive
endif
restore context
return (*rte*)
```

Figure 5.3-21 Network-port interrupt-service routine.

```
Receive

nbyte := Nport                 (* input byte from Nport                 *)
if Nport status OK then        (* otherwise ignore byte                 *)
  if RBF = 0 then              (* if RBUF is empty                      *)
    if BYR = 0 and nbyte = PRE then     (* if first byte, and it       *)
                                        (* is the "preamble" byte      *)
      BYR := 1                 (* change NL's state to "receive"        *)
    elseif BYR = 1 then        (* if NL is in the "receive" state       *)
      if nbyte = EOT then      (* if last byte of frame received        *)
        DP := 1                (* request frame display                 *)
        RBF := 1               (* RBUF became full                      *)
        BYR := 0               (* end receiving, change NL's state to   *)
                               (* "ready"                               *)
        rbend := rbnxt         (* prepare RBUF pointers for AL routines *)
        rbnxt := rborg
      else
        rbnxt^ := nbyte        (* save byte in RBUF                     *)
        rbnxt := rbnxt+1       (* increment buffer pointer              *)
      endif
    endif
  endif
endif
return.
```

Figure 5.3-22 Network layer Receive routine.

```
Transmit

if tbnxt = tbend then (* if all bytes from TBUF already transmitted *)
  BYS := 0            (* change NL's state to "ready"               *)
  TBF := 0            (* TBUF became empty                          *)
  tbnxt := tborg+1    (* reinitialize tbnxt pointer for AL routines *)
  Enable_receive
else
  Nport := tbnxt^     (* write next byte from TBUF to Nport         *)
  tbnxt := tbnxt+1
endif
return.
```

Figure 5.3-23 Network layer Transmit routine.

```
Enable_receive     (* clear pending receive interrupts, then enable *)
                   (* them                                           *)
wait until Nport receives new byte
nbyte := Nport
wait until Nport receives new byte
nbyte := Nport
wait until Nport receives new byte
nbyte := Nport
enable receive and disable transmit interrupts at Nport
return.
```

Figure 5.3-24 Network layer Enable_receive routine.

5.3-22) inputs one byte at a time from the network port to the RBUF buffer. The appending of received bytes to the RBUF starts when the PRE byte is received, provided that RBUF is free and NL is not already busy, and terminates when the EOT is received. At this time, the message display is requested. The Transmit routine (Fig. 5.3-23) outputs one byte at a time from the TBUF buffer to the network port. The outputting terminates when all bytes from the TBUF have been transmitted. The Enable_receive routine (Fig. 5.3-24) is then called to clear the network port from bytes inadvertently received during transmission. Recall the explanation given in section 4.3.2.

An assembly-language program for Lab 3 nodes is given in Appendix I.

5.3.5 Demonstrations

1. Use two bidirectional nodes (A and B). Send a message from A to B. Send a reply from B to A.
2. Demonstrate broadcast effects.
3. Demonstrate network collision.
4. Use three nodes operating at low network and terminal-data rates. Demonstrate message loss. (Send two messages quickly, one after another, from two nodes).
5. At a low network rate, show that you cannot enter a new message before the previous one has been transmitted.

5.3.6 Problems

1. Reduce the number of logical variables (flags) used by the algorithm. To achieve that goal, use an integer variable to encode current state.
2. Create multiframe buffers.
   (a) In the receive direction only
   (b) In both directions
   In what situations will there be more than one frame in the buffers?
3. Is it better to keep the PRE and EOT in the TBUF or to append them "on the fly" during frame transmission?

4. Use different forms for controlling the frame length. Instead of an EOT character terminating the frame, use a COUNT byte in the frame header. After receiving the COUNT byte, the receiver will accept only as many of the following bytes as indicated by the value of COUNT. If only one byte is used for COUNT, the frame length is limited to 256 bytes plus header.

5. Implement error detection methods.

   (a) Use the check sum byte appended to the frame.

   (b) Use the cyclic redundancy check (CRC) method. See [3].

   (c) Reject frames received with errors.

   (d) Replace frames received with errors by a BAD FRAME message.

5.4 LAB 4—ADDRESSED FRAME BROADCAST AND RECEPTION

5.4.1. Purpose

This experiment, an extension to experiment 3, introduces a very important concept, called *packet addressing*. In all previous experiments, if a node transmitted a byte or string of bytes to the network cable, this information was accepted by all other nodes present in *receive* states on the network. From the transmitter's point of view, packet addressing implies the need to include packet's destination information in the packet itself. From the receiver's point of view, packet addressing implies the need to analyze incoming packets and reject those whose addresses do not match that of a receiving node. On the other hand, since there is no possibility of forseeing if a packet is to be accepted before at least part of it is received, all packets transmitted to the network have to be monitored by all receivers. One can imagine a forgotten node that does not receive any packets—nobody sends packets addressed to this node—but has to spend nearly all its time monitoring all other packets, constantly expecting one of them to have its address.

From the algorithm-design point of view, this experiment is a modified version of Experiment 3. Although the complete algorithm for Lab 4 is explained, only the new or modified routines are shown in detail. The complete list of all routines necessary to implement Lab-4, some of them taken from Lab 3 without any change, is given in Fig. 5.4-6.

5.4.2 Operation

To cut the monitoring time to a minimum, the destination-address information is located at the beginning of the packet frame. Thus, receiving nodes can quickly quit monitoring packets with wrong addresses. In this experiment, the data-packet format of Lab 3 is slightly modified:

PRE , DID , SID , . . . data . . . , EOT

Note that the CR and LF bytes are not specified here. They still are used as last characters of our keyboard-to-screen messages, but they really belong to the data field and their only importance is for the AL and, finally, the human user of the network.

From the receiver's point of view, all packets begin with PRE byte, and the PRE byte always marks the beginning of a packet. Then, the first byte after PRE always contains the address information, the DID. The next byte after the DID always represents the information about the source of the packet, the source ID (SID). Then, all bytes after the SID are data, until the EOT byte. Finally, the EOT always marks the end of a packet.

From the transmitter's point of view, all that has to be done is to stuff a byte representing the DID into second position in the packet frame and a byte representing the SID into the third position in the packet, that is, into second and third bytes of the TBUF buffer, respectively. The destination of a message is decided at the time when the message is created. Also, the SID is known at this moment, too. Therefore, in this experiment, the DID and SID byte positions in the TBUF frame are filled by the AL. Actually, from the AL point of view, the DID and SID can be regarded as a part of the whole message. It is assumed that the first character pressed on the keyboard for each message always represents the ID of the destination node. Thus the AL from Lab 3 needs to be modified to stuff the SID byte into the third byte position in the TBUF buffer. Note that the SID is always equal to MID, the node's own ID. The modification is very simple and affects only the Input routine, presented in Section 5.4.4.

Only the receiving part of the NL has to be modified. The transmit part stays the same as the Lab 3 because it is designed to output data from TBUF as it is prepared by the AL. The receive part has to be upgraded to be able to analyze incoming byte strings to determine which packets should be accepted and which should be rejected.

5.4.3 Algorithm Design

The concept of the NL as a state machine must be slightly modified with respect to the NL from Lab 3. Lab 3 distinguished the *idle* state, in which the NL was doing nothing. In fact, even in the *idle* state, the NL was always invoked (activated) by every byte transmitted on the network cable. Every time a byte was transmitted by some node, all nodes with NL in the *idle* state would receive this byte and compare it with the PRE code. In fact, there were only two states of the NL, the *transmit* state and the *receive* state. Within the *receive* state we can distinguish two substates, a *receive idle* state, when bytes arriving from network are compared with PRE code, and a *receive active* state, when bytes arriving from the network are accepted and placed in the RBUF buffer.

For the NL state machine of this experiment, the following states are recognized: *transmit, receive waiting for PRE* (labeled R0), *receive expecting MID* (labeled R1), and *receive active* (labeled R2). In the following experiments the NL state machine becomes more and more complicated. Therefore, it will be very convenient to represent it as a two-level state machine: that is, first, analyze general states and then consider details of state changes within the *receive* state. The state diagram for Lab 4 NL state machine is given in Figs. 5.4-1 and 5.4-2. Figure 5.4-3(a) presents state encoding for NL using the BYS flag. Note that the BYR flag is not used anymore. Instead, the *rstate* integer variable is used to encode receive substates (Fig. 5.4-3(b)). The complete definition of state machine is given by the state-transition tables in Figs. 5.4-4 and 5.4-5.

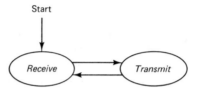

Figure 5.4-1 Network layer of a Lab 4 node as a state machine.

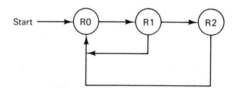

Figure 5.4-2 Receive state substates and transitions.

FIGURE 5.4-3 NL STATE ENCODING.

(a) General States	
State	BYS
Receive	0
Transmit	1
(b) *Receive Substates*	
Receive substates	rstate
R0	0
R1	1
R2	2

FIGURE 5.4-4 DEFINITION OF THE NL STATE MACHINE FOR THE LAB 4 NODE.

(a) General state machine

Current state	Next state	Condition	Action
Receive	*Transmit*	SP = 1 and rstate = 0	BYS := 1
Transmit	*Receive*	EOT sent	BYS := 0, rstate := 0

(b) *Receive* state machine

Current state	Next state	Condition	Action
Rx	R1	Byte received = PRE	rstate := 1
R1	R0	Byte received <> MID	rstate := 0
R1	R2	Byte received = MID and RBF = 0	rstate := 2
R2	R0	Byte received = EOT	rstate := 0, DF := 1 RBF := 1, rbend := rbnxt, rbnxt := rborg

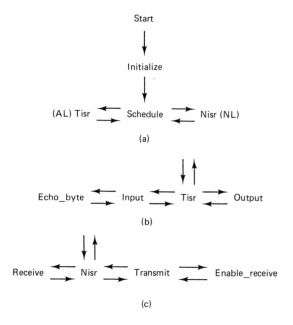

Start

Initialize

(AL) Tisr   Schedule   Nisr (NL)

(a)

Echo_byte   Input   Tisr   Output

(b)

Receive   Nisr   Transmit   Enable_receive

(c)

Figure 5.4-5 Program flow: (a) General program flow, (b) Detailed program flow for AL routines, (c) Detailed program flow for NL routines.

5.4.4 Algorithm Implementation

Lab 4 node layers are implemented in a very similar way to Lab 3. Figure 5.4-5 defines the program flow and Fig. 5.4-6 lists all routines used in Lab 4. Some of these routines were defined in Lab 3 and are used here without any change. Some of the routines are similar to those of Lab 3 but are modified (Main, Input, Nisr, Receive, Transmit), some are completely new (Input_MID, Display, End_display, PRE_received, DID_received, Accept). New and modified routines are explained in Figs. 5.4-7 through 5.4-16. Most of the Lab 4 routines are used again in following experiments. The assembly-language code for modified routines is given in Appendix I.

      The Main routine (Fig. 5.4-7) shows the general logic of the Lab 4 node program. First, stack pointers are initialized to allow for subroutine calls and interrupt

```
Main segment              Application layer      Network layer

Main                      *Tisr        (3)       Nisr
*Clear_flags    (3)       Input                  Receive
*Initialize     (3)       *Echo_byte   (3)       Transmit
*Schedule       (3)       *Output      (3)       *Enable_receive (3)
*Start_send     (3)                              PRE_received
*Start_display  (3)                              DID_received
Input_MID                                        Accept
Display
Input_byte
End_display

* Routines defined in Lab 3
```

Figure 5.4-6   Lab 4 node routines.

```
Main

const
  inpmid = 'input MID',0 : character string
  rborg, tborg  : integer
  PRE,EOT,CR,LF : character
var
  TBF,RBF,BYD,BYI,SP,DP : logical
  rstate : integer
  txtptr : pointer
  MID : character
  tbyte,nbyte : character

begin

  initialize user and system stack pointers
  Input_MID
  Initialize
  enable CPU interrupts and enter user mode
  repeat
    Schedule
  until reset

end.
```

Figure 5.4-7   Main routine.

handling. Then the MID is entered by node's operator (see the Input_MID routine, Fig. 5.4-8). Next, logical variables, buffers, and ports are initialized and CPU interrupts are enabled. Finally, an infinite loop is entered, in which the schedule routine is executed.

The Input_MID routine first displays the message "input MID" on the terminal's screen and then accepts a byte corresponding to a key pressed on terminal's keyboard by the node's operator. The byte, an ASCII code for the key, is placed in the MID variable and, from now on, represents node's ID. Finally, the cursor is moved to the beginning of next line on terminal's screen. The Display routine (Fig. 5.4-9) simply displays a message selected by the txtptr pointer until a 0 byte is found in the message string. A byte representing a key pressed on the terminal's keyboard is inputted using the Input_byte routine (Fig. 5.4-10). The cursor is moved to the start of the next line by the End_display routine (Fig. 5.4-11).

The algorithm for the Input routine is given in Fig. 5.4-12. This routine is used to input a data packet from the terminal's keyboard to the TBUF buffer. It is assumed that the first key pressed represents the DID for the packet. Every time the first key is pressed (BYI = 0), two bytes are saved in the RBUF buffer—the DID byte that corresponds to the ASCII code of the first key pressed and the SID byte that is equal to the MID byte. For each key pressed, the Echo_byte routine is called to display the character corresponding to the key on the terminal's screen. The inputting of data packet

```
Input_MID

txtptr := inpmid (* initialize txtptr for 'input MID' string *)
Display          (* display the 'input MID' string             *)
Input_byte       (* input MID                                  *)
MID := tbyte     (* establish node id number, MID              *)
End_display      (* move cursor to start of next line          *)
return.
```

Figure 5.4-8   Input_MID routine.

```
Display

while txtptr^ <> 0 do    (* while byte pointed by txtptr is nonzero *)
  wait until Tport ready for output
  Tport := txtptr^       (* output byte pointed by txtptr           *)
  txtptr := txtptr+1     (* increment txtptr                        *)
enddo
return.
```

Figure 5.4-9   Display routine.

```
Input_byte

wait until Tport receives new byte    (* from keyboard *)
tbyte := Tport                        (* input byte    *)
return.
```

Figure 5.4-10   Input_byte routine.

```
End_display
wait until Tport ready for output        (* test port status *)
Tport := tbyte                           (* output byte       *)
wait until Tport ready for output        (* test port status *)
Tport := CR                              (* output CR         *)
wait until Tport ready for output        (* test port status *)
Tport := LF                              (* output LF         *)
return.
```

Figure 5.4-11 End—display routine.

```
Input                      (* application layer routine      *)

tbyte := Tport             (* input byte from Tport          *)
if Tport status OK then    (* otherwise ignore byte          *)
  if TBF = 0 then          (* if TBUF empty                  *)
    if BYI = 0 then        (* if first byte from keyboard    *)
      BYI := 1             (* change AL's state to "input"   *)
      Echo_byte            (* send DID  to screen            *)
      tbnxt^ := tbyte      (* save DID  in TBUF              *)
      tbnxt := tbnxt+1     (* increment tbnxt pointer        *)
      byte := MID          (* define SID byte                *)
      tbnxt^ := tbyte      (* save SID  in TBUF              *)
      tbnxt := tbnxt+1     (* increment tbnxt pointer        *)
    endif
    Echo_byte              (* send byte to screen            *)
    tbnxt^ := tbyte        (* save byte in TBUF              *)
    tbnxt := tbnxt+1       (* increment tbnxt pointer        *)
    if byte = CR then      (* if last byte of message        *)
      byte := LF
      Echo_byte            (* send NL to screen              *)
      tbnxt^ := tbyte      (* save NL in TBUF                *)
      tbnxt := tbnxt+1
      tbnxt^ := EOT        (* save EOT in TBUF               *)
      tbnxt := tbnxt+1
      SP := 1              (* request message transmission   *)
      TBF := 1             (* TBUF became full               *)
      BYI := 0             (* change AL's state to "ready"   *)
      tbend := tbnxt       (* prepare TBUF pointers for      *)
      tbnxt := tborg       (* the NL routines                *)
    endif
  endif
endif
return.
```

Figure 5.4-12 Input routine.

bytes, one at a time, continues until the Input routine recognizes the CR byte. When the CR key is pressed, the data packet is terminated by appending the LF and EOT bytes. The LF is also sent to the terminal's screen to move the cursor to the next line. When the Input routine terminates data-packet input, it also changes the AL state to *ready,* requests packet transmission (SP: = 1) and asserts the TBF flag. Since the next operation to be performed on the TBUF buffer is packet transmission by the NL layer, the buffer pointers tbnxt and tbend are prepared so that they define the boundries of the buffer in memory.

All processing of bytes arriving from the network medium through the network port is done by the Receive routine together with PRE_received, DID_received, and the Accept routines. The Receive routine (Fig. 5.4-13) is called by the Nisr routine whenever a network-port interrupt happens while the network layer is expecting a byte arrival. The Receive routine always inputs a byte from the network port. Even if the byte were to be rejected, it has to be read from the network port to clear its interrupt request. If there are any errors, the byte is ignored. If a PRE byte is received, the PRE_received routine (Fig. 5.4-14) is called, which changes the rstate to 1—in other words, makes the NL start expecting the second byte in a packet. If an unexpected PRE byte arrives from the network and the RBUF buffer is empty, the rbnxt pointer is reinitialized. The DID_received routine (Fig. 5.4-15) is called from the Receive routine whenever a byte is received while a second byte of a packet is expected (rstate = 1). If the byte is equal to the node's MID and the RBUF buffer is empty, the NL starts accepting the packet (rstate: = 2). If the byte is different, the NL returns to waiting for a PRE byte (rstate: = 0). The Accept routine (Fig. 5.4-16) is called whenever a byte

```
Receive                        (* network layer routine          *)

nbyte := Nport                 (* input byte from Nport           *)
if Nport status OK then        (* otherwise ignore byte           *)
    if nbyte = PRE then        (* if first byte of packet received *)
      PRE_received
    elseif rstate = 1 then     (* if next byte after PRE received *)
      DID_received
    elseif rstate = 2 then     (* if already receiving a packet   *)
      Accept
    else
      rstate := 0              (* clear receive state             *)
    endif
endif
return.
```

Figure 5.4-13   Receive routine.

```
PRE_received

if rstate <> 0 and RBF = 0 then (* if unexpected PRE byte received  *)
    rbnxt := rborg              (* reinitialize RBUF buffer pointer *)
endif
rstate := 1                     (* start waiting for DID byte       *)
return.
```

Figure 5.4-14   PRE_received routine.

```
DID_received

if nbyte=MID and RBF=0 then    (* if MID recvd and RBUF buffer free *)
    rstate := 2                (* start accepteing the packet       *)
else
    rstate := 0                (* start waiting for a PRE byte       *)
endif
return.
```

Figure 5.4-15   DID_received routine.

```
Accept

if nbyte = EOT then            (* if last byte of frame received  *)
    DP := 1                    (* request message display         *)
    RBF := 1                   (* RBUF became full                *)
    rstate := 0                (* start waiting for a PRE byte    *)
    rbend := rbnxt             (* prepare RBUF pointers for       *)
    rbnxt := rborg             (* AL routines                     *)
else
    rbnxt^ := nbyte            (* save byte in RBUF               *)
    rbnxt := rbnxt+1           (* increment RBUF buffer pointer   *)
endif
return.
```

Figure 5.4-16 Accept routine.

arrives from the medium while rstate = 2. If the byte is an EOT byte, it marks the end of the data packet. In such a case, a request to display the packet is made to the AL by asserting the DP flag. Also, the NL starts awaiting another PRE byte marking another packet being transmitted through network medium. When the Accept routine determines that the byte received is not an EOT byte, such a byte is unconditionally appended to the RBUF buffer.

5.4.5 Demonstrations

1. Use three nodes (*A,B,* and *C*). Exchange messages between nodes.
2. Stop the program in node *C*. Send a message from *A* to *C*. Send a message from *A* to *A*. Send a message from *A* to *B*. What happens?
3. Make nodes *B* and *C* have identical IDs. Demonstrate multicast.

5.4.6 Problems

1. Implement multicast in the algorithm.
2. Implement automatic message acknowledgement (an ACK frame sent back from destination node to the source node).
3. Implement error detection and ACK/NAK response. (ACK is a positive acknowledge, sent when the packet is received without errors; NAK is a negative acknowledge, sent when the packet is received with errors.)
4. Implement multipacket messages.
5. If the COUNT is used in packet header instead of an EOT terminator should it be placed before or after the DID field in the packet frame? Why?

5.5 LAB 5—CSMA MEDIUM-ACCESS SCHEME

5.5.1 Purpose

This experiment illustrates the concept of a medium-access scheme based on a CSMA technique. The purpose of any medium-access scheme is to prevent collisions, for example, prevent situations in which more than one node transmits to the network medium (the cable) simultaneously. The principle of the CSMA is simple: if a node wants to transmit, it should first watch the medium to decide if some other node is using it (carrier sense). Only if a node determines that medium is free (no carrier) can transmission begin. However, once a transmission is started, it continues until completion, disregarding possible collisions and assuming that all other nodes will follow this principle and collisions will not happen. This technique prevents most—but not all—collisions. For example, if two nodes decide to start transmissions at the same time, both of them will find the medium free and start transmitting simultaneously.

5.5.2 Operation Principles

This experiment integrates the AL developed in Lab 4 with a modified NL implementing the CSMA medium-access technique. Messages are created and consumed in exactly the same way as they were in Lab 4. Frame format, given in Fig. 5.5-1, is the same as that used in Lab 4. Also, the operations and structure (Fig. 5.5-2) of the interlayer interface are identical to those used in Lab 3 and Lab 4 (see Figs. 5.3-2 and Fig. 5.3-6). Only the transmitting part of NL is modified. Data frames are received in the same way as in Lab 4.

In the transmit direction, the NL is activated whenever the AL completes a message creation and requests frame transmission by asserting the SP flag. At this point, the NL has to determine whether the network medium is free. This is achieved by testing the network-port operations in the receive direction during a period of time equivalent to a time used to transmit 2 bytes on the network medium. With 2400 bytes per second, using 1 start bit and 1 stop bit, it takes $\frac{1}{240}$ to send 1 byte, that is, $\frac{1}{120}$ of a second to send 2 bytes. A byte arrival means that some other node is transmitting, that is, that the medium is busy. If there is no byte arrival during the waiting time, the NL can assume that the medium is free. Two-byte waiting time is used because the network port—implemented using ACIA or an equivalent integrated circuit—can report new byte arrivals only at the moment when all bits of a byte have been received. If a 1-byte waiting time were used, a byte could arrive during the waiting time, but it reception by the ACIA would not be completed until after the expiration of the waiting time.

```
packet

PRE,DID,SID,.. data .. ,EOT
```
Figure 5.5-1 Packet format.

```
buffers in memory :


              TBUF                        RBUF

TBORG   --> PRE        RBORG   --> SID
            DID                     .
            SID                     .
             .                      d
             .                      a
             .                      t
            d                       a
            a         RBEND   -->
            t
            a
             .
             .
            EOT
TBEND   -->
```

Figure 5.5-2 Buffers in memory.

If this were the case, the NL would assume that the medium was free whereas, in fact, it was busy. Longer waiting times could be used, but this is not necessary. Assuming that there are no significant delays in the stream of bytes transmitted as a frame to the medium, a 2-byte waiting time guarantees detection of medium activity.

If the network medium is found to be busy, the process of testing its activity, as previously described, is repeated until the medium becomes free. Then, frame transmission begins, and, once started, is carried on unconditionally until all bytes of the frame have been transmitted. At that moment, the AL is informed that the message transmission has been completed.

It is possible and can easily be demonstrated that 2 nodes will find the medium free simultaneously and will start to transmit their frames. In such a case, the frames will collide in the medium. This experiment does not deal with the problem of such collisions, which is illustrated in Lab 7 and solved in Lab 9. In this experiment, if a collision happens, destination nodes receive distorted messages. It is also possible that the collided frames are not received at all if the destination fields in collided frames are distorted.

5.5.3 Algorithm Design

Only the NL is modified in this experiment as compared to Lab 4. The NL is implemented as a two-level state machine, shown in Fig. 5.5.-3. Two general states are defined, similar to Experiment 4. In the *receive* state, the node monitors transmissions occurring in the medium and accepts only the data packets that have destination fields equal to the node's ID. In the *transmit* state, the node outputs a data packet (prepared by the AL) to the network medium. A logical variable BYS is used to encode the current state of the NL (Fig. 5.5-3). If BYS = 0, the NL is in the *receive* state. When BYS = 1, the NL is in the *transmit state*. The state transitions for NL general states are defined in Figs. 5.5-4 (a) and 5.5-5(a). For most of time, the node is in the *receive* state. The state is changed to *transmit* when a packet transmission is requested by the

FIGURE 5.5-3 STATE ENCODING USING LOGICAL VARIABLE BYS.

State	BYS
Receive	0
Transmit	1

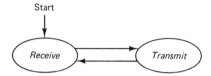

(a) State diagram — NL only, AL as in experiment 3.

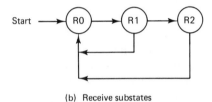

(b) Receive substates

Figure 5.5-4 NL of the Lab 5 node as a state machine.

FIGURE 5.5-5 DEFINITION OF THE NL STATE MACHINE FOR THE LAB 5 NODE.

State-transition tables			
(a) General state machine			
Current state	Next state	Condition	Action
Receive	*Transmit*	SP = 1 and rstate = 0 and medium free	BYS := 1, SP := 0
Transmit	*Receive*	Packet frame sent	BYS := 0, start timer
(b) *Receive* state machine			
Current state	Next state	Condition	Action
R0	R1	Byte received = PRE	rstate := 1
R1	R0	Byte received <> MID	rstate := 0
R1	R2	Byte received = MID	rstate := 2
R2	R0	Byte received = EOT	rstate := 0, DP := 1, RBF := 1
Rx	R1	Byte received = PRE	rstate := 1

AL, provided that the medium is found to be free. The NL's state is changed from *transmit* to *receive* when the NL completes packet transmission.

Three receive substates are used in the same way as in Lab 4. The transitions between the receive substates are shown in Figs. 5.5-4(b) and 5.5-5(b). Comparing the NL state machines used in this experiment and in Lab 5, the only difference is in the condition under which NL's state can be changed from *receive* to *transmit*.

5.5.4 Algorithm Implementation

The basic structure of the software implementing Lab 5 node layers is shown in Fig. 5.5-6, and the list of routines used is given in Fig. 5.5-7. The pseudocode algorithms for new routines are given in Fig. 5.5-8, 5.5-9, and 5.5-10.

The Main routine given in Fig. 5.5-8 is nearly identical to the Main routine used in Lab 4. The only modification is the addition of a logical variable network busy (NBY). This flag is used by the Start_send routine (Fig. 5.5-9) to determine whether the network medium is free. Initially, the NBY flag is cleared. If, after waiting for 2 byte times the flag is still 0, it means that there was no activity on the network, and packet transmission can begin. If the NBY flag is found set to 1 after the waiting time, it means that the Receive routine (Fig. 5.5-10) was invoked in the meantime by an Nport interrupt. Such an interrupt could mean only that a byte arrived from the network medium—in other words, that the medium is busy. The Receive routine used in this experiment is again very similar to that used in Lab 4. The only modification is that the Lab 5 routine sets the NBY flag to 1 every time it is invoked. The assembly-language code for new routines used in Lab 5 is given in Appendix I.

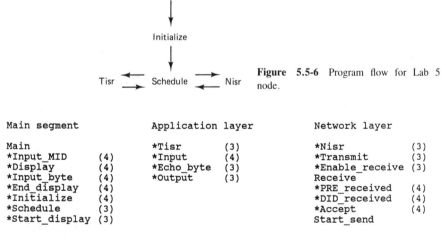

Figure 5.5-6 Program flow for Lab 5 node.

Main segment		Application layer		Network layer	
Main		*Tisr	(3)	*Nisr	(3)
*Input_MID	(4)	*Input	(4)	*Transmit	(3)
*Display	(4)	*Echo_byte	(3)	*Enable_receive	(3)
*Input_byte	(4)	*Output	(3)	Receive	
*End_display	(4)			*PRE_received	(4)
*Initialize	(4)			*DID_received	(4)
*Schedule	(3)			*Accept	(4)
*Start_display	(3)			Start_send	

* Routines as defined in Lab 3 or Lab 4

Figure 5.5-7 Lab 5 node routines.

```
Main

const
  PRE,EOT,CR,LF : character
  ERI,ETI,DI      : integer
  tborg,rborg    : integer
  inpmid = 'input MID',0 : character string
var
  SP,DP : logical
  RBF,TBF : logical
  BYS,BYD,BYI, : logical
  NBY : logical
  MID,DID : integer
  rstate : integer
  rbnxt,rbend,tbnxt,tbend : pointer
  tbyte,nbyte : character
begin
  initialize stack pointers
  Input_MID
  Initialize
  enable interrupts  (* clear interrupt mask and enter user state *)
  repeat
    Schedule
  until reset
end.
```

Figure 5.5-8   Main routine.

```
Start_send

NBY := 0              (* assume that the medium is free     *)
wait 2 byte times     (* loop                               *)
if NBY = 0 then       (* if medium is still free then       *)
  BYS := 1            (* enter "transmit" state             *)
  SP := 0             (* clear packet transmission request  *)
  enable transmit and disable receive interrupts at Nport
endif
return.
```

Figure 5.5-9   Start_send routine.

```
Receive                          (* network layer routine          *)

nbyte := Nport                   (* input data from Nport          *)
NBY := 1                         (* declare network medium busy    *)
if Nport status OK then          (* otherwise ignore byte          *)
  if nbyte = PRE then            (* if first byte of packet received *)
    PRE_received
  elseif rstate = 1 then         (* if next byte after PRE received  *)
    DID_received
  elseif rstate = 2 then         (* if already receiving a packet   *)
    Accept
  else
    rstate := 0                  (* clear receive state            *)
  endif
endif
return.
```

Figure 5.5-10   Receive routine.

5.5.5 Demonstrations

1. Use three nodes (*A*,*B*, and *C*). Make the network busy by sending a continous stream of PRE bytes from node *C*. Enter a message at node *A*. Show that it waits until the stream of bytes from *C* ends (until the network becomes free) and then is automatically and correctly transfered from *A* to *B*. You will have to write a short program that will transmit the stream of bytes from node *C*.

2. Use a low data rate on the network bus. Demonstrate message distortion due to a collision.

3. Use two nodes (*A* and *B*). Send messages across (from *A* to *B* and from *B* to *A*) simultaneously. Do they collide? Use high and low network data rates. Request message transfers by simultaneously pressing the CR keys at both nodes.

5.5.6 Problems

1. In the CSMA method, a node waits before transmitting until the network bus becomes free. In this experiment, the waiting is implemented as a loop with a fixed wait time between tests of the state of network bus (busy or free). In the experiment description, the wait time is set to 2 byte times at 2400 b/s. Can it be changed? Does it depend on the network data rate?

2. Is it possible in this medium-access method to receive and accept (that is, in our experiment, display) corrupted messages? When can such an event happen? How would the message look on receiver's screen? Could one corrupted message lead to loss or corruption of the following one?

3. Implement positive (ACK) and negative (NAK) acknowledgements as well as a timeout at the source node. If, after transmitting a message, the source node receives the ACK, it assumes that the destination received the message correctly. If an NAK is received or no acknowledgement arrives within a time limit (timeout), the source node should transmit the message again. Is such a method any improvement of network reliability over the method implemented in Experiment 5? Does it solve all reliability problems?

4. Change the wait time to be proportional to a node's ID. Would it eliminate all or most collisions?

5. Add additional wait time after network is found to be free. For example:

       repeat
               wait until network free
               wait a time proportional to node's ID
       until network free
       transmit

Would such an approach eliminate all (most) collisions?
Would it make some nodes more priviledged than others?

5.6 LAB 6—TOKEN-BUS MEDIUM-ACCESS SCHEME

5.6.1 Purpose

This experiment is designed to illustrate the operation of a token-bus LAN. The scope of token-bus implementation is limited and does not include token-recovery and network-reconfiguration operations. These functions are developed in Lab 8. In this experiment, the logical ring is created "manually" with the help of node operators. However, token passing along the logical ring as well as message transfers should occur automatically. The network, as implemented in this experiment, will be operational only until the token is lost. Since token recovery is not supported, a token loss stops network operations. Therefore, token loss should be reported to each node's operator by displaying appropriate text on the terminal screen.

Another very important goal of this experiment is to illustrate benefits of layered protocol design. In Lab 5, the NL implemented a CSMA medium–access scheme. Here, a token-bus medium-access is used. Nevertheless, both experiments share identical ALs. This is also true for all remaining experiments. The particular details of NL change from experiment to experiment, but the application–network interface remains the same, as does the overall function of the NL. In all experiments, the NL provides the same service. It transfers data packets from source to destination nodes and guarantees that the packets will be transferred without collisions. Error–free transfers should be provided, according to the OSI recommendation mode. In our experiments, error detection is limited. Further enhancements are suggested for more advanced projects in Chapter 6.

5.6.2 Operation

A passive logical ring is initially created manually by entering both the MID and the NID to each node. This way, every node on the network knows not only its own network address but also the address of the node next in logical ring. No node is initially given the right to transmit. To activate the ring, that is, to start token passing, one of the nodes (and only one) has to be given the token. When the first token pass occurs, all other nodes that are intended to participate in the logical ring must be waiting for the token. Otherwise, the token is immediately lost.

Token loss is detected by measuring the time since the last token posession. Due to the ring operation, the token has to be back at a node within a limited time. This time depends on the total number of active nodes on the network as well as on the maximum length of a data packet. Each node that is in possession of a token can transmit a packet and then has to transmit the token. The token turnaround time also depends on data transmission rate used on the network. In this experiment, as in all other experiments in this chapter, the data field of the data–packet frame is limited to 82 characters (80

```
frame structures

packet

        PRE,DID,SID, .. data .. ,EOT

token

        PRE,DID,EOT
```
                                              Figure 5.6-1 Frame formats.

characters of message text plus CR and line feed). Thus, as shown in Fig. 5.6–1, the
maximum size of a data packet is 86 bytes. The token frame, also shown in Fig. 5.6–1,
is composed of 3 bytes. Altogether, whenever a node has the right to transmit (possesses the token), it may take up to 89 byte times until the token is passed to the next
node. With a 2400–b/s data rate, it takes $1/240$ s to transmit 1 byte. Thus, it may take up
to 89 ($1/240$) or approximately 0.37 s, to pass the token to the next node along the logical
ring.

A node loses the token at the moment when it has completed token transmission.
Thus if there are N nodes on the network, waiting time is proportional to $N–1$, not to N.
For example, if there are four nodes in the ring, the wait–for–token time for each of
them will be 3 (0.37) = 1.11 s. If the token is not received within 1.11 s from the
moment when it was passed to the next node in the ring, the token was lost. Since
token recovery is not implemented in this experiment, a token loss should be reported
on the node's screen, and node operation should be stopped. Initially, when the network is started up in this experiment, several nodes have to begin waiting for a token
even before the logical ring is activated. Most probably, it will take more than 1.11 s to
start up all nodes and enter the token to one of them. Thus none of the waiting nodes
should begin measuring the token–return time until it obtains the token for the first
time.

5.6.3 Algorithm Design

The algorithm design is based on multilayer approach with AL and interlayer interface
taken from Lab 4. As shown in Fig. 5.6-1, in addition to data packets, the NL in this
experiment also transmits and receives token frames. Packets to be transmitted are
stored in the TBUF and received packets are stored in the RBUF. The token frame is
kept in a buffer, from which it is transmitted when the node passes the right to use the
medium to the next node in the logical ring. Therefore, the second byte in the token-
frame buffer contains the NID. When a token frame is received, its bytes are analyzed,
but there is no need to store it in memory. All three frame buffers are shown in Fig.
5.6-2.

Three states in the NL operations can be recognized: *receive, send packet,* and
send token (Fig. 5.6-3(a)). In the *receive* state, the NL monitors the frames arriving
from the network medium and awaits a token or a packet frame. If a packet is received,
the application layer is informed about it, but the NL remains in the *receive* state, ready
to accept another packet or the token frame. If the token is received, it means that the

```
                 TBUF                              RBUF
                 -----                             -----

TBORG     --> PRE                   RBORG -->    SID    ( part of data )
TBORG+1   --> DID                                 .
TBORG+2   --> SID = MID                           .
                .                                  d
                .                                  a
                d                                  t
                a                                  a
                t                  RBEND   -->
                a
                .
                .
                EOT
TBEND     -->


                 TOKEN FRAME

TFORG     --> PRE
TFORG+1   --> DID = NID
              EOT
TFEND     -->
```

Figure 5.6-2 Buffers in memory.

node obtained the right to transmit. If a packet is waiting to be transmitted, the state is changed to *send packet,* and packet transmission begins. The request to send a packet is signaled in the application-network interlayer interface by the send-packet flag (SP = 1). After packet transmission has been completed, state is changed to *send token,* and token transmission begins. The NL can also change its state to *send token* directly from *receive* if, at the moment of token-frame arrival, there is no request from the AL to transmit a packet (SP = 0). The definition of the general NL state machine describing state changes discussed previously is given in Fig. 5.6-4.

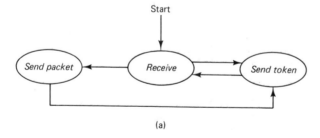

(a)

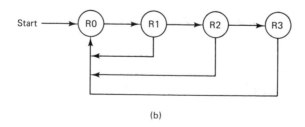

(b)

Figure 5.6-3 NL of the Lab 6 node as a state machine: (a) General states, (b) Receive substates. (Note: AL as defined in Lab 3 (4).)

FIGURE 5.6-4 STATE-TRANSITION TABLE—GENERAL STATES.

Current state	Next state	Condition	Action
Receive	*Send token*	Token received and SP = 0	BST := 1, stop timer
Receive	*Send packet*	Token received and SP = 1	BYS := 1, SP := 0, stop timer
Send token	*Receive*	Token frame sent	BST := 0, start timer
Send packet	*Send token*	Packet frame sent	BYS := 0, BST := 1

The *receive* state is partitioned into several substates, as indicated in Fig. 5.6-3(b). The reasons for state transitions within the *receive* substates are summarized in Fig. 5.6-5. In the R0 state, the network layer awaits a first byte of a frame, that is, it expects the PRE byte to arrive. When this happens, the state is changed to R1, in which the NL awaits the second byte of a frame that began with the PRE byte. The second byte of every frame in this experiment represents the DID. When a byte arrives while the Network layer is in the R1 state, it is compared to the MID. If they are equal, it means that the frame is addressed to this node and should be accepted. Thus the state is changed to R2, and a third byte is awaited. If the byte received in R1 state does not match the MID, the frame is rejected. The state is changed to R0 and the PRE byte is awaited again.

As seen in Fig. 5.6-1, the third byte position may have two different meanings. If the third byte is equal to the EOT, it means that the token was just received. In such a case, waiting for a token terminates, the general state is changed to either *send packet* or *send token*, and the receive substate is changed back to R0. If the third byte is not an

FIGURE 5.6-5 DEFINITION OF THE NL STATE MACHINE—RECEIVE SUBSTATES.

Current state	Next state	Condition	Action
R0	R1	Byte received = PRE	rstate: := 1
R1	R0	Byte received <> MID	rstate := 0
R1	R2	Byte received = MID	rstate := 2
R2	R0	Byte received = EOT	rstate := 0, stop timer (*)
R2	R3	Byte received <> EOT and DP = 0 and BYD = 0	rstate := 3
R3	R0	Byte received = EOT	rstate := 0, DP := 1
Rx	R1	Byte received = PRE	rstate := 1

(*) Token frame received, if SP = 1 then BSP := 1 else BST := 1

EOT byte, than the frame being received is regarded to be a data-packet frame and the third byte (the byte received in state R2) is regarded as the SID. The *receive* substate is then changed to R3, in which bytes arriving from the medium are accepted and placed in consecutive locations of the RBUF buffer until the EOT is received. The EOT received in state R3 marks the end of the data packet. The AL is informed about packet arrival and the *receive* substate is changed back to R0.

5.6.4 Algorithm Implementation

The algorithm for Lab 6 nodes is implemented using three groups of routines, as illustrated in Figs. 5.6-6 and 5.6-7. The AL routines, invoked by the terminal interrupt, are taken without changes from Lab 3 and Lab 4. Some of the NL routines and most of the main segment routines, marked by an asterisk in Fig. 5.6-7, are also taken from Lab 3 and Lab 4. Most NL routines are either new or modified. Except for the Timer_isr routine, which is invoked by timer interrupt, all NL routines are invoked by the network-port interrupt, through the Nisr routine.

The pseudocode algorithms for new or modified routines of the main segment are given in Figs. 5.6-8 through 5.6-14. New NL routines are defined in Figs. 5.6-15

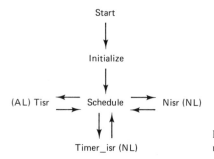

Figure 5.6-6 Program flow for the Lab 6 node.

```
Main segment                 Application layer        Network layer

Main                         *Tisr      (3)           Nisr
*Input_MID        (4)        *Input     (4)           Send
Input_NID                    *Echo_byte (3)           Send_token
Input_token                  *Output    (3)           *Enable_receive (3)
*Display          (4)                                 Receive
*Input_byte       (4)                                 PRE_received
*End_display      (4)                                 DID_received
Clear_flags                                           Token_received
Initialize                                            Start_transmit
Schedule                                              *Accept          (4)
*Start_display    (3)                                 Timer_isr
Disp_token_lost
Start_timer_to_wait_for_token

* Routines defined in Labs 3 & 4
```

Figure 5.6-7 Lab 6 node routines.

through 5.6-24. The assembly-language code for new routines used in Lab 6 is given in Appendix I.

The Main routine (Fig. 5.6-8) performs the following groups of operations: First, stack pointers are initialized to allow the use of subroutines and interrupts. Then, the MID and the NID are inputted by the operator from the terminal's keyboard. These two steps are performed by the Input_MID (previously defined) and the Input_NID (Fig. 5.6-9) routines. Then, logical variables are all cleared by the Clear_flags (Fig. 5.6-10) routine, and buffers and ports are initialized by the Initialize routine (Fig. 5.6-11).

```
Main

const
  CR,LF,EOT,PRE : character
  tborg,rborg,tforg,tfend : integer
  inpmid = 'input MID',0 : character string
  inpnid = 'input NID',0 : character string
  inptok = 'input token (Y/N)',0 : character string
  tlost = 'token lost',0 : character string
var
  TR,TL,SP,DP : logical
  RBF,TBF : logical
  BYS,BYD,BYR,BYI,BST : logical
  MID,NID,DID : integer
  rstate : integer
  txtptr,tfnxt,tbnxt,tbend,rbnxt,rbend : integer
  tbyte,nbyte : character
begin
  initialize stack pointers
  Input_MID
  Input_NID
  Clear_flags         (* clear logical variables            *)
  Input_token         (* yes/no                             *)
  Initialize          (* init. buffers, ports, and variables *)
  enable CPU interrupts
  if TR = 1 then      (* if token was input                 *)
    BST := 1          (* start sending token                *)
    enable transmit and disable receive interrupts at Nport
  endif
  repeat
    Schedule
  until TL = 1        (* until token lost                   *)
  Display_token_lost  (* display 'token lost' message       *)
end.
```

Figure 5.6-8 Main routine.

```
Input_NID

txtptr := inpnid  (* display text 'input NID'                      *)
Display           (*                                               *)
Input_byte        (* input a one-character NID code                *)
NID := byte       (* regard byte just input as  ID of the node     *)
                  (* next in logical ring                          *)
End_diplay        (* move cursor on sreen to start of next line    *)
return.
```

Figure 5.6-9 Input_NID routine.

```
Clear_flags

TR  := 0;  TL  := 0
SP  := 0;  DP  := 0
BYS := 0;  BYR := 0;  BST := 0
BYI := 0;  BYD := 0
return.
```
                                        Figure 5.6-10   Clear_flags routine.


```
Initialize

tforg^ := PRE        (* load PRE into first byte of TFBUF     *)
tforg+1^ := NID      (* load NID into second byte of TFBUF    *)
tforg+2^ := EOT      (* load EOT into third byte of TFBUF     *)
tfnxt := tforg       (* initialize tfnxt pointer for NL routine *)
tborg^ := PRE        (* load PRE into first byte of TBUF      *)
tbnxt := tborg+1     (* initialize tbnxt pointer for AL routines *)
rbnxt := rborg       (* initialize rbnxt pointer for NL routines *)
initialize vector for timer interrupt
initialize vector for Tport interrupt
initialize vector for Nport interrupt
select mode for Tport (* data rate, byte frame, interrupts    *)
clear Nport           (* clear possible pending interrupts    *)
select mode for Nport (* data rate, byte frame, interrupts    *)
return.
```
                     Figure 5.6-11   Initialize routine.


```
Input_token

txtptr := inptok  (* display text 'input token (Y/N)'         *)
Display           (*                                          *)
Input_byte        (* input a 'Y' or 'N' character             *)
End_display       (* move cusror on screen to start of next line *)
if tbyte = 'Y' then
   TR := 1        (* assume that token was input to this node   *)
endif
return.
```
                     Figure 5.6-12   Input_token routine.

Next, the operator decides whether or not this particular node is the one that will initiate token circulation around the logical ring. The Input_token routine (Fig. 5.6-12) is called to allow the operator to enter (or not to enter) the token. After this decision is made, the CPU interrupts are enabled, and, if the node has the token, token transmission is initiated by setting the BYS flag and enabling transmit interrupts at the network port. Finally, the Main routine enters a loop in which the Schedule routine (Fig. 5.6-13) is called. The loop is repeated until the token loss (TL = 1) is detected. When this happens, a token-loss message is displayed on terminal's screen by the Display_token_lost routine (Fig. 5.6-14). Several new NL routines are introduced in this experiment. The Nisr routine (Fig. 5.6-15) is a modified version of the identically named routine used in Lab 4. This routine is invoked by the network-port interrupt when the port becomes ready for output (while transmitting) or when a new byte

```
Schedule

if DP=1 and BYD=0 and BYI=0 then (* if packet display requested    *)
                                 (* and AL is in the "ready" state  *)
  Start_display
endif
return.
```

Figure 5.6-13 Schedule routine.

```
Disp_token_lost

txtptr := tlost    (* initialize txtptr pointer to point to *)
                   (* 'token lost' string                   *)
Display
End_display
return.
```

Figure 5.6-14 Display—token—lost routine.

```
Nisr                 (* network port interrupt service routine *)

save context
if BYS = 1 then      (* if busy sending packet               *)
  Send
elseif BST = 1 then  (* if busy sending token                *)
  Send_token
else                 (* assume that it is a receive interrupt *)
  Receive
endif
restore context
return.
```

Figure 5.6-15 Network interrupt-service routine.

arrives at the port from the network medium (while receiving). Two transmitting states are distinguished in this experiment. When the interrupt happens while BYS = 1, it is assumed that the node is transmitting a data packet, and the Send routine is called. The Send_token routine is called by the nisr routine if it is invoked while the NL is busy sending a token (BST = 1).

The Send routine (Fig. 5.6-16) transmits a next byte from the TBUF buffer to the network medium through the network port. When the Send routine is called after all bytes from TBUF have already been transmitted, the TBUF buffer is released for the AL, and token transmission is initiated. The token frame is transmitted by the Send_token routine (Fig. 5.6-17). This routine outputs a next byte of the token frame to the network port every time it is called. When all bytes of the token frame have been transmitted, the timer is started to measure the wait-for-token time and the network-port receive interrupts are enabled to allow the NL to receive token or data-packet frames from the network medium.

```
Send

if tbnxt = tbend then    (* if packet transmission completed      *)
   BYS := 0              (* clear BYS flag                        *)
   TBF := 0              (* TBUF became empty                     *)
   tbnxt := tborg+1      (* reinit. tbnxt pointer for AL routines *)
   BST := 1             (* request transmission of token         *)
else
   Nport := tbnxt^       (* output next byte from TBUF to Nport   *)
   tbnxt := tbnxt+1      (* increment the TBUF pointer            *)
endif
return.
```

Figure 5.6-16   Send routine. (Note: The Send routine is similar to that of Lab 5 (csma) but modified to set BST flag at the end of packet transmission. Also, Send should not enable receive interrupts at the Nport.)

```
Send_token

if tfnxt = tfend then    (* if token frame transmission completed   *)
   BST := 0              (* signal the end of token transmission    *)
   tfnxt := tforg        (* reinit. tfnxt for next token transmission *)
   Start_timer_to_wait_for_token    (* to wait for token come back   *)
   Enable_receive       (* clear Nport and enable its receive interrupt *)
else
   Nport := tfnxt^       (* output next byte of token frame from TFBUF *)
   tfnxt := tfnxt+1      (* increment token frame pointer           *)
endif
return.
```

Figure 5.6-17   Send_token routine.

The Receive routine, together with PRE_received, DID_received, Token_received, and Accept routines, is responsible for handling all bytes arriving from the network medium while the node is not transmitting itself. The operation of the Receive routine (Fig. 5.6-18) is similar to Lab 4. The new operations result from the use of two different frames in the network protocol: the token and data-packet frames. The first two bytes of a frame, the PRE and the DID bytes, are handled in the same way for both types of frames (Figs. 5.6-19 and 5.6-20). When the third byte of a frame is expected (rstate = 2) and the Receive routine is called, the Token_received routine (Fig. 5.6-21) is invoked to decide whether the token frame has been received. If the byte received from the medium as a third byte in the frame (while rstate = 2) is the EOT byte, it means that the token frame has been received. In this case, the timer is stopped and transmission of a data packet or a token frame is initiated by calling the Start_transmit routine. If the byte received while rstate = 2 is not the EOT byte, then a data packet is being received. If the RBUF buffer is empty, the byte is appended to the buffer as the SID byte, and packet acceptance begins (rstate: = 3). Data packet bytes are appended to the RBUF buffer by the Accept routine (defined in Lab 4) until the EOT byte is received, which marks the end of the packet.

```
Receive

nbyte := Nport                (* input byte from Nport                   *)
if Nport status OK then       (* otherwise ignore byte received          *)
  if nbyte = PRE then         (* if byte received = PRE                   *)
    PRE_received
  elseif rstate = 1 then      (* if byte recvd while NL is in state R1 *)
    DID_received
  elseif rstate = 2 then      (* if byte recvd while NL is in state R2 *)
    Token_received
  elseif rstate = 3 then      (* if byte recvd while NL is in state R3 *)
    Accept
  endif
endif
return.
```

Figure 5.6-18   Receive routine.

```
Fig. 5.6-16 The Send routine.
```

```
PRE_received

rstate := 1                       (* change NL's state to R1              *)
return.
```

Figure 5.6-19   PRE_received routine.

```
DID_received

if nbyte = MID then       (* if byte received = MID                       *)
  rstate := 2             (* change NL's state to R2                       *)
else
  rstate := 0            (* change NL's state to R0, in other words, *)
                         (* abort packet reception                        *)
endif
return.
```

Figure 5.6-20   DID_received routine.

```
Token_received

if nbyte = EOT then       (* if last byte of token frame received    *)
  rstate := 0            (* change NL's state to R0                      *)
  stop timer
  Start_transmit         (* activate possible packet transmission   *)
else
  if RBF = 0 then        (* if RBUF empty                                *)
    rbnxt^ := nbyte      (* save byte in RBUF                            *)
    rbnxt := rbnxt+1     (* as SID                                       *)
    rstate := 3          (* change NL's state to R3                      *)
  else
    rstate := 0          (* change NL's state to R0                      *)
  endif
endif
return.
```

Figure 5.6-21   Token_received routine.

The Start_transmit routine (Fig. 5.6-22) is called whenever the NL receives the token. At this point a decision is made whether a data packet prepared by the AL is awaiting transmission (SP = 1). If this is the case, the packet transmission is initiated (BYS := 1) and the packet-transmission request is cleared (SP := 0). If no data packet is awaiting transmission, token transmission is initiated (BST := 1). In both cases, network-port transmit interrupts are enabled to start actual transmit operations via the Nisr and Send or Send_token routines.

Two timer-related routines are used in this experiment. The Start_ timer_to_wait_for_ token routine (Fig. 5.6-23) is called from the Send_token routine at the end of token transmission. At this moment, the timer is initialized to start measuring the waiting time. The timer can be stopped by the Token_received routine when the token frame is received. If this does not happen soon enough, the timer will timeout, signaling the loss of token on the network. The constant value *time until token* (WFT) has to be so chosen to reflect the maximum token-turnaround time. If WFT is too small, the timer times out before the token has a chance to come back to the node. The WFT should take into consideration that the maximum token-turnaround time depends on the number of nodes on the network, the size of token frames and data packets, and the data-transfer rate used in the network medium.

The Timer_isr routine (Fig. 5.6-24) is invoked by the timer interrupt when the timer times out. In this experiment a timeout means token loss and terminates the node's operation. The Timer_isr routine sets the *token-lost* (TF) flag, stops the timer, and clears its interrupt. The TF flag is tested by the Main routine (Fig. 5.6-8). When TL = 1 is detected, a "token lost" message is displayed, and the node program terminates.

```
Start_transmit

if SP = 1 then        (* if request to send packet asserted  *)
   SP := 0            (* request to send packet accepted      *)
   BYS := 1           (* change NL's state to "send packet"   *)
else
   BST := 1           (* change NL's state to "send token"    *)
endif
enable transmit and disable receive interrupts at Nport
return.
```

Figure 5.6-22   Start_transmit routine.

```
Start_timer_to_wait_for_token

stop timer
load timer preload regs with WFT   (* WFT : wait for token time *)
start timer
return.
```

Figure 5.6-23   Start_timer_to_wait_for_token_routine.

```
Timer_isr

TL := 1                         (* signal token loss      *)
stop timer
clear timer interrupt
return.
```

Figure 5.6-24   Timer-interrupt-service routine (Timer-ISR).

5.6.5 Demonstrations

1. Create a ring of three nodes. Send messages, one at a time, between all nodes.
2. In a ring of three nodes (A, B, and C), enter three messages and press the CR keys at all nodes simultaneously. If the messages follow a pattern: A → B, B → C, C → A, all messages should arrive at their destination. Explain the sequence of arrivals.
3. In the same ring, simultaneously request transmission of messages in the following pattern: A → B, B → A, C → A. Will any message be lost? Why?
4. Break the ring. Recreate the ring using different set of node IDs.
5. Try to create a ring with two of the nodes having identical IDs.

5.6.6 Problems

1. Compute the waiting time (wait for token) for different network data rates, different numbers of nodes on the network, and different packet lengths.
2. Implement multipacket messages.
3. Implement token acknowledgement.
4. Implement packet error-detection and acknowledgement.

5.7 LAB 7—COLLISION DETECTION

5.7.1 Purpose

The purpose of this experiment is to illustrate network collisions and their detection. Collision detection is one of fundamental operations involved in the CSMA/CD medium-access scheme. CSMA operations were described in experiment 5. Full CSMA/CD protocol is implemented in experiment 9. As explained in Chapter 4, medium collisions in our laboratory network can be detected by LAN nodes equipped with collision detectors implemented in hardware. A collision is detected whenever two or more nodes are simultaneously outputting a signal level representing logical 0. To illustrate collision detection, we have to create a collision situation on the network. Also, the NL has to be able to react to collisions, and the fact of collision has to be signaled to the human operator of the network node.

5.7.2 Operation

In Experiment 4, we implemented a multilayer network software, which allowed for bidirectional, addressed frame transfers but did not provide any medium-access technique. Any node in which the AL completed a message creation would immediately start sending this message to the medium. To avoid collisions, human operators had to communicate directly to share the medium for their message transmissions. Otherwise, collisions occurred. This is exactly what is needed to illustrate collisions. Thus, for the most part, solutions developed for Experiment 4 are used here.

Messages are created and consumed by the AL exactly as in Lab 4. After a message has been created, its transmission begins immediately and unconditionally. However, should a collision occur during frame transmission, the transmission is aborted and the user is informed about it by the word *collision* appearing on terminal screen. In this experiment message retransmissions are not implemented. If a collision happens, the message is lost.

Network collisions create a problem not only for transmitting nodes but also for receiving nodes. If a collision happens, say halfway through frame transmission, the destination node will have started frame reception. As a result of the collision, frame transmission is aborted, and the destination node is stuck waiting for the remaining portion of aborted transmission. To avoid this problem, on each collision, reception of frames is also aborted.

5.7.3 Algorithm Design

For the most part, the algorithm for this experiment is taken from Experiment 4. The only modifications result from implementing collision-related operations. Figure 5.7-1 represents a state transition table defining NL operations for Lab 7. Note that it is a

FIGURE 5.7-1 DEFINITION OF THE NL STATE MACHINE FOR THE LAB 7 NODE.

(a) General state machine			
Current state	Next state	Condition	Action
Receive	*Transmit*	SP = 1 and rstate = 0	BYS := 1
Transmit	*Receive*	EOT sent or collision	BYS := 0, rstate := 0 tbnxt := tbnxt + 1, TBF := 0

(b) Receive-state machine			
Current state	Next state	Condition	Action
Rx	R1	Byte received = PRE	rstate := 1
R1	R0	Byte received <> MID	rstate := 0
R1	R2	Byte received = MID and RBF = 0	rstate := 2
R2	R0	Byte received = EOT	rstate := 0, DF := 1, RBF := 1, rbend := rbnxt, rbnxt := rborg
Rx	R0	Collision	rstate := 0, rbnxt := rborg

modified version of the state-transition table given in Fig. 5.4-4. State change from *transmit* to *receive* can happen either because of transmission completion (EOT sent) or because of a collision. This state change, if due to collision, is equivalent to an aborted transmission. Also, whenever a collision occurs, the *receive* substate is changed to R0 and the RBUF pointer (rbnxt) is reinitialized to point to the beginning of the RBUF buffer (rborg). This operation results in an abort of the frame reception.

Whenever a collision happens, the word *collision* appears on the node's terminal screen. Since the purpose of this experiment is to illustrate collisions, the text will appear in both transmitting and receiving nodes.

5.7.4 Algorithm Implementation

As illustrated in Figs. 5.7-2 and 5.7-3, the Lab 7 algorithm is implemented using many Lab 4 routines and preserving overall partition of software into main segment and NL and AL groups of routines. One routine, the Collision-interrupt service routine (Col_isr) is added to the network layer group. This routine is invoked by an interrupt generated by a collision detector whenever a collision situation occurs in the medium. Some of the main segment routines, the Main and Initialize, are modified to support collision detection and signalization. Algorithms for modified routines are given in Figs. 5.7-4 and 5.7-5. An algorithm for the Col_isr routine is shown in Fig. 5.7-6. Assembly-language code for new and modified routines is given in Appendix I.

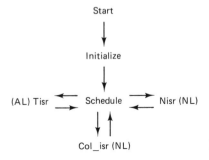

Figure 5.7-2   Program flow.

```
Main segment              Application layer         Network layer

Main                      *Tisr       (3)           *Nisr            (4)
*Clear_flags   (3)        *Input      (4)           *Receive         (4)
Initialize                *Echo_byte  (3)           *Transmit        (4)
*Schedule      (3)        *Output     (3)           *Enable_receive (3)
*Start_send    (3)                                  Col_isr
*Start_display (3)
*Input_MID     (4)
*Display       (4)
*End_display   (4)

* Routines defined in previous labs
```

Figure 5.7-3   Lab 7 node routines.

```
Main

const
  inpmid = 'input MID',0 : character string
  coltxt = 'collision',0 : character string

var
  BYS, BYD, BYI, SP, DP : logical
  TBF,RBF : logical
  rstate : integer
  txtptr : pointer
  MID : character
  tbyte,nbyte : character

begin
  initialize user and system stack pointers
  Input_MID
  Clear_flags
  Initialize
  enable interrupts and enter user mode
  repeat
    Schedule
  until reset
end.
```

Figure 5.7-4 Main routine.

```
Initialize

rbnxt := rborg      (* initialize rbnxt pointer                *)
tbnxt := tborg+1    (* initialize tbnxt pointer                *)
tborg^ := PRE       (* load "preamble byte" into first byte of TBUF *)
initialize interrupt vectors for Tport and Nport
initilaize byte frame, data rate for Tport and Nport
enable receive interrupts for Tport and Nport
initialize interrupt vector for collision detector   (* section 4.3 *)
initialize collision detector                        (* section 4.3 *)
return.
```

Figure 5.7-5 Initialize routine.

```
Col_isr                   (* invoked by collision interrupt      *)

disable Nport interrupts
clear collision interrupt
txtptr := coltxt
Display                     (* display 'collision' text            *)
End_display                 (* move cursor on screen to next line  *)
if BYS = 1 then             (* if collision while transmitting     *)
    BYS := 0                (* abort transmission                  *)
    tbf := 0                (* release TBUF buffer                 *)
    tbnxt := tborg+1        (* reinitialize TBUF pointer           *)
elseif rbnxt = 2 then       (* if collision while accepting a frame *)
    rbnxt := rborg          (* reinitialize RBUF pointer           *)
    rstate := 0             (* abort frame acceptance              *)
endif
clear Nport
enable receive  interrupts at Nport
return.
```

Figure 5.7-6 Col_isr routine.

The Main (Fig. 5.7-4) routine is nearly identical to the Main routine used in Lab 5. The only difference is the addition of the collision, 0 character string. Similarly, the Initialize routine (Fig. 5.7-5) is derived from the Initialize routine used in Lab 5. The only addition is the initialization of the collision detector and its interrupt vector. The Col_isr routine is invoked by an interrupt generated by the collision detector. On collision, network-port interrupts are disabled to prevent further transmission or reception of data. Then, the collision interrupt is cleared and a collision message is displayed on the screen. If a collision happens while the NL is transmitting a data packet, the transmission is aborted and the TBUF buffer is released for the AL. If a collision happens while the node is receiving a data packet from the network medium, the packet is rejected by reinitializing the RBUF buffer pointer and changing the rstate to 0.

5.7.5 Demonstrations

1. Use three nodes (A, B, and C). Enter long messages at A and B, both with node C as destination. Press CR at A and B simultaneously. Show collision messages on all three nodes.
2. Show that messages A → C and B → C can be transferred without collision if transfers are not requested simultaneously. How much time should you allow between message-transfer requests?
3. Demonstrate that, in case of a collision, both message transmission in the source node and message reception at the destination node are aborted and both nodes are ready for next message transfer.

5.7.6 Problems

1. Can collision situation be detected in transmitting and receiving nodes by software rather than by hardware? (*Hint:* Consider network-port ACIA feed-back property (see Chapter 4).) Implement software collision detection. Is it a better solution than hardware collision detector?
2. Does the hardware collision detector guarantee 100% collision detection? If not, under what circumstances would medium collisions be undetected?
3. If a $FF byte were used instead of the $00 byte in frame preamble, would collisions be detected in PRE time?
4. The network port ACIA can set the TxD line to a *space* (0) state for a prolonged time (see Appendix G). Would the use of this property (as an attention signal) instead of sending the PRE be a better solution? Implement and verify your algorithm.

5.8 LAB 8—TOKEN RECOVERY AND RING RECONFIGURATION

5.8.1 Purpose

The objective of this experiment is to illustrate token recovery and logical ring reconfiguration necessary to implement a full token-bus network. Token passing and packet transmission in the token-bus network were illustrated in Lab 6. In this experiment, the AL is not used at all. The NL should be able to create a logical ring automatically, without human operator's help. If a node wants to join the network, it somehow has to inform all other nodes on the network that the ring reconfiguration is needed. If a node quits the network, the ring is broken and the token is lost. Again, all nodes remaining on the network should act to reconstruct the logical ring. All these operations, for the purpose of this experiment, should be signaled to node operators.

5.8.2 Operation

When the first node is started on the network, there are no other nodes, and it is impossible to create a logical ring. Nevertheless, from the point of view of this first node, it is not known whether there are any other nodes on the network or not. Also, it is not possible to predict which node will be the first one to attempt to join the network. Therefore, each node, when joining the network, makes an attempt to perform network reconfiguration. A reconfiguration fails if there are no other nodes. Otherwise, the reconfiguration is successful. At the end of a successful reconfiguration process, each node has established an NID, thus creating a logical ring. Also, once the ring has been created, the token is passed along it. Whenever an NID is established, a text defining a new NID value appears on the screen. If a reconfiguration attempt is not successful, a text informing the operator that there are no other nodes on the network is displayed.

To enforce network reconfiguration, the new node begins its network activities by jamming the network medium. As a result, if a logical ring was operating before, token transmissions are distorted, and all nodes on the ring lose the token. This fact should be also reported on the terminal screen of each node that detected a token loss.

Any node that loses the token should begin a network-reconfiguration attempt. Network reconfiguration is achieved by *polling* the network. A polling node sends the token frame to the network using all possible network addresses, except for its own, in a token-frame DID field. If a node with an ID equal to the one used in the token frame exists on the network, it responds by beginning its own polling activity. The network address used in the token frame sent by the polling node just before a new node started the polling is used as an NID until next reconfiguration.

5.8.3 Algorithm Design

Only one kind of frame is used in this experiment, the token frame (Fig. 5.8-1). The network layer is implemented as a state machine that is considerably more complex than those used in previous experiments. State diagrams representing the *general*-state machine and the *receive*-state machine are shown in Figs. 5.8-2 and 5.8-3, respec-

```
token frame buffer in memory

TFORG    -->    PRE
                NID
                EOT
TFEND    -->
```

Figure 5.8-1 Token-frame buffer. (Note: No other buffers are used in this lab.)

State diagram

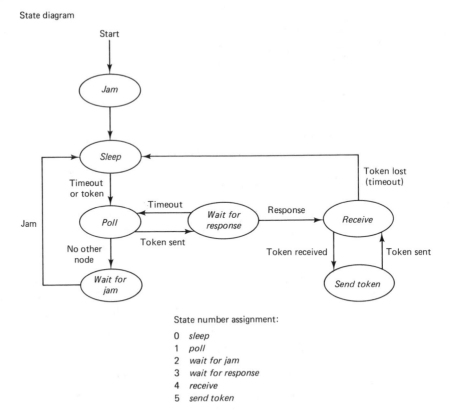

State number assignment:

0 *sleep*
1 *poll*
2 *wait for jam*
3 *wait for response*
4 *receive*
5 *send token*

Figure 5.8-2 NL of the Lab 6 node as a state machine—general states.

Receive substates

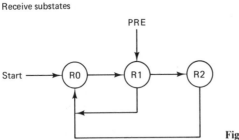

Figure 5.8-3 Receive substates.

tively. The reasons for state transitions as well as actions taken on state-change occurences are defined in Figs. 5.8-4 and 5.8-5.

When the node starts up, it enters the jam state, in which a jamming sequence is sent unconditionally to the network medium to cause token loss for all currently operating nodes. The jamming sequence has to be long enough to destroy a token. In

FIGURE 5.8-4 DEFINITION OF THE NL STATE MACHINE—GENERAL STATES.

State-transition tables			
Current state	Next state	Condition	Action
0 Sleep	1 Poll	Timeout or token frame received	state := 1, NID := MID
1 Poll	2 Wait for jam	Poll completed and no response from the network	state := 0
1 Poll	3 Wait for response	Token frame sent to next node	state := 3, Start timer
2 Wait for jam	0 Sleep	Jam detected (a byte received)	state := 0, Start timer
3 Wait for response	1 Poll	Timeout	state := 1
3 Wait for response	4 Receive	Response detected (a byte received)	Stop timer, state := 4, Start timer
4 Receive	0 Sleep	Timeout	state := 0, Start timer
4 Receive	5 Send token	Token frame received	state := 5, Stop timer
5 Send token	4 Receive	Token frame sent	state := 4, Start timer

FIGURE 5.8-5 DEFINITION OF THE NL STATE MACHINE—RECEIVE SUBSTATES.

Receive-state transition table			
Current state	Next state	Conditions	Action
R0	R1	Byte received = PRE	Rstate := 1
R1	R0	Byte received <> MID	rstate := 0
R1	R2	Byte received = MID	rstate := 2
R2	R0	Byte received = EOT	rstate := 0, (*)
Rx	R1	PRE received	rstate := 1

this experiment, only token frames are sent. Therefore, if the jamming sequence consists of four PRE bytes, token destruction is guaranteed. In Lab 10, where packets are sent as well, jamming sequence has to be longer than the sum of a longest packet and token frame to guarantee token destruction.

After completion of the jamming sequence, the node enters a *sleep* state. The length of time that the node will remain in the *sleep* state is computed as a product of node's ID and a sleep-time unit. In the *sleep* state, the node is still able to monitor network activity. Specifically, it is able to recognize a token frame possibly sent to it by some other node. When the sleep time expires or when the token frame is received, the node changes its state from *sleep* to *poll*. Note that since the sleep time is proportional to node's ID and all nodes fall asleep more or less simultaneously, only one node wakes up first—the node with the lowest ID.

Every time the NL enters the *poll* state, a new value of NID is computed. Then a token frame is sent to the medium and the state is changed to *wait for response*. A node remains in this state for a short and fixed period of time. If network activity is observed during this time, it is assumed that a node with an ID equal to the ID used as DID in the last-sent token frame has awakened and started polling on its own. Thus this ID is assumed to be the NID from now on, and the state is changed to receive. The change of state from *wait for response* to *receive* marks the end of network reconfiguration operations for this node. If no response is observed on the network in the *wait for response* state, the state is changed back to *poll* and next token frame is sent.

If all possible values for NID are tried in the *poll* state and there is no network response, it is assumed that there are no other nodes on the network, and state is changed to *wait for jam*. A node can remain in this state indefinitely, until some other node jams the network to begin the network reconfiguration process. When this happens, the state is changed to *sleep,* and reconfiguration begins.

Once a node enters the *receive state,* its normal operation on the logical ring begins. Since no packets are used in this experiment, a node in the *receive* state awaits the token frame with its ID in the DID field. When such a frame arrives, the state is changed to *send token*. In this state, the token frame with previously established NID as destination address is sent, and the state is changed back to *receive*. Until next reconfiguration, the node oscillates between the *receive* and *send token* states. If the token is not received back in time, it is assumed that it has been lost. The state is changed to sleep and reconfiguration begins.

5.8.4 Algorithm Implementation

The range of node IDs is limited because only 1 byte is used in a packet for both DID and SID. Also, some of the codes—for example, the PRE or EOT bytes—cannot be used as node IDs. For the purpose of this experiment, a node ID range of $<1,..,9>$ is completely sufficient. NL states are represented using two integer variables: *state* and *rstate*. A program-flow diagram is given in Fig. 5.8-6. No application layer routines are used in this experiment. A list of routines for Lab 8 is shown in Fig. 5.8-7. Pseudocode algorithms for new routines are given in Figs. 5.8-9 through 5.8-22.

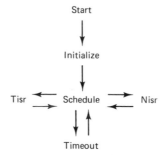

Figure 5.8-6 Program flow for the Lab 8 node.

```
Main segment        Application layer     Network layer

Main                                      Start
Schedule                                  *Enable_receive        (3)
*Input_MID    (4)                         Start_timer_to_sleep
*Display      (4)                         Timer_isr
*Input_byte   (4)                         Poll
*End_display  (4)                         Nisr
Initialize                                Receive
Display_NID                               Send
Display_Tlost                   Start_timer_to_wait_for_response
Display_nonodes                *Start_timer_to_wait_for_token (6)


* Routines defined in previous labs
```

Figure 5.8-7 Lab 8 node routines.

In the Main routine (Fig. 5.8-8), the node is initialized (by routines given in Figs. 5.8-9 and 5.8-10) and then unconditionally jams the network medium by calling the Start routine (Fig. 5.8-11). The start_timer_to_sleep routine (Fig. 5.8-12) loads timer preload registers with a value equal to the product of the node's ID and a sleep-time unit (STU). Note that the Initialize routine puts the NL in the *sleep* state. After

```
Main

const
  CR,LF,BL,PRE,EOT : character
  MINID,MAXID : integer
  STU,WFR,WFT,N : integer
  inpnid = 'input NID',0 : character string
  newnid = 'new NID =',0 : character string
  tlost  = 'token lost',0 : character string
  nonodes = 'no other nodes on network',0 : character string
var
  BYD, BYI, TBF, RBF, SP, DP : logical
  DNID,DTL,DNN : logical
  MID,NID : integer    (* NID equivalent to tforg+1^ *)
  state,rstate : integer
  frnxt,frend : pointer
  txtptr : pointer
  tbyte,nbyte : character
begin
  initialize stacks
  Input_MID
  Clear_flags
  Initialize
  Start                                        (* jam *)
  enable interrupts and enter user mode
  repeat
    Schedule
  until reset.
```

Figure 5.8-8 Main routine.

```
Clear_flags

DNID := 0;   DTL := 0;   DNN:=0
BYD  := 0;   BYI := 0
TBF  := 0;   RBF := 0
SP   := 0;   DP  := 0
return
```

Figure 5.8-9 Schedule routine.

```
Initialize

state  := 0            (* clear NL state encoding variables    *)
rstate := 0            (*                                      *)
tforg^ := PRE          (* load preamble byte to token frame    *)
frnxt  := tforg        (* initialize frame pointers            *)
frend  := tfend        (*                                      *)
tforg+1^ := MID        (* load MID byte to token frame         *)
initialize timer interrupt vector
initialize Nport interrupt vector
initialize Nport       (* receive and transmit interrupts disabled! *)
return.
```

Figure 5.8-10 Clear_flags routine.

```
Start

for k := 1 to N do
   wait until Nport ready for output  (* jam network medium by    *)
   Nport := PRE                       (* transmitting N PRE bytes *)
enddo
Enable_receive         (* clear Nport and enable receive interrupts *)
Start_timer_to_sleep
return.
```

Figure 5.8-11 Initialize routine.

```
Start_timer_to_sleep

stop timer
load timer preload registers with MID x STU
start timer
return.
```

Figure 5.8-12 Start routine.

jamming the network and falling asleep, the node enters an infinite loop, in which the
Schedule routine (Fig. 5.8-13) is executed. The Schedule routine monitors the state of
three flags: display NID (DNID), display token last (DTL), and display no nodes
(DNN). If any one of these flags is found to be set, a display routine is called to display
one of three messages informing node operator on new NID, token loss, or that no
other nodes are presently active on the network. The display routines are defined in
Figs. 5.8-14 through 5.8-16.

```
Schedule

if DNID = 1 then        (* if new NID established             *)
    DNID := 0           (* clear request to display new NID    *)
    Display_NID         (* display new NID                     *)
elseif DTL = 1 then     (* if token lost                       *)
    DTL := 0            (* clear request to display 'token lost' msg. *)
    Display_Tlost       (* display 'token lost' message        *)
elseif DNN = 1 then     (* if no other nodes on network        *)
    DNN := 0            (* clear request to display 'no nodes' msg.  *)
    Display_Nonodes     (* display 'no nodes' message          *)
endif
return.
```

Figure 5.8-13   Start_timer_to_sleep routine.

```
Display_NID

txtptr := newnid        (* initialize text pointer      *)
Display                 (* display the new NID message  *)
tbyte := SP             (* display space character and  *)
End_display             (* move cursor to next line     *)
return.
```

Figure 5.8-14   Display_NID routine.

```
Display_Tlost

txtptr := tlost         (* initialize text pointer        *)
Display                 (* display the token lost message *)
tbyte := SP             (* display space character and    *)
End_display             (* move cursor to next line       *)
return.
```

Figure 5.8-15   Display_token_lost routine.

```
Display_nonodes

txtptr := nonodes       (* initialize text pointer        *)
Display                 (* display the 'no nodes' message *)
tbyte := SP             (* display a space character and  *)
End_display             (* move cursor to next line       *)
return.
```

Figure 5.8-16   Display_nonodes routine.

The Timer_isr (Fig. 5.8-17) is invoked by an interrupt whenever the timer times out. For example, if the timer is started by the Start_timer_to_sleep routine (Fig. 5.8-12) and this node is the first node on network to wake up, the timer times out after the sleep time elapses. The state diagram given for the NL of a Lab 8 node (Fig. 5.8-2) shows that the timeout can occur when NL is in one of three states: *sleep, wait for response,* or *receive.* If the timer times out while NL is in the *sleep* or *wait for response*

```
Timer_isr                      (* on timer interrupt             *)

save context
stop timer
if state = 3 or state = 0 then  (* if sleeping or waiting for    *)
                                (* response                      *)
  state := 1                    (* change NL state to "poll"     *)
  Poll                          (* poll for next id              *)
elseif state = 4 then           (* token lost, fall asleep       *)
  state := 0                    (* change NL state to "sleep"    *)
  DTL := 1                      (* signal token loss             *)
  Start_timer_to_sleep
  NID := MID       (* prepare first value of NID for Poll routine *)
endif
restore context
return.
```

Figure 5.8-17   Timer—interrupt routine.

```
Poll

NID := NID+1               (* increment the NID                 *)
if NID > MAXID then        (* if all higher IDs polled          *)
  NID := MINID             (* start polling lower IDs           *)
endif
if NID = MID then          (* if all nodes polled               *)
  DNN := 1                 (* signal lack of other nodes on network *)
  state := 2              (* enter "wait for jam" state         *)
else                       (* if still polling                  *)
  frnxt := tforg           (* initialize frame pointers for token *)
  frend := tfend           ( *                                   *)
  enable transmit and disable receive interrupts at Nport
                           (* start token transmission          *)
endif
return.
```

Figure 5.8-18   Poll routine.

state, the state should be changed to *poll* and the Poll routine (Fig. 5.8-18) should be called. If the timeout happens when the NL is in the *receive* state, it means that the token is lost. In such a case, the state is changed to *sleep* and the timer is started to measure the sleep time.

    In the Poll routine, the NID byte in the token frame is incremented to allow trying to pass the token to another node. If all NID values that are higher than the MID of the polling node have already been used, the NID is assigned the lowest-possible ID value. When the NID value reaches that of the MID of the polling node, it means that all possible NIDs have already been tried and there was no response from the network. The conclusion in such a case is that there are no other nodes active on the network. NL's state is changed to *wait for jamming* and the DNN flag is set to request display of the ''no nodes'' message for the node operator. If the newly established value for the NID does not equal that of polling node's MID, the transmission of a token frame addressed by the new NID is initiated.

    The Nisr (Fig. 5.8-19) is invoked by network port interrupt. If the interrupt happens while the NL is in the *sleep, wait for response,* or *receive* state, the Receive rou-

```
Nisr                              (* on Nport interrupt          *)

save context
if state = 0 or state = 3 or state = 4 then
  Receive
elseif state = 2 then             (* other node jams, fall asleep *)
  state := 0
  Start_timer_to_sleep
else                              (* transmit token frame         *)
  Send
endif
restore context
return.
```

Figure 5.8-19   Network_port_interrupt_routine.

tine (Fig. 5.8-20) is called to handle the reception of a byte that arrived from the network medium. If the interrupt happens when the NL is in the *wait for jamming* state, the NL's state is changed to *sleep,* and the timer is started to measure the sleep time. The Send routine (Fig. 5.8-21) is called when the Nport interrupt happens while the NL is in the *poll* or in the *send token* state.

The Receive routine inputs a byte from the network port and checks the port status. If there are any errors in the received byte, the byte is ignored. If the Nport status indicates no errors, the byte is analyzed. The PRE byte always results in changing the *receive* substate (the rstate) to 1. If the PRE byte is received while the NL is in the *wait for response* state, it means that another node on the network woke up

```
Receive

nbyte := Nport                  (* input byte from Nport          *)
if status OK then               (* otherwise ignore byte          *)
  if nbyte = PRE then           (* if first byte of a frame received *)
    rstate := 1                 (* start waiting for second byte  *)
    if state = 3 then           (* response received while polling *)
      state := 4                (* enter the "receive" state      *)
      DNID := 1                 (* request display of new NID     *)
      Start_timer_to_wait_for_token
    endif
  elseif rstate = 1 and nbyte = MID then    (* if MID received    *)
    rstate := 2                 (* start accepting the frame      *)
  elseif rstate = 2 and nbyte = EOT then    (* if token received  *)
    if state = 0 then           (* if sleeping                    *)
      state := 1                (* start polling                  *)
      NID := MID                (* establish initial NID          *)
      Poll
    elseif state = 4 then       (* if in the "receive" state      *)
      state := 5                (* start transmitting             *)
    endif
    stop timer                  (* stop sleeping or waiting for token *)
    frnxt := tforg              (* initialize frame pointers for  *)
    frend := tfend              (* token                          *)
    rstate := 0                 (* start waiting for  a PRE byte  *)
    enable transmit and disable receive interrupts at Nport
  else
    rstate := 0                 (* start waiting for a PRE byte    *)
  endif
endif
return.
```

Figure 5.8-20   Receive routine.

```
Send

if frnxt = frend then            (* if all bytes of frame transmitted *)
  if state = 1 then              (* if polling                         *)
    state := 3                   (* start waiting for response         *)
    Start_timer_to_wait_for_response
  elseif state = 5 then          (* if transmitting                    *)
    state := 4                   (* change NL state to receive         *)
    Start_timer_to_wait_for_token  (* start waiting for token          *)
  endif
  Enable_receive          (* clear Nport and enable receive interrupts *)
else
  Nport := frnxt^                (* output next byte of frame          *)
  frnxt := frnxt+1               (* increment frame pointer            *)
endif
return.
```

Figure 5.8-21   Send routine.

from its *sleep* state as a result of this node's polling. Therefore, from the polling node's standpoint, the NID has been established and the token has already been passed. NL's state is changed to *receive,* the timer is started to measure the wait-for-token time, and the DNID flag is set to request the display of the 'new NID' message for node's operator. A byte equal to the MID received when the NL awaits the second byte of a frame (rstate = 1) means that the arriving frame is addressed to this particular node and should be accepted. In this case, the rstate is changed to 2. In this experiment, only token frames are used. Therefore, with rstate = 2, the node awaits the last byte of the token frame, the EOT byte. When this happens, it means that the token frame has been received. A token frame can be received by a node in either the *sleep* or *receive* state. If the token frame is received in the *sleep* state, the polling sequence is started. When the token frame is received in the *receive* state, the state is changed to *send token.* In both cases, the reception of the last byte of the token frame terminates the measurement of the sleep or wait time. Thus, the timer is stopped. Also, when the NL state is changed to *poll* or to *send token,* the transmission of the token frame is initialized.

The Send routine (Fig. 5.8-21) is called from the Nisr routine if the Nport interrupt happens while the NL is in the *poll* or in the *send token* state. In both cases, the task of the Send routine is to transmit the next byte of the token frame to the network medium through the network port. The end of token transmission is detected by the Send routine when both frame pointers, frnxt and frend, have equal values. If the node is polling (state = 1), the state is changed to *wait for response,* and the timer is started to measure the wait-for-response time. If the node is transmitting (state = 5), the state is changed to *receive* and the timer starts to measure the wait-for-token period.

The timer starts to measure the wait-for-response time as a result of the Start_timer_to_wait_for_response routine (Fig. 5.8-22). A constant value, wait-for-response (WFR), is loaded to the timer's preload registers by this routine. The WF determines the waiting time. The wait-for-response time should be chosen so that it is longer than the time necessary to transmit a token message from the polling node to any other node present on the network. Otherwise, the timer times out before any node has

```
Start_timer_to_wait_for_response

stop timer
load timer preload regs with WFR  (* WFR : wait for response time *)
start timer
return.
```

Figure 5.8-22   Start—timer—to— wait—for—response routine.

a chance to respond. The wait-for-response time should not be too long, because it determines the ring-reconfiguration time.

Assembly-language code for new routines used in Lab 8 nodes can be found in Appendix I.

5.8.5 Demonstrations

1. Start one node only on the network. Demonstrate the 'no other nodes' display.
2. With first node running, start another node. Show that the logical ring has been established.
3. Stop the program in one of the two nodes. Show token-loss detection.
4. Establish a two-node ring again. Then start a third node. Show token-loss detection and network reconfiguration.
5. With a three-node ring running, stop one of the nodes. Show that the ring reconfigures automatically.
6. With a three-node ring running, stop two nodes. Show that the one remaining node detects its loneliness.
7. With a three-node ring running, change IDs of all three nodes, one at a time. In effect, you should have a three-node ring again.

5.8.6 Problems

1. Could the token recovery time be shortened? If yes, implement all necessary changes in the algorithm.
2. Compute token recovery time for the following cases:
   (a) Maximum 1024 nodes, maximum packet length 2048 bytes
   (b) Maximum 16 nodes, maximum packet length 512 bytes
3. List all possible design errors that would result in an oscillating reconfiguration attempt, that is, in a situation where nodes keep trying to close the ring but either cannot do it or give up and restart the reconfiguration attempt too early.
4. If token frames were acknowledged, modify algorithm to speed up token-recovery and network-reconfiguration processes.
5. Modify the algorithm to use the start-reconfiguration (or fall asleep) frame broadcast by the node that detected token loss due to the lack of acknowledge frame.

5.9 LAB 9—CSMA/CD PROTOCOL

5.9.1 Purpose

This experiment integrates the CSMA technique developed in Lab 5 with collision-detection methods illustrated in Lab 7 to create a complete CSMA/CD LAN model. The principles of the CSMA/CD medium-access scheme are discussed in Section 2.3. Collisions are allowed but their frequency is limited due to the CSMA technique. When a collision happens, the collided frame is retransmitted. The frame-retransmission attempts are repeated until the frame is successfully (without collision) transmitted to the medium. Collisions should not be signaled to the operator.

5.9.2 Operation

Full CSMA/CD protocol is implemented in this experiment, with back-off time proportional to node's ID. A node wishing to transmit a packet first defers its transmission until the medium is found to be idle. Should a collision happen during frame transmission, the transmitting node aborts it and then backs off for a period of time. This time is computed as a product of the node's ID and a back-off time unit that is equal to 2-byte transmission time. As in Lab 8 the range of node IDs is limited to $<1,..,9>$. Thus, if node 1 is involved in a collision, it backs off for $1(1/120)$ s. When the back-off time expires, the aborted transmission is repeated, but it cannot start immediately. First, the medium has to be tested. If, right after the back-off time, the medium is found to be busy, the frame retransmission has to be defered until medium becomes free again.

　　　　The CSMA/CD should be implemented in the network layer with AL operations as defined in experiment 4.

5.9.3 Algorithm Design

The algorithm for this experiment is based on Lab 5 (CSMA) with modifications similar to those used in Lab 7 necessary to implement collision detection. Additionally, back-off time computations and frame retransmission are implemented. A state-transition table defining NL operations for Lab 9 is given in Fig. 5.9-1. One new state, *back-off*, is added to the state machine used in Lab 5. The NL enters this state from the *transmit* state on collision. The change from *back-off* to *transmit* occurs when the back-off time expires. On collision, frame transmission is aborted. To obtain the frame retransmission, the SP flag is set, which is equivalent to a repeated request to transmit the frame from the TBUF buffer.

FIGURE 5.9-1 DEFINITION OF THE NL STATE MACHINE FOR THE LAB 9 NODE.

State-transition tables

(a) General state machine

Current state	Next state	Condition	Action
Receive	*Transmit*	SP = 1 and rstate = 0	BYS := 1, SP := 0
Transmit	*Receive*	Packet frame sent	BYS := 0, TBF := 0
Transmit	*Back-off*	Collision	SP := 1, BYS := 0 tbnxt := tborg
Back-off	*Transmit*	Timeout	SP := 0, BYS := 1

(b) *Receive*-state machine

Current state	Next state	Condition	Action
Rx	R1	Byte received = PRE	rstate := 1
R1	R0	Byte received <> MID	rstate := 0
R1	R2	Byte received = MID and RBF = 0	rstate := 2
R2	R0	Byte received = EOT	rstate := 0, DP := 1, RBF := 1
R2	R0	Collision	rstate := 0, rbnxt := rborg

5.9.4 Algorithm Implementation

The program flow and a list of routines used in this experiment are given in Figs. 5.9-2 and 5.9-3, respectively. Only two routines are new. The Col_isr routine (Fig. 5.9-4) is similar to a routine with the same name used in Lab 7. This routine is invoked by an interrupt generated by the collision detector. If a collision is detected while the node is transmitting, the back-off is performed and the packet transmission request is reissued (SP := 1). Therefore, a node attempts to send the packet for an unlimited number of times until a success is achieved. A successful packet transmission is marked, in this experiment, by the lack of collision during packet transmission. Collisions can also be detected by a node with NL in the *receive* state. In this case, collisions matter only when the node has already started to accept a packet (rstate = 2). Such a packet has to be rejected. It is achieved by reinitializing the receive buffer pointer (rbnxt) and changing the rstate to 0.

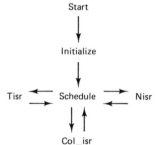

Figure 5.9-2 Program flow for Lab 9 node.

```
Main segment               Application layer           Network layer

*Main            (7)        *Tisr        (3)            *Nisr            (5)
*Input_MID       (4)        *Input       (4)            *Send            (5)
*Display         (4)        *Echo_byte   (3)            *Enable_receive  (3)
*Input_byte      (4)        *Output      (3)            *Receive         (5)
*End_display     (4)                                    *PRE_received    (5)
*Initialize      (7)                                    *DID_received    (5)
*Schedule        (5)                                    *Accept          (5)
*Start_display   (3)                                    *Start_send      (5)
*Clear_flags     (5)                                    Col_isr
                                                        Back_off
```

* Routines as defined previous labs

Figure 5.9-3 Lab 9 node routines.

```
Col_isr                        (* invoked by collision interrupt      *)

clear collision interrupt
disable Nport interrupts
if BYS = 1 then                (* if collision while transmitting      *)
   Back_off
   tbnxt := tborg              (* reinitialize TBUF pointer            *)
   SP := 1                     (* request packet transmission          *)
elseif rstate = 2 then         (* if collision while accepting a packet *)
   rbnxt := rborg              (* reinitialize RBUF pointer,           *)
                               (* in other words, reject the packet    *)
   rstate := 0                 (* start waiting for a PRE byte          *)
endif
clear Nport                    (* clear possible pending interrupts     *)
enable receive interrupts at the Nport
return.
```

Figure 5.9-4 Col_isr routine.

The Back_off routine (Fig. 5.9-5) implements computation of the back-off time and a delay loop. In this experiment, the back-off time is proportional to the MID. Therefore, the node with the lowest ID in a given collision always wins the contest for the network medium.

Assembly-language code for two new routines of Lab 9 is given in Appendix I.

```
Back_off

delay for MID * ( 1/120 of a second )
return.
```
                                                        Figure 5.9-5 Back_off routine.

5.9.5 Demonstrations

1. Use two nodes. Send messages across, hitting CR on both nodes simultaneously. Both messages should be transferred without errors. Repeat several times. Does the collision occur? Why? Does the same node always win the contention? Why?

2. Use two nodes. Write a little program for a third node unconditionally sending some bytes to the network and thus making it permanently busy. Enter messages and press CR on both CSMA/CD nodes. Then, stop the third node. As a result, both messages that were waiting for free network are transmitted. Does collision happen? Why? Should a node with a lower ID always win the contest?

3. Use three nodes. Enter messages in one of the following patterns:

   - $A \rightarrow B$, $B \rightarrow C$, $C \rightarrow A$
   - $A \rightarrow B$, $B \rightarrow A$, $C \rightarrow B$

   Any messages lost? Why?

4. Use four nodes. Show all cases when a message may be lost.

5.9.6 Problems

1. If back-off time were proportional to the sum of the frame length and node's ID, could a deadlock (repetitive, never-ending collisions) occur?

2. Which mechanism, wait before sending or back off and wait, prevents more collisions? Which one of the two prevents deadlocks?

3. Modify the algorithm using software collision detection. See Section 5.7.7.

5.10 LAB 10—TOKEN-BUS PROTOCOL

5.10.1 Purpose

Lab 6 and Lab 8 are integrated here to create a full token-bus protocol network. Logical ring reconfiguration and data packet transfers should be demonstrated. Again, it is important to realize that Lab 9 and Lab 10 have identical ALs and interlayer interfaces. NLs, however, are very different. The NL of Lab 9 implements CSMA/CD protocol, whereas the NL in this experiment implements the token-bus protocol. From the point of view of the node's user, both networks provide the same services. Nevertheless, due to the differences in the NL, only nodes with one kind of NL may cooperate on a network segment.

5.10.2 Operation

Operation of a Lab 10 node is defined by functions introduced in Lab 6 and Lab 8. Initially, when the node wants to join the network, network reconfiguration is automatically performed (see Lab 8). Then, once the logical ring has been established, the token is passed along it, and users can enter and transfer messages between any pair of nodes (see Lab 6). If the token is lost due to error or addition or removal of a node, network reconfiguration is automatically performed, and a new logical ring is established. During network reconfiguration, data packets (messages) can be entered in the network node, but their transmissions are deferred until reconfiguration is completed.

5.10.3 Algorithm Design

Lab 10 nodes use frame formats identical to those used in Lab 6 (Figs. 5.10-1 and 5.10-2). The algorithm for a Lab 10 node is basically the same as for a Lab 8 node with one additional state: *Send packet* (Figs. 5.10-3 and 5.10-4). State transitions for the general-state machine and *receive*-state machine are defined in Figs. 5.10-5 and 5.10-6, respectively.

```
packet
        PRE,DID,SID, ... data ... ,EOT
token
        PRE,DID,EOT                          Figure 5.10-1  Frame formats.
```

```
                TBUF                    RBUF
                -----                   -----

     TBORG    --> PRE        RBORG -->  SID    ( part of data )
     TBORG+1  --> DID                    .
     TBORG+2  --> SID = MID              .
                  .                      d
                  .                      a
                  d                      t
                  a                      a
                  t        RBEND   -->
                  a
                  .
                  EOT
     TBEND    -->


                TOKEN FRAME

     TFORG    --> PRE
     TFORG+1  --> DID = NID
                  EOT
     TFEND    -->
```

Figure 5.10-2   Buffers in memory.

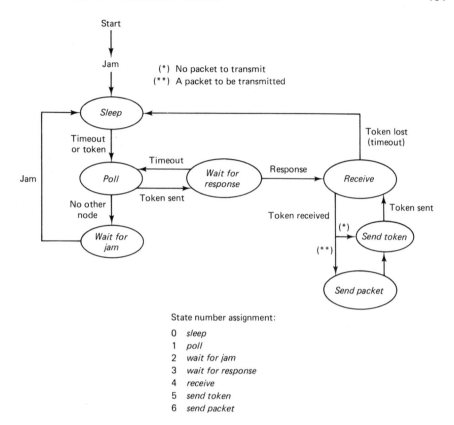

State number assignment:

0 *sleep*
1 *poll*
2 *wait for jam*
3 *wait for response*
4 *receive*
5 *send token*
6 *send packet*

Figure 5.10-3 NL for Lab 10 node as a state machine—general states.

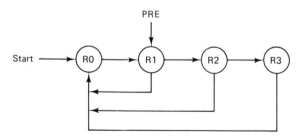

Figure 5.10-4 NL state machine—receive substates.

FIGURE 5.10-5 DEFINITION OF THE NL STATE MACHINE—GENERAL STATES.

State-transition tables			
Current state	Next state	Condition	Action
0 Sleep	1 Poll	Timeout or token frame received	state := 1, NID := MID
1 Poll	2 Wait for jam	Poll completed and no response from the network	state := 0
1 Poll	3 Wait for Response	Token frame sent to next node	state:= 3, Start timer
2 Wait for jam	0 Sleep	Jam detected (a byte received)	state := 0, Start timer
3 Wait for response	1 Poll	Timeout	state := 1
3 Wait for response	4 Receive	Response detected (a byte received)	Stop timer, state := 4, Start timer
4 Receive	0 Sleep	Timeout	state := 0, Start timer
4 Receive	5 Send packet	Token frame received and SP = 1	state := 5, Stop timer
4 Receive	6 Send token	Token frame received and SP = 0	state := 6, Stop timer
5 Send packet	6 Send token	Packet frame sent	state := 6
6 Send token	4 Receive	Token frame sent	state := 4, Start timer

FIGURE 5.10-6 DEFINITION OF THE NL STATE MACHINE—RECEIVE SUBSTATES.

Receive-state transition table

Current state	Next state	Conditions	Action
R0	R1	Byte received = PRE	rstate := 1
R1	R0	Byte received <> MID	rstate := 0
R1	R2	Byte received = MID	rstate := 2
R2	R0	Byte received = EOT or (byte received <> EOT and (DP = 1 or BYD = 1))	rstate := 0
R2	R3	Byte received <> EOT and DP = 0 and BYD = 0	rstate := 3
R3	R0	Byte received = EOT	rstate := 0, DP := 1
Rx	R1	PRE received	rstate := 1

5.10.4 Algorithm Implementation

Program flow is given in Fig. 5.10-7 and a list of routines is found in Fig. 5.10-8. Most of the routines have been defined in previous experiments. Algorithms for new routines are given in Figs. 5.10-9 through 5.10-20. Assembly-language code for new routines is given in Appendix I.

The logic of the Main routine (Fig. 5.10-9) is identical to that of the Main routine used in Lab 8. The difference is that both the AL and NL are integrated here, and therefore more variables have to be used. Similarly, the Schedule routine (Fig. 5.10-10) is a modified version of the Schedule routine used in Lab 8. In Lab 10, the message displays can be initiated only if the terminal is free in order to avoid a mix-up of packet and error messages on the terminal screen. The Clear_flags (Fig. 5.10-11) and the Initialize (Fig. 5.10-12) routines, as with the Main routine, are different from their Lab 8 counterparts only in that more variables have to be initialized.

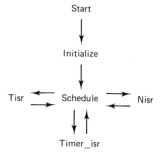

Figure 5.10-7 Program flow for Lab 10 node.

Main segment	Application layer	Network layer	
Main	*Tisr (3)	*Start	(8)
Schedule	*Input (4)	*Enable_receive	(3)
*Input_MID (4)	*Output (3)	*Nport_Interrupt_routine	(8)
*Display (4)	*Echo_byte (3)	Receive	
*Input_byte (4)		PRE_received	
*End_display (4)		DID_received	
Clear_flags		Token_received	
Initialize		Accept_SID	
*Display_NID (8)		Packet_received	
*Display_Tlost (8)		Accept_byte	
*Display_nonodes (8)		Send	
		*Start_timer_to_sleep	(8)
		*Start_timer_to_wait_for_response	(8)
		*Start_timer_to_wait_for_token	(8)
		*Timer_isr	(8)
		*Poll	(8)

* Routines defined in previous labs

Figure 5.10-8 Lab 10 node routines.

```
Main

const
  CR,LF,SP,PRE,EOT : character
  MINID,MAXID : integer
  STU,WFR,WFT,N : integer
  inpnid = 'input NID',0 : character string
  newnid = 'new NID =',0 : character string
  tlost = 'token lost',0 : character string
  nonodes = 'no other nodes on network',0 : character string
var
  MID,NID : integer                    (* NID equivalent to tforg+1^ *)
  DNID,DTL,DNN : logical
  SP,DP : logical
  BYI,BYD : logical
  RBF,TBF : logical
  RBUF,TBUF : array
  state,rstate : integer
  frnxt,frend : pointer
  txtptr : pointer
  tbyte,nbyte : character
begin
  initialize stacks
  Input_MID
  Clear_flags
  Initialize
  Start                                (* jam *)
  enable interrupts and enter user mode
  repeat
    Schedule
  until reset.
```

Figure 5.10-9 Main routine.

```
Schedule

if BYD = 0 and BYI = 0 then    (* if terminal free               *)
  if DNID = 1 then             (* if new NID established          *)
    DNID := 0                  (* request to display accepted     *)
    Display_NID                (* display info about new NID       *)
  elseif DTL = 1 then          (* if token lost                   *)
    DTL := 0                   (* request to display accepted     *)
    Display_Tlost              (* display info about token loss    *)
  elseif DNN = 1 then          (* if no other nodes on network    *)
    DNN := 0                   (* request to display accepted     *)
    Display_Nonodes     (* display info about lack of other nodes *)
  elseif DP = 1 then           (* display received packet          *)
    DP := 0                    (* request to display  accepted    *)
    BYD := 1                   (* AL enters "output" state         *)
    enable transmit and disable receive interrupts
  endif
endif
return.
```

Figure 5.10-10 Schedule routine.

```
Clear_flags

DNID := 0;  DTL := 0;  DNN := 0
SP   := 0;  DP  := 0
BYD  := 0;  BYI := 0
TBF  := 0;  RBF := 0
return.
```

Figure 5.10-11 Clear__flags routine.

```
Initialize

state := 0                (* clear NL state encoding         *)
rstate := 0               (* variables                       *)
tforg^ := PRE             (* load the PRE byte to token frame *)
frnxt := tforg            (* initialize frame pointers for    *)
frend := tfend            (* token                           *)
tforg+1^ := MID           (* load the MID byte to token frame *)
initialize timer interrupt vector
initialize Nport interrupt vector
initialize Nport          (* Nport interrupts disabled!      *)
return.
```

Figure 5.10-12 Initialize routine.

The Receive routine (Fig. 5.10-13) is called from the Nport_interrupt routine (defined in Lab 8) when the network port interrupt happens while the network layer is in the *sleep, wait for response,* or *receive* state. If the byte received from the network port is received without errors (Nport status OK), the Receive routine decides what the NL's reaction should be to the just-received byte. The PRE_received routine (Fig. 5.10-14) is called if the byte received is the PRE byte. If the PRE byte is received while the NL is in the *wait for response* state, it means that the polled node on the network has awakened, and, in effect, that the polling node has just established the

```
Receive

nbyte := Nport              (* input byte from Nport              *)
if Nport status OK then     (* otherwise ignore byte             *)
   if nbyte = PRE then      (* if a preamble byte received       *)
      PRE_received
   elseif rstate = 1        (* DID received                      *)
      DID_received
   elseif rstate = 2 then   (* if accepting a frame              *)
      if nbyte = EOT then   (* if end of frame character received *)
         Token_received
      elseif RBF = 0 then   (* if RBUF free                      *)
         Accept_SID
      else
         rstate := 0        (* reject packet                     *)
      endif
   elseif rstate = 3 then   (* if accepting a packet             *)
      if nbyte = EOT then   (* if last byte of packet            *)
         Packet_received
      else
         Accept_byte
      endif
   else
      rstate := 0           (* start waiting for next frame      *)
   endif
endif
return.
```

Figure 5.10-13 Receive routine.

```
PRE_received

rstate := 1            (* start waiting for a second byte of a frame *)
if state = 3 then      (* if waiting for response                    *)
   state := 4          (* change NL state to "receive"               *)
   DNID := 1           (* request display of 'new NID' message       *)
   Start_timer_to_wait_for_token
endif
return.
```

Figure 5.10-14 PRE_received routine.

NID value and passed the token on to the next node on logical ring. Therefore, NL's state is changed to *receive,* and a request is made to display the new NID message (DNID := 1). Whenever the PRE_received is executed, the rstate is changed to 1 and the NL begins to await an arrival of the second byte of a frame from network medium.

The DID_received routine (Fig. 5.10-15) is called from the Receive routine whenever the second byte of a frame is received. If this byte proves to be equal to MID, then frame acceptance begins (rstate := 2); otherwise, the frame is rejected (rstate := 0). If the EOT byte is received while the NL is expecting the third byte of a frame (rstate = 2), the Token_received routine (Fig. 5.10-16) is called. The token frame can be received while the NL layer is in the *sleep* or in the *receive* state. In the first case, the state is changed to *poll,* and the polling process is initiated. In the second case, the send packet (SP) flag is tested. The SP being set means that there is a pending request from the AL to transmit a data packet. Therefore, the state is changed to *send*

```
DID_received

if nbyte=MID then        (* if MID received          *)
   rstate := 2           (* start accepting a frame *)
else
   rstate := 0           (* reject the frame         *)
return.
```

Figure 5.10-15 DID_received routine.

packet, and packet transmission is initiated. If the SP flag is found to be cleared, there is no need to transmit a data packet, and token transmission is initiated. Whenever the token frame is received, the rstate is changed to 0, so that the receiving part of the NL begins waiting for a PRE byte from the network medium. The Accept_SID routine (Fig. 5.10-17) is called when the third received byte of a frame is not the EOT byte, provided the RBUF buffer is free (RBF = 0). According to the frame formats defined for this experiment in Fig. 5.10-1, such a situation means that a data packet is being received and the Accept_SID routine places the just-received byte in the RBUF buffer as the SID byte. The rstate is changed to 3, and acceptance of remaining bytes of the data packet begins. If the RBUF buffer is full, the data packet is rejected, and the rstate is changed to 0 by the Receive routine.

When the node is already accepting a data packet (rstate = 3) and the EOT byte is received, the Packet_received routine (Fig. 5.10-18) is called. This routine terminates packet acceptance (rstate := 0), issues a display-packet request to the AL (DP := 1), and prepares RBUF buffer pointers for AL routines. If the byte received while rstate = 3 is not the EOT byte, the Accept_byte routine (Fig. 5.10-19) is called. This routine simply appends the newly arrived byte to the RBUF buffer.


```
Token_received

if state = 0 then        (* if sleeping                      *)
   state := 1            (* start polling                    *)
   NID:=MID              (* establish initial NID            *)
   Poll
   frnxt := tforg        (* initialize frame pointers for    *)
   frend := tfend        (* token                            *)
elseif state = 4 then    (* if receiving                     *)
   stop timer            (* stop waiting for token           *)
   if SP = 1 then        (* if packet transmission requested *)
      SP := 0            (* clear 'send packet' flag         *)
      state := 6         (* change NL state to "send packet" *)
      frnxt := tborg     (* initialize frame pointers for    *)
      frend := tbend     (* packet                           *)
   else
      state := 5         (* change NL state to "send token"  *)
      frnxt := tforg     (* initialize frame pointers for    *)
      frend := tfend     (* token                            *)
   endif
endif
rstate := 0
enable transmit and disable receive interrupts at Nport
return.
```

Figure 5.10-16 Token_received routine.

```
Accept_SID

rstate := 3              (* start accepting the packet *)
rbnxt^ := nbyte          (* save byte as SID in RBUF    *)
rbnxt := rbnxt+1         (* increment RBUF pointer      *)
return.
```

Figure 5.10-17 Accept__SID routine.

```
Packet_received

DP := 1                 (* signal packet reception       *)
RBF := 1                (* protect data in RBUF buffer   *)
rbend := rbnxt          (* initialize RBUF pointers for  *)
rbnxt := rborg          (* AL routines                   *)
rstate := 0             (* start waiting for a new frame *)
return.
```

Figure 5.10-18 Packet__received routine.

```
Accept_byte

rbnxt^ := nbyte         (* store byte in the RBUF buffer *)
rbnxt := rbnxt+1        (* increment RBUF buffer pointer *)
return.
```

Figure 5.10-19 Accept__byte routine.

The Send routine (Fig. 5.10-20) is called from the Nport_interrupt routine when an Nport interrupt happens while the NL is in the *poll, send token,* or *send packet* state. If the Send routine is called when all bytes of a frame have already been transmitted (frnxt = frend), it marks the end of frame transmission. Otherwise, the next byte of the frame being transmitted is sent to the network port. Two types of frames can be transmitted: data packets and tokens. Token frame can be transmitted during normal operation of the ring (state = 5) or during polling (state = 1). If a data-packet transmission is completed (Send routine called while state = 6), the TBUF buffer is released, and token transmission is initiated. When token transmission ends while the node is polling (state = 1), the state is changed to *wait for response*, the timer is started, and receive interrupts of the network port are enabled. When the token transmission is completed during normal operation of the logical ring (state = 5), NL's state is changed to *receive* and the timer is started to measure the wait-for-token time. Also, the receive interrupts of the network port are enabled to allow the node to monitor frames arriving from the network medium.

```
Send

if frnxt = frend then      (* if all bytes of a frame transmitted    *)
   if state = 6 then        (* if a packet transmission completed     *)
      state := 5            (* start token transmission               *)
      TBF := 0              (* allow write operations to TBUF buffer  *)
      frnxt := tfnxt        (* initialize frame pointers for          *)
      frend := tfend        (* token                                  *)
      enable transmit and disable receive interrupts at Nport
   elseif state = 1 then    (* if polling                             *)
      state := 3            (* start waiting for response             *)
      Start_timer_to_wait_for_response
      Enable_receive        (* clear Nport and enable its rcv intrpts *)
   elseif state = 5 then    (* if a token transmission completed      *)
      state := 4            (* change NL state to "receive"           *)
      Start_timer_to_wait_for_token
      Enable_receive        (* clear Nport and enable its rcv intrpts *)
   endif
else
   Nport := frnxt^          (* transmit next byte of frame            *)
   frnxt := frnxt+1         (* increment frame pointer                *)
endif
return.
```

Figure 5.10-20   Send routine.

5.10.5 Demonstrations

1. Create a logical ring with three nodes. Exchange messages between all nodes.

2. Send a message to a nonexisting node. What happens?

3. Change the ID of one of the three nodes and put it back into the ring.

4. Send these messages, pressing the CR keys simultaneously:

   • $A \rightarrow B,\ \ B \rightarrow C,\ \ \ C \rightarrow A$
   • $A \rightarrow B,\ \ B \rightarrow A,\ \ \ C \rightarrow A$

   Explain the sequence of message arrivals. Are any messages lost? Why?

5. Write a small program monitoring the network, for example, displaying all characters transmitted on the network bus. Show message and token frames.

5.10.6 Problems

1. Assume that multiple-packet messages are used. What should be done if the token is lost before all packets of a message are transferred from source to destination? Solve this problem for both transmit and receive directions.

2. Can token loss be detected during packet reception?

3. Consider the following modification of the token-bus algorithm:

   A node in posession of a token does not pass it on but polls all possible node IDs to find a node willing to send a packet. The token is passed to the first node found to be willing to transmit. As long as no nodes have packets to transmit, the token remains at the original node.

Would such a mechanism do any of the following?

(a) Prevent token losses

(b) Slow down or speed up the network

(c) simplify or complicate the algorithm

6

Laboratory LAN Extension

In this chapter additional projects that can be developed for the LAN laboratory are discussed. Only general descriptions for networking functions are given, assuming the student's familiarity with algorithm design and implementation methods introduced in Chapter 5. The projects are more complex but many of the routines developed for experiments 1 through 10 can be directly implemented. The projects are presented in a logical sequence that allows the software developed in the earlier projects to be utilized in the more advanced projects. This technique is known as the *layered network protocol design* approach. The proposed projects by no means exhaust all possibilities and are selected to represent the most important networking functions that were not covered in Chapter 5.

The projects include a network traffic monitor, which can be used to analyze network performance, a gateway node, which can connect two network segments operating with different protocols, and a set of projects involving more advanced functions of LAN protocols. These include multiple-frame and message buffering, frame-acknowledge methods, and error detection. The last two projects deal with some aspects of the presentation and application layers.

6.1 LAN TRAFFIC MONITOR

The objective of this project is to develop a program for one unique node that will not participate in network operations but will monitor and analyze all frames being sent through the network medium. Two versions of this project can be developed, one for the CSMA/CD LAN and one for the token-bus LAN. In both cases, the overall objective is to monitor network traffic in real time and display performance parameters on the terminal screen.

The network monitor for CSMA/CD protocol should specifically analyze network collisions. Interesting performance parameters are the number of collisions per minute and the average number of collisions per packet transmission. Also, overall performance indicators such as medium utilization are very interesting. Medium utilization can be defined as a ratio between the time used for packet-transmission attempts and the total network time. A better utilization indication is given by the ratio of time used for successful data transmissions to the total network operation time.

Network performance for the token-bus LAN is indicated by frequency of token losses and the time used for token-recovery operations. Also, the ratio of time used for token transfers and the time used for data transfers is a good indicator of network performance.

For both traffic monitors, measurements displayed on the screen should include both current and long-term performance indicators. Also, traffic-simulation programs should be developed for network nodes to allow testing network-performance limits. Traffic simulators should reside on normal network nodes and should generate—randomly, if possible—packet-transmission requests.

6.2 GATEWAY NODE

This project requires the use of the specialized network node described in Chapter 4. The gateway node operates between two network segments and therefore has to be equipped with two network ports. In this project this additional hardware is exploited to ensure communication between network nodes belonging to different segments and using different medium-access schemes. On one side, the gateway node implements the CSMA/CD protocol; on the other side, it uses the token-bus protocol.

One of the primary functions of the gateway node is address translation. Data packets addressed to network nodes belonging to the other segment must have destination fields indicating this fact. All such packets have to be received by the gateway node and then retransmitted, possibly with changed destination field, on the other side of the gateway node. Packets with destination fields indicating that they are addressed to one of the nodes on their own network segment are not processed by the gateway at all. Since many nodes may be sending packets to the other segment, the gateway node has to provide appropriate buffering.

The gateway node has to implement both the CSMA/CD and token-bus protocols, one for each of its network ports. Therefore, it must perform all functions of NLs as defined in Lab 9 and Lab 10, respectively. There is no need for an AL in the gateway node. The NL routines from Lab 9 and Lab 10 can be used almost without any change.

6.3 MULTIPLE FRAME AND MESSAGE BUFFERING.

In all experiments from Chapter 5, only one transmit buffer and one receive buffer per network node were used. As a result, each node could operate on only one data packet at a time. Therefore, all messages were restricted in size to one packet. Moreover, only one packet—and thus one message—could be buffered at a time. This was not much of a problem in the transmit direction because all messages were created by typing them in, which was relatively slow. In the receive direction, the use of only one buffer could result in packet (message) loss if two or more nodes transmitted to the same destination node simultaneously. In such a case, for both Lab 9 and Lab 10, the packet would be transmitted through the medium correctly but would be lost anyway because of receiver's inability to accept it.

The purpose of this project is to create multiple buffers allowing use of long messages, with many packets per message. Also, several messages should be able to be accepted simultaneously. For example, if two nodes are transmitting long messages to one destination node, the packets belonging to separate messages arrive at the destination node interleaved in time. Not only should all packets be accepted, but the messages should also be reconstructed properly. Of course, if messages are to be transferred in many packets, they have to be first partitioned in the transmit direction. This problem refers to the *fragmentation* concept (Chapter 1).

A suggestion about how to organize multiple buffers occurs in Sections 3.4 and 3.5 describing chained-buffer concept used by both LAN coprocessor and LAN controller VLSI devices.

6.4 MESSAGE ACKNOWLEDGEMENT AND FREE-BUFFER INQUIRY

One of the major functions performed by the lower layers of an OSI network is to support error-free transfer of messages. A combination of two methods is used to ensure this function: message (or packet) acknowledgement and error detection through the CRC code. This project is concerned with packet acknowledgement, and error detection using CRC code is the subject of the following project.

The concept of packet acknowledgement stems from the fact that if a packet is received with an error, it should be retransmitted. The transmitting node will not know whether a packet was received error-free unless it is somehow informed about it by the receiving node. Two types of acknowledgment frames are used: ACK and NAK. If a packet is received with an error, a NAK frame is sent. If no errors are detected in the received packet, the ACK frame is sent. It can also happen that a transmitted packet is not received at all, for example, due to an error in the destination address field. In such a case, no acknowledgment frame is sent. Therefore, a time limit has to be set during which an acknowledgment frame must be received. A lack of any acknowledgment frame in this time means that there was some problem with packet transmission and the packet has to be retransmitted. In both the CSMA/CD and token-bus cases, the next packet in multiple-packet messages cannot be transmitted unless an ACK frame has been received by the source node, confirming error-free reception of the previous packet by the destination node.

There are different requirements for the form of acknowledgment frames in the CSMA/CD and token-bus networks. In the token-bus network, a packet can be sent only by a node in possession of a token. Therefore, if an acknowledgment frame is sent by a receiving node immediately after packet reception, this frame does not have to be addressed. At this moment, the token is still at the node that transmitted the packet and, before passing the token along, waits for the acknowledgment frame. In the CSMA/CD case, the problem is more complicated. Nodes can use the network medium at random and collisions are allowed. Therefore, an acknowledgment frame may have to be deferred (due to another node winning the contention) or may have to be repeated several times (due to collisions). Other packets can be transmitted on the medium in the meantime. As a result, acknowledgment frames for the CSMA/CD network have to be addressed both by the source and destination addresses.

If a packet is lost due to receive buffer overflow, a NAK frame can be sent to request packet retransmission. Such a solution guarantees error-free transfer of messages, but the time used to transmit a packet for which there was no room in the destination node is lost. This problem can be avoided by asking the destination node about its buffering capabilities before sending a data packet. Such a technique can easily be used for a token-bus network. When a source node obtains the token, before sending a data packet it can send a *free-buffer-enquiry* frame to the destination node. An ACK frame (identical to the frame used to acknowledge data packets) received from the destination node means that a source node has enough room in its receive buffer to accept one packet. In this case, the packet is sent. Otherwise, the source node passes the token on and tries to transmit the packet on next token possession.

The buffer-enquiry technique cannot be used directly in the CSMA/CD network because of its random medium-use characteristics. However, a buffer reservation method in which the source node can request buffer space to be reserved in the destination node before sending the packet can be implemented. Again, reservation request and acknowledgment frames have to be addressed by both destination and source IDs.

6.5 CRC GENERATION AND TESTING

The CRC code is used in most computer networks, including LANs, to support error-detection and error-correction functions. It is a relatively simple and standard, if tedious, operation and therefore was not included in the experiments in Chapter 5. Nevertheless, it is a fundamental ingredient of any network protocol, so it is worthwhile to implement it as a project.

CRC bytes are computed in the transmitting node and attached to a data packet as its trailer field. Usually, only the data field of packets is covered by a CRC. In the receiving node, the CRC bytes are computed again using the data field as received. If there are no errors during packet transmission, the CRC bytes received in the packet's trailer field are identical to the computed ones. Any mismatch means an error and the need for packet retransmission.

The CRC bytes are computed using a standard algorithm based on the concept of a *generating polynomial*. The CRC computation algorithm is published in several books. A clear presentation that can be readily adapted for this project is given in [3].

6.6 UPPER LAYERS—MESSAGE ENCODING

This project is concerned with functions prescribed by the OSI model for the presentation layer, that is with text transformations. In terms of complexity, the project is very similar to the previous project on CRC generation. Again, the purpose of additional segments of software that have to be written for this experiment is to encode a given sequence of bytes (a message) into another form.

Two types of text transformations may be used. Data compression, where messages created in source nodes have to be encoded in order to shorten their length, is used to reduce the time necessary for their transmission. Another form of text transformation may require that messages be encoded in order to prevent unauthorized use. In this case, only a user knowing the key (password) can decode received messages. In both cases, messages are encoded in the source node before transmission and decoded (transformed back to their original form) after reception in the destination node.

6.7 DISTRIBUTED DATA BASE

This project illustrates some concepts of a distributed processing system implemented in a LAN and is the most ambitious of the projects. The actual level of complexity of this project varies, but it is best if fundamental elements of all previous experiments and projects are used—thus creating a model of a complete, multilayer OSI network.

A model of a distributed data base consists of several files scattered through LAN nodes and a central directory located in one of the nodes. For the purpose of illustration, we limit the files to one type only and regard them all as text messages. A file may be created at a node by simply giving it a name and typing in a text at the node's terminal. Whenever a file is created, the application layer in this node should automatically update the central file directory. This can be achieved by sending a message from the node where the file was created to the node that contains the central directory. This message should be created and automatically sent by the AL without human-user intervention. Also, the user should be able to delete files located in his or her node. In such a case, an appropriate message should be sent by the AL to remove the information about the deleted file from the central directory.

The user should be allowed to create files to be stored in his or her own node and to obtain files located at other nodes. Also, the user should be allowed to view, but not modify, a part of the central file directory to find out which files are available. The actual location of these files should be of no concern to the user. To obtain a file, the user should type in a command specifying the file name. The file should be located automatically by the AL using the central file directory. Then, the AL should initiate file transmission from the node where it is located to the node where the file request originated. Finally, the received file should be displayed on the user's screen, thus completing the execution of the user's command by the network operating as a distributed system. Note that as a result, the networking operations (transferring of request messages and the files) are transparent to the user, the true property of a distributed system.

Summarizing, the user should have four commands available: create a file, delete a file, obtain a file, and view the directory. All files in the system should have a form of text files, that is, should appear as strings of characters. For simplicity, the file size may be limited to one screen—for example, 20 lines and 80 characters per line. Each file has to be given a name, and the AL will have to solve the problem of not allowing multiple files with identical names. Actually, such a function does not really belong to the OSI network model and more properly should be a part of a distributed operating system. The problem may be solved by searching the directory every time a create a file command is entered. Message exchanges necessary to verify the validity of a file name have to be transparent to the user.

Bibliography

1. Tannenbaum, Andrew S. *Computer Networks*. Englewood Cliffs, N.J.: Prentice-Hall, 1981.

2. Stallings, William. *Local Networks, An Introduction*. New York, N.Y.: Macmillan, 1984.

3. Lane, Malcolm G. *Data Communications Software Design*. Boston, Mass.: Boyd and Fraser, 1985.

4. Nagvi, S., et al. "A Versatile VLSI Controller for Local Area Networks", in *VLSI Solutions for Local Area Networks*. Professional Session Record 10, Electro/83, New York, N.Y., April 19-21, 1983.

5. Stieglitz, Mark. "LSI Implements Efficient Token Protocol", in *VLSI Solutions for Local Area Networks*. Professional Session Record 10, Electro/83, New York, N.Y., April 19-21, 1983.

6. Dixon, R. C., et al. "A Token-ring Network for Local Data Communications", in *IBM Systems Journal*, 22, no 1 and 2 (1983): 47–62.

7. *Carrier Sense Multiple Access with Collision Detection—ANSI/IEEE Std 802.5-1985*. Piscataway, N.J.: IEEE Computer Society Press, 1985.

8. *Token-Passing Bus Access Method—ANSI/IEEE Std 802.5-1985*. Piscataway, N.J.: IEEE Computer Society Press, 1985.

9. *Token Ring Access Method—ANSI/IEEE Std 802.5-1985*. Piscataway, N.J.: IEEE Computer Society Press, 1985.

10. *LAN components User's Manual*. Santa Clara, Calif.: Intel Corporation, 1984.

11. *Network Products Handbook*. Irvine, Calif.: Western Digital Corp., 1983.

12. *MC68000 16-bit Microprocessor User's Manual*. Austin, Tex.: Motorola Inc., 1982.

13. *Motorola Microprocessors Data Manual*. Austin, Tex.: Motorola Inc., 1981.

14. Triebel, Walter A. and Singh Avtor. *The 68000 Microprocessor, Architecture, Software, and Interfacing Techniques*. Englewood Cliffs, N.J.: Prentice-Hall, 1986.

15. *Motorola MC68000 Educational Computer Board User's Manual*. Austin, Tex.: Motorola, Inc., 1981.

A

intel®

82586
LOCAL COMMUNICATIONS CONTROLLER

- ■ Fully Implements the Ethernet* and Proposed IEEE 802 Specifications
- ■ User Configurable for Non-Ethernet Applications
  - —From 0 to 6 Bytes of Address Generation/Checking
  - —16- or 32-Bit CRC Generation/Checking
  - —Optional Priority Function
  - —Variable Preamble Length
  - —Serial Transmission from 100 Kbps to 10 Mbps
  - —8- or 16-Bit Data Bus

- ■ 4 On-Chip DMA Channels for Efficient, High-Speed Transfer of Data, Status and Commands
- ■ Complete Set of Diagnostics for Reliable Network Operation
- ■ Fully Implements the CSMA/CD Access Method Including Retries and Random Backoff (Wait) Time
- ■ Two Methods of Frame Delimiting: Ethernet and HDLC Flags/Bit Stuffing
- ■ Independent 8-MHz System Clock Input

Designed as an intelligent peripheral, the 82586 manages the entire process of transmitting and receiving frames, thereby relieving the host processor of the tasks of managing the communications peripheral. The major functions performed by the 82586 include:

—direct transfer of frames to and from external memory using four on-chip DMA channels.
—executes commands from lists residing in external shared memory.
—automatically reports the status of both transmitted and received frames, including error conditions.
—fully integrates the CSMA/CD access method including automatic retries after collisions and random backoff (wait-time) generation.
—diagnostic commands to identify and isolate faults.

In order to take full advantage of the LAN concept and CSMA/CD access method, the 82586 architecture is also configurable under program control. This allows the 82586 to be "customized" for other applications requiring high-speed serial transmission including serial backplanes (serial peripheral interconnection) and low-cost, short-distance LANs.

*Ethernet is a trademark of Xerox Corporation.

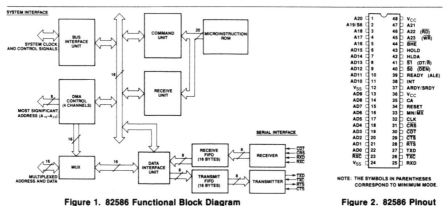

Figure 1. 82586 Functional Block Diagram   Figure 2. 82586 Pinout

OCTOBER 1982
ORDER NUMBER: 210783-001

intel®   **82586**   ADVANCE INFORMATION

Controlling the 82586

From the user's point of view, the 82586 consists of two independent, though communicating units: the Command Unit (CU) and the Receive Unit (RU) as shown in Figure 3. The CU executes commands given by the host CPU and manages frame transmissions. The RU handles all activities related to frame reception such as buffer management, frame and address recognition, and CRC checking. The two units are controlled and monitored by the host CPU via a shared memory structure called the System Control Block (SCB). All logical communication between the CPU and 82586 takes place through the SCB. The two other memory structures used by the 82586 are the Command Block List (CBL) and Receive Frame Area (RFA). These are used to hold

the list of commands to be executed by the 82586 and hold all received frames, respectively. Pointers to the CBL and RFA are in the SCB, along with status registers and counters for certain tallies maintained by the 82586, and control commands for the 82586. The only direct control lines between the CPU and the 82586 are the interrupt to the CPU and Channel Attention to the 82586.

82586 Memory Structures

The three primary memory structures used by the host CPU and the 82586 to pass control, status and data are the System Control Block (SCB), Command Block List (CBL) and the Receive Frame Area (RFA), Figure 4.

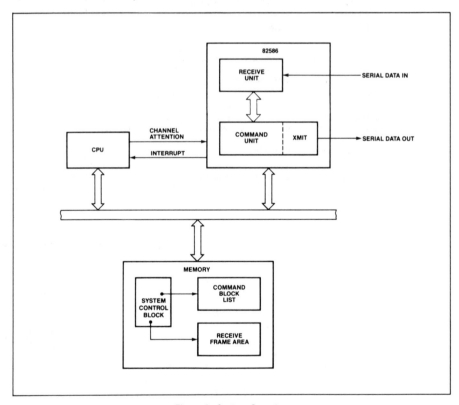

Figure 3. System Overview

4-2

AFN-00864A

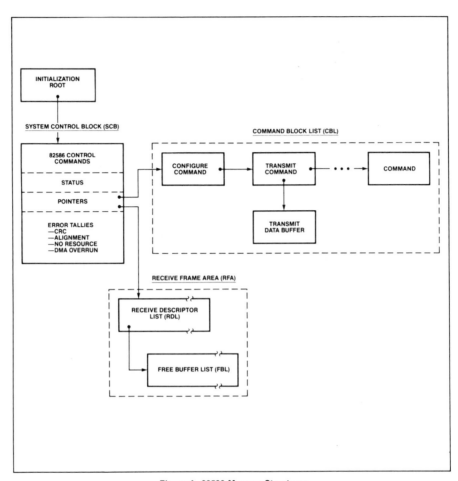

Figure 4. 82586 Memory Structures

Upon initialization, the 82586 obtains the address of its System Control Block through the Initialization Root which begins at location 0FFFFF6H. The SCB contains control commands, status register, pointers to the Command Block List (CBL) and Receive Frame Area (RFA), and tallies for CRC, Alignment, DMA Overrun and No Resource errors. Through the SCB, the 82586 is able to provide status and error counts for the host CPU, execute "programs" contained in the Command Block List (CBL) and receive incoming frames in the Receive Frame Area (RFA).

Both the Command Block List and the Receive Frame Area are first configured by the host CPU and then passed to the 82586 via the SCB. As commands are executed by the 82586, it returns status information back to the CPU, which may, in turn, update the CBL with additional commands. As frames are received by the 82586 and stored in the RFA, the 82586 will return the appropriate status to the CPU. The CPU retrieves the received frames from the RFA and returns free buffers to the Receive Descriptor and Free Buffer lists.

The 82586 has a 22-bit memory address range in minimum mode and 24-bit memory address range in maximum mode. All memory structures, the System Control Block, commands in the Command Block List, Receive Descriptor List, and all buffer descriptors (see Figure 6), must reside within one 64K-byte memory segment. The Data Buffers can be located anywhere in the memory space.

Transmitting Frames

The 82586 executes commands from the Command Block List in external memory. These commands are fetched and executed in parallel with the host CPU's operation, thereby significantly improving system performance potential. The general format for such commands is

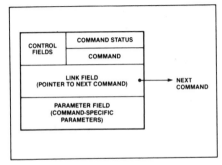

Figure 5. Action Command Format

Via the Link Field, commands can be linked together to form a list of commands for execution by the 82586.

One such command is the Transmit command. A single Transmit command contains, as part of the command-specific parameters, the destination address and type field for the transmitted frame along with a pointer to a buffer area in memory containing the data portion of the frame. The data field is contained in a memory data structure consisting of a Buffer Descriptor (BD) and Data Buffer (or a linked list of buffer descriptors and buffers) as seen in Figure 6. The BD contains a Link Field which points to the next BD on the list and a 24-bit address pointing to the Data Buffer itself. The length of the Data Buffer is specified by the Actual Count field of the BD.

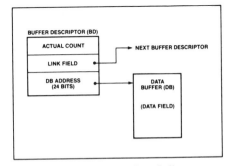

Figure 6. Transmit Data Buffer

Using the BDs and Data Buffers, multiple Data Buffers can be "chained" together. Thus, a frame with a long Data Field can be transmitted using multiple (shorter) Data Buffers chained together. This chaining technique allows the system designer to develop efficient buffer management policies.

When transmitting a frame as shown below:

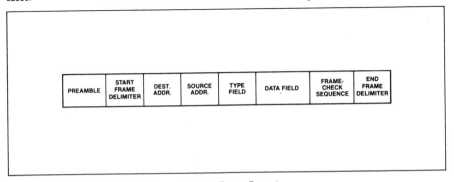

Figure 7. Frame Format

AFN-00864A

The 82586 automatically generates the preamble (alternating 1s and 0s) and start frame delimiter, fetches the destination address and type field from the Transmit command, inserts its unique address as the source address, fetches the data field from buffers pointed to by the Transmit command, and computes and appends the CRC at the end of the frame.

The 82586 can be configured to generate either the Ethernet or HDLC start and end frame delimiters. In the Ethernet mode, the start frame delimiter is two consecutive 1 bits and the end frame delimiter indicated by the lack of a signal after transmitting the last bit of the frame-check sequence field. When in the HDLC mode, the 82586 will generate the 01111110 "flag" for the start and end frame delimiters and perform the standard "bit stuffing/stripping." In addition, the 82586 will optionally pad frames that are shorter than the specified minimum frame length by appending the appropriate number of flags to the end of the frame.

In the event of a collision (or collisions), the 82586 manages the entire jam, random wait and retry pro-

cess, reinitializing DMA pointers without CPU intervention. Multiple frames can be sent by linking the appropriate number of Transmit commands together. This is particularly useful when transmitting a message that is larger than the maximum frame size (1518 bytes for Ethernet).

Receiving Frames

In order to minimize CPU overhead, the 82586 is designed to receive frames without CPU supervision. The host CPU first sets aside an adequate amount of receive buffer space and then enables the 82586's Receive Unit. Once enabled, the 82586 "watches" for any of its frames which it automatically stores in the Receive Frame Area (RFA). The RFA consists of a Receive Descriptor List (RDL) and a list of free buffers called the Free Buffer List (FBL) as shown in Figure 8. The individual Receive Frame Descriptors that make up the RDL are used by the 82586 to store the destination and source address, type field and status of each frame that is received. (Figure 9.)

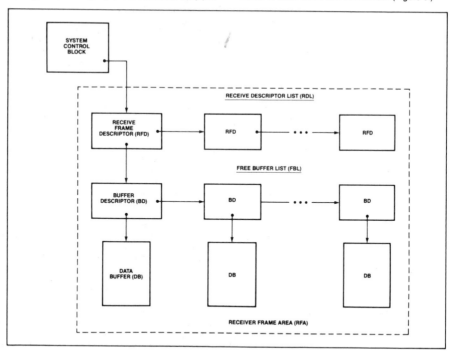

Figure 8. Receive Frame Area Diagram

AFN-00864A

intel   82586   ADVANCE INFORMATION

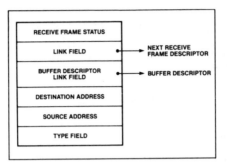

Figure 9. Receive Frame Descriptor

The 82586, once enabled, checks each passing frame for an address match. The 82586 will recognize its own unique address, one or more multicast addresses or the broadcast address.

If a match occurs, it stores the destination and source address and type field in the next available RFD. It then begins filling the next free Data Buffer on the FBL (which is pointed to by the current RFD) with the data portion of the incoming frame. As one DB is filled, the 82586 automatically fetches the next DB on the FBL until the entire frame is received. This buffer chaining technique is particularly memory efficient because it allows the system designer to set aside buffers that fit a frame size that may be much shorter than the maximum allowable frame. Without buffer chaining, all receive data buffers would have to be as long as the maximum allowable frame.

Once the entire frame is received without error, the 82586 performs the following housekeeping tasks:

—Updates the Actual Count field of the last Buffer Descriptor used to hold the frame just received with the number of bytes stored in its associated Data Buffer.
—Fetches the address of the next free Receive Frame Descriptor.
—Writes the address of the next free Buffer Descriptor into the next free Receive Frame Descriptor.
—Posts a "Frame Received" interrupt status bit in the SCB.
—Interrupts the CPU.

In the event of a frame error, such as a CRC error, the 82586 automatically reinitializes its DMA pointers and reclaims any data buffers containing the bad frame. As long as Receive Frame Descriptors and data buffers are available, the 82856 will continue to receive frames without further CPU help.

82586 Action Commands

The 82586 executes a "program" that is made up of action commands in the Command Block List. As shown in Figure 5, each command contains the command field, status and control fields, link to the next action command in the CBL, and any command-specific parameters. The 82586 has a repertoire of 8 commands.

NOP
Set Up Individual Address
Configure
Set Up Multicast Address
Transmit
TDR
Diagnose
Dump

NOP:
This command results in no action by the 82586 other than the normal command processing such as fetching the command and decoding the command field.

Individual Address Set Up:
This command is used to load the 82586's unique address. The unique address is contained in the parameter field of the command.

Configure:
The Configure command is used to load the 82586 with its operating parameters. Upon reset, the 82586 initializes to the Ethernet-based parameters. If the user wishes to use any other values, the Configure command is used.

Multicast Address Set Up:
This command allows the programmer to set up one or more multicast addresses into the 82586. The multicast addresses to be set up are located in the parameter field of the command.

Transmit:
One Transmit command is used to send a single frame. If more than one frame is to be sent, the host CPU can link multiple Transmit commands together. The destination address, type field and pointer to buffers containing the data field are contained in the parameter field of the Transmit command.

TDR:
This command performs the Time Domain Reflectometry test on the coaxial cable. The TDR command is used to detect and locate cable faults caused by either short or open circuits on the coaxial cable.

AFN–00864A

82586 ADVANCE INFORMATION

Diagnose:
The Diagnose command puts the 82586 through a self-test procedure and reports on the success or failure of the internal test.

Dump:
This command causes the 82586 to dump its internal registers into memory. The registers included are those loaded by the Configure and Address Set-Up commands, plus status and other internal working registers.

PROGRAMMABLE NETWORK PARAMETERS AND DIAGNOSTICS

Network Parameters

The Ethernet specification represents a complete description of the physical and data link layers of a local-area network. As such, items such as address and preamble length, maximum distance between two stations, and frame-check sequence length are fixed to assure that stations connecting to the network are compatible. Through the Configure command, the 82586 can also be tailored to achieve maximum efficiency in other network configurations. The following parameters can be specified in the Configure command:

PARAMETER	LENGTH
Source/Destination Address	0 to 6 bytes
CRC	16 or 32 bits
Preamble Length	16, 32, 64, or 128 bits
Frame Delimiter	Ethernet or HDLC (Flags and bit stuffing)
Slot Time	11 bits to specify number of transmit clock times

The Slot time is a period slightly longer than the maximum round-trip delay time through the network, i.e., the round-trip delay between the two most distant stations. The Slot time is used in the CSMA/CD Backoff calculation where the random time is defined in increments of the Slot Time. Shorter networks, such as a serial backplane within a cabinet would have a very short Slot Time compared to a 2500-meter Ethernet Network, for example.

Priority can also be assigned via a field in the Configure command. This field specifies the amount of time the particular 82586 must wait after the cable has been quiet before attempting to transmit its frame. By assigning lower-priority stations a longer wait time, the high-priority (shorter wait-time)

stations will have better access to the cable during peak busy periods.

Diagnostics

In addition to specifying network parameters, the Configure command is also used to call up a powerful set of diagnostic functions through individual fields within the command.

Save Bad Frame:
Under normal operation, the 82586 automatically discards frames with errors, such as a CRC error. Frames can be saved for later examination by requesting it through this field.

Address/Type Field Location:
This field informs the 82586 that the destination and source addresses and type field are the first entries in the Transmit Data Buffer rather than in the parameter field of the Transmit command (destination address and type field) and Individual Address register of the 82586 (source address).

Loopback:
Two Loopback modes are available on the 82586. The Internal Loopback moves the transmitted frame from memory into the 82586 FIFO, through the bit transmitter, back into the bit receiver and back to memory without going through the external serial drivers and receivers of the 82586. Note that the data moves at one-fourth the normal bit rate when the 82586 is in Internal Loopback.

External Loopback is identical to the Internal Loopback except that the frame does move out through the serial drivers and back in through receivers of the 82586 at the normal bit rate. This allows external components, such as the 82501 ESI chip and Ethernet transceivers, to be tested independently of the coaxial cable or remote station.

Promiscuous Receive:
The 82586 can be made to receive all good frames, regardless of address, using this field. This is useful as a monitor or diagnostic mode for a station.

Broadcast Disable:
This field is used to disable the reception of all broadcast messages by the 82586.

Minimum Frame Length:
The 82586 automatically rejects received frames which are shorter than the minimum frame length as specified in this field. This 9-bit field allows the minimum frame length to range from 1 to 511 bytes. (For Ethernet the minimum frame is 64 bytes.)

AFN–00864A

No CRC Insertion:
This field disables the automatic CRC insertion and terminates the frame after last byte of the data field is transmitted. Using this option, frames with the wrong CRC can be generated in order to test a receiving station's CRC checking circuitry.

As an aid to monitoring the operation of the network and tracking its "vital signs," the 82586 also reports the following conditions after each received and transmitted frame.

RECEIVED FRAME
—No errors
—Short Frame (less than minimum frame length)
—DMA Overrun; FIFO overflow before DMA service
—CRC error
—Alignment error
—No resources (buffers) to store frame

TRANSMITTED FRAME
—Frame transmitted
—Number of collisions encountered
—Transmission aborted, too many collisions
—DMA underrun; FIFO empty before DMA service

—Channel busy; 82586 deferred before frame transmission
—CTS (Clear To Send) lost
—CRS (Carrier Sense) lost
—Collision Test Status (Heartbeat Test)

System Interface

The 82586 operates as a bus master. Through its HOLD/HLDA signals, it is able to request bus cycles, transfer data and release the bus. Two internal 16-byte FIFOs are used to buffer data to and from the system bus through the four DMA channels on the 82586. Therefore, once the DMA request is granted, the 82586 is able to transfer multiple bytes of data (to fill or empty the FIFO) with each DMA request.

The 82586 system interface is a standard multiplexed bus that can be used with any of the popular 8- and 16-bit microprocessors. It is optimized for minimum-interface support logic when used with the iAPX 186 (Figure 10). When combined with the 82501 ESI chip, the Ethernet interface is complete from the CPU to the transceiver cable.

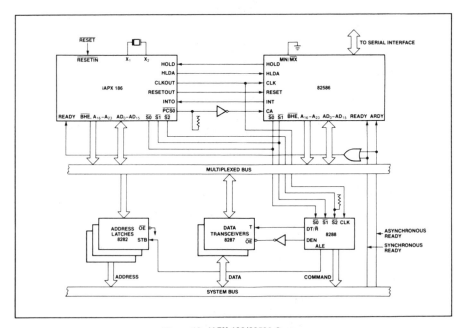

Figure 10. iAPX 186/82586 System

AFN-00864A

For 8086/8088-based systems, the 82285 is used as a clock generator for the 82586 system clock and the 8259A as an interrupt controller. The 8288 Bus Controller is common as both the CPU and the 82586

have the same data transfer timing. A bus arbiter is also needed to convert to/from the 82586 HOLD/HLDA from/to the 8086/8088 RQ/GT. This configuration is shown in Figure 11.

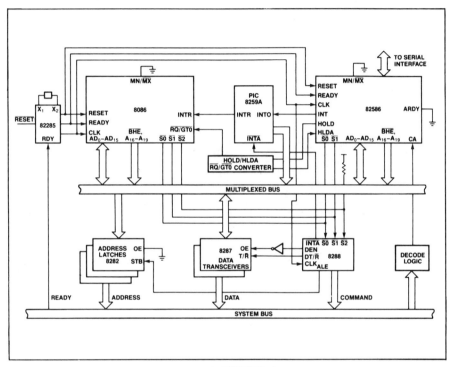

Figure 11. 8086/82586 System

intel   **82586**   ADVANCE INFORMATION

A third system configuration shown in Figure 12 is a dual-port RAM-based system. In this configuration, the bus traffic between the 82586 and shared memory (via port B) is isolated from system bus traffic. Using such a configuration, high-bandwidth pe-

ripherals like the 82586 can operate with shared memory using its own local bus, leaving the system bus free for the CPU and other peripherals such as a display controller, with access to shared memory via Port A.

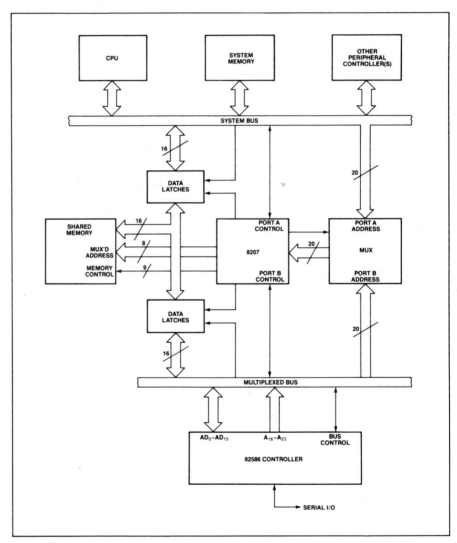

Figure 12. Dual-Port RAM-Based System

AFN-00864A

B

WESTERN DIGITAL
C O R P O R A T I O N

WD2840

WD2840 Local Network Token Access Controller

FEATURES

- Broadcast Medium Oriented (Coax, RF, CATV, IR, etc.)
- Up to 254 nodes
- Dual DMA/Highly efficient Memory Block Chaining
- Token based protocol
- Acknowledge option on each datagram
- Adjustable fairness, stations may be prioritized
- Frame format similar to industry standard HDLC
- Supports Global Addressing
- Diagnostic Support: Self-Tests, System and Network
- TTL Compatible

APPLICATIONS

The WD2840 is a general purpose Local Network Token Controller applicable to virtually all types of multi-point communications applications. The token protocol allows the sharing of one bus by up to 254 nodes. WD2840's will be designed into process control equipment, micro-computers, mini-computers, personal computers, proprietary micro-processor based applications, intelligent terminals, front-end processors, and similar equipment.

The great advantage for the design engineer is the ease with which he can implement a local network function. The WD2840 handles autonomously all major communications tasks as they relate to the local network function.

GENERAL DESCRIPTION

The WD2840 is a MOS/LSI device intended for local network applications, where reliable data communications over a shared medium is required. The device uses a buffer chaining scheme to allow efficient memory utilization. This scheme minimizes the host CPU time requirements for handling packets of data. The WD2840 frees the host CPU from extensive overhead by performing network initialization, addressing, coordination, data transmission, acknowledgements and diagnostics.

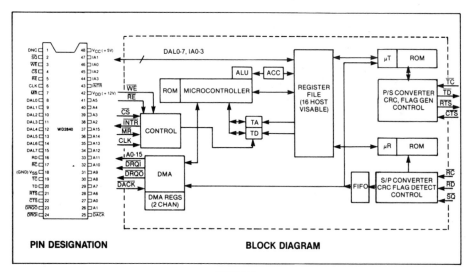

PIN DESIGNATION **BLOCK DIAGRAM**

Figure 1.1

179

**WD2840 LOCAL NETWORK
TOKEN ACCESS CONTROLLER**

INTRODUCTION

The WD2840 is a single LSI device which gives systems designers the ability to include networking capabilities into their unique products simply and economically.

A general and fundamental advantage to the use of complex LSI in a given system is the partitioning of required technical expertise. A successful user of the WD2840 need not be a data-communications expert, and further, he need not be at all concerned with low level network details (though these details are documented and available to him if he is interested). The potential user of the WD2840 must simply evaluate the communications facilities provided by the device to determine its suitability for the intended use.

The WD2840 is designed to logically interconnect 2 to 254 user devices over a shared communications medium. Examples of expected mediums include coax cable, twisted pair bus, RF, and CATV. All network control functions, such as data framing and error checking, destination filtering, fair and adjustable transmission scheduling, and network initialization and fault recovery (caused by noise for example) are handled completely by the WD2840.

The protocol implemented allows guaranteed station access intervals allowing applications in factory automation and other critical communications environments where "statistical delays" are not acceptable. The WD2840 token protocol also allows the addition and/or removal of stations to a network at anytime, including while operating.

Serious attention has also been given to the user's interface to the device. The interface is a combination of conventional I/O registers and an elaborate DMA buffer chaining interface. This chaining feature allows the user much more efficient use of his system memory, particularly in situations where the maximum message sent over the network is much longer than the average size. This feature also allows the automatic queueing of messages independently of the user's consumption rate, in effect, speed decoupling the user's CPU and processing requirements from the network.

The WD2840 has several parameters (registers) that allow tailoring to the user's requirements. In this way, network priority and access ordering, to name two, can be manually set if desired.

Using an integrated version of these network algorithms saves not only the development costs already mentioned, but further, the total processing power required for the user's application is not increased. In other words, a CPU upgrade can likely be avoided by "distributing" the network processing task into LSI devices such as the WD2840.

SCOPE

This document differs from traditional LSI data sheets in that it details not only the LSI implementation of a function, but also defines the overall function in detail. Specifically, this document includes de-

tails of the communications protocol implemented by the WD2840 Token Access Controller.

The document is organized into three main sections:

SECTION ONE is much like a traditional data sheet including register descriptions, pin definitions, and hardware architecture.

SECTION TWO describes the interfaces to the WD2840. The network side is conventional, the host side consists of an elaborate DMA interface with control blocks and WD2840/host handshaking.

SECTION THREE details the network protocol implemented by the device. Normal operation, initialization, and the handling of error conditions are described.

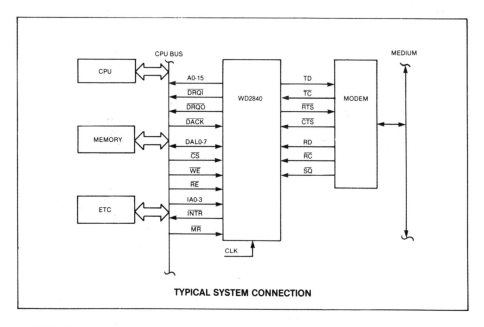

TYPICAL SYSTEM CONNECTION

1.2 DEVICE ARCHITECTURE

A detailed block diagram of the WD2840 is shown in Figure 1.1.

Mode control and monitor of status by the user's CPU is performed through the Read/Write Control circuit, which reads from or writes into registers addressed by IA0-IA3.

Transmit and receive data are accessed through DMA control. Serial data is generated and received by the bit-oriented controllers.

Internal control of the WD2840 is by means of three internal micro-controllers; one for transmit, one for receive, and one for overall control.

Parallel transmit data is entered into the Transmitter Holding Register (THR), and then presented to the Transmitter Register (TR) which converts the data to a serial bit stream. The Frame Check Sequence (FCS) is computed in the sixteen bit CRC register, and the results become the transmitted FCS.

Parallel receive data enters the Receiver Holding Register (RHR) from the 24 bit serial Receive Register (RR). The 24-bit length of RR prevents received FCS data from entering the RHR. The receiver CRC register is used to test the validity of the received FCS. A three level FIFO is included in the receiver.

The WD2840 sends all information, network control and user data, in blocks called frames. Each frame starts and ends with a single flag (binary pattern 01111110). In between flags, data transparency is provided by the insertion of a zero bit after all sequences of five contiguous one bits. The receiver will strip the inserted zero bits. (See section on frame format for location of address, control, and FCS fields.)

1.3 REGISTER DEFINITION

The WD2840 is controlled and monitored by sixteen 8 bit registers. This set of registers consists of two Control Registers, three Status Registers, an In-terrupt Event Register, a Counter Register and a variety of Parameter Registers. In general the host is responsible for defining these registers (except certain host read-only registers: SR0-2, IR0, CTR0 and NA) to contain proper and meaningful values prior to entering Network Mode from Isolate State. Furthermore, while the WD2840 is in Network Mode, the CBP (H,L) and MA registers must not be changed by the host. Register NAR may be changed arbitrarily but will only be considered by the WD2840 in response to the NEWNA (CR10) control bit being set. The two Control Registers and the TA, TD, AHOLT, TXLT registers may change dynamically to control the behavior of the WD2840.

REG [1]	NAME	DESCRIPTION
0	CR0	Control Register 0
1	CR1	Control Register 1
2[2]	SR0	Status Register 0
3[2]	IR0	Interrupt Event Register
4[2]	SR1	Status Register 1
5[2]	SR2	Status Register 2
6[2]	CTR0	Counter Register 0
7[2]	NA	Next Address
8	TA	ACK Timer
9	TD	Net Dead Timer
A	CBPH	Control Block Pointer (MSB)
B	CBPL	Control Block Pointer (LSB)
C	NAR	Next Address, Request
D	AHOLT	Access Hold-off Limit
E	TXLT	Transmit Limit
F	MA	My Address

[1] = Hexadecimal representation of IA0-IA3.
[2] = CPU read only, write not possible.

Control, status, and interrupt bits will be referred to as CR, SR, or IR, respectively, along with two digits. For example, SR21 refers to status register #2 and bit 1, which is "STATE."

181

1.4 DIAGNOSTIC AIDS

There are three levels of diagnostics supported by the WD2840; those that are associated with the network as a whole, those associated with the in-

DIAGNOSTIC MODE CONTROL			
CR00 ISOL	CR17 DIAGC	SR21 STATE	DEFINITION
1	0	0	WD2840 "Isolated." Power-up condition or isolate request.
0	0	0	WD2840 active.
1	0	1	Isolate request function confirmed.
1	1	0	Host request to enter diagnostic mode.
1	1	1	Diagnostic mode confirmed. Diagnostic functions of CR1 apply.
0	0	1	Illegal.
0	1	0	Illegal.
0	1	1	Illegal.

dividual node, and those that are limited to the WD2840 as a device. These tests are Network Diagnostics, System Diagnostics and Self Diagnostics respectively. The Network Diagnostics can be performed while the WD2840 is in the logical ring, but the System Diagnostics and the Self Diagnostics may be used only while the WD2840 is in the diagnostic mode.

Diagnostic mode may be entered after power-up or from the network mode by manipulation of the mode control bits. The mode transition is confirmed by the WD2840 via the STATE status bit.

Once in diagnostic mode, the desired test is selected via CR1. Because most of registers 8 through F are interpreted differently for each test, only one of the diagnostic test bits should be set at a time. In conjunction with setting the diagnostic bits, the NUDIAG (CR10) bit must be set to perform the diagnostic test requested.

At the completion of the selected test NUDIAG is cleared by the WD2840. Therefore the host can initiate a diagnostic by entering the diagnostic mode, initializing the proper registers, setting the desired diagnostic bit, and setting NUDIAG. The host then moniters CR1 for NUDIAG going to zero, indicating the completion of the requested diagnostic.

DIAGNOSTIC STATE FLOW CHART

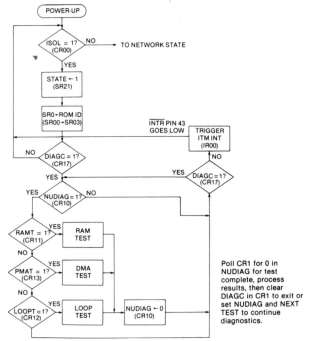

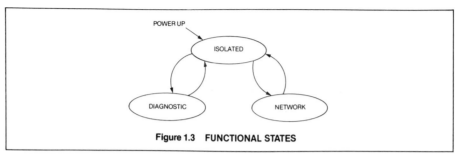

Figure 1.3   FUNCTIONAL STATES

1.4.1 SELF DIAGNOSTICS

Internal Ram and Interrupt Test

There are nine eight bit registers in the WD2840 which are not directly accessable by the users CPU. This test provides a means to check those registers and the interrupt register. The contents of register A are placed into the interrupt register and five even internal registers, and the contents of register B in four odd internal registers. The nine registers are then added together without carry and the result is placed in registers 2, 5, 6, 7.

Use the following procedure to initiate the RAM test:

1. Enter diagnostic mode.

2. Set up registers A and B

3. Set RAMT.

4. Set NUDIAG (can be set with RAMT bit together).

5. Wait for NUDIAG to be cleared.

6. Read registers 2, 5, 6, 7. Clear RAMT.

Note that the setting of any bit in the interrupt register while NOINT is clear will generate a hardware interrupt (INTR , pin 43 goes true).

1.4.2 SYSTEM DIAGNOSTICS

DMA Test

This test verifies proper operation of the DMA subsystem by reading the value from a register and writing it into the user memory. The test continues by reading the value from the same location in memory and writing it into another register.

The value is read from register C. Using the transmitter DMA sub-system, it is written into memory location addressed by register A and B (location N; register A is the MSB). The receiver DMA sub-system is used and contents of the same address is read and it is stored into the register 7. Next the receiver dma is used and the contents from register D is written into location N + 1. The transmitter dma reads the value from location N + 1 and stores it into register 6.

It is the host's responsibility to check if the contents of registers C and register 7 and memory location N

match. The same is true for registers D and 6 and memory location N + 1.

Loop-Back Test

The host can test the WD2840 parallel to serial, serial to parallel converters, CRC, and framing logic by setting LOOPT (CR12) bit of the WD2840, while in the diagnostic mode. The host has the responsibility of initializing a transmit buffer with a known pattern and then verifying its correct reception. The pattern is looped internally to the device if ILOOP (CR03) = 1, or may be looped externally (with outside logic) if ILOOP = 0.

The following procedure should be followed in order to run the loop-back test:

1. Enter diagnostic mode.

2. Set up register A and B to point to a buffer that is initialized with a pattern for transmission.

3. Set up register C and D to point to a buffer to receive the frame. (It is a good practice to initialize this buffer with all '00' or all 'FF' value bytes.)

4. Set up the buffer size in bits 3-0 of register E. (NOTE: In this test the last two bytes of the buffer will not be transmitted.)

5. Set ILOOP bit (CR03). (This is optional, if internal loop-back test is desired.)

6. Set LOOPT bit (CR12).

7. Set NUDIAG (CR10).

8. Wait for NUDIAG (CR10) to be cleared.

9. Compare the two buffers to verify correct reception of the frame.

NOTE:

If this test frame is allowed onto the network, transmission collisions may occur. Further, the first three bytes of the transmit buffers will be interpreted as TC, DA and SA, respectively, by the other stations. Therefore in case this test is initiated while this node is in the logical ring, care should be taken for choosing these three values for external loop-back test.

For proper operation of the internal loop-back test the CTS and SQ pins of the WD2840 should be either tied to ground or tied to RTS pin of the WD2840.

1.4.3 NETWORK DIAGNOSTICS

Duplicate Station Detection

Duplicate stations (more than one station with the same address) can result from the faulty programming of internal register MA (due to wrong address switch settings on the user's device, for example). This is expected to occur often enough to warrant the addition of a detection algorithm in the users WD2840 initialization procedure.

After initializing all required parameters, the user places the WD2840 in network mode (by setting ISOL false). The WD2840 monitors all frames on the network, and, if one is observed as having been transmitted by its address (source address of the frame equals the value in register MA) an event counter is incremented.

The user should monitor the SA = MA event counter at least long enough for the token to have circulated all the way around the access ring (time is configuration dependent) before enabling the WD2840's transmitter.

It is useful to note that this constraint requiring each node which is participating in the network logical ring to have a unique address does not extend to nodes which are "listening" but not "in the ring." It might be useful to a network designer to have groups of receive only nodes which have the same node address but do not participate in the network token passing (see GIRING - CR13). Data frames transmitted to such clusters must not request acknowledgement since all nodes in the cluster would simultaneously respond.

Copy Mode

The COPY Mode is selected by setting the COPY control bit (CR02). Normally the WD2840 receives (DMA's into the receive buffer chain) data frames only if they contain the general broadcast destination address or if they are specifically addressed to the WD2840. This occurs when the frame's destination address (DA) matches the WD2840 my address (MA, set by the host).

However, when COPY mode is selected data frames which are specifically addressed to other nodes will be treated as broadcast frames by this node. The COPY mode allows a specific node to "evesdrop" on data frame traffic on the network.

Nak Response

The WD2840 sends negative acknowledgements (NAK's) on response to received frames under several circumstances. The NAK prevents the transmitting node from wasting bandwidth retrying indiscriminately, and further, lends visibility to individual network node problems. The NAK includes a reason code which is available to the transmitter's software (via the TFSB).

Each data frame to be transmitted can be specifically marked (via the FCB) by the host to require an ACK/NAK response from the receiving WD2840. In the absence of errors, an acknowledge (ACK) frame will be returned to the transmitter as confirmation. However, several circumstances cause a Negative Acknowledge (NAK) to be returned:

1. Insufficient buffer space

2. Receiver not enabled (RXEN - CR05 cleared)

3. Receiver overrun

4. Frame exceeded 16 buffers in length

This information is placed in the transmitted frames's FSB. See section 2.1.2 for more details on the Transmit Frame Status Byte (TFSB).

2.0 INTERFACES

There are two interfaces to the WD2840: the host computer side, and the network side. The network side is conventional from an electrical point of view, the WD2840 performs all logical functions required to ensure communications capability on broadcast media (such as coax or RF).

The host interface involves two separate functional interfaces: the status/control registers described in section one, and a DMA interface that is described in the following subsection.

2.1 HOST

The WD2840 uses a complex memory buffer architecture allowing it to respond in real time to its network obligations (e.g., to meet network data rate and processing delay requirements). These memory structures are managed cooperatively by the host and the WD2840.

Memory management functions requiring real time response (e.g., traversing chains) are completely handled by the WD2840. Other important, but not time critical operations are the responsibility of the host software (such as removing used buffers from the transmit chain).

All memory references by the WD2840 are pointed to by memory locations (and internal registers) initially defined and set up by the host software. Initial values and memory based registers are grouped together and called the WD2840 Control Block.

The location of this control block is written into the registers CBPH and CBPL anytime the WD2840 is in Isolate State. This control block has the following structure:

CBP →	+0	NXTR (H)	Receive Buffer Chain (MSByte)
	+1	NXTR (L)	Receive Buffer Chain (LSByte)
	+2	NXTT (H)	Transmit Buffer Chain (MSByte)
	+3	NXTT (L)	Transmit Buffer Chain (LSByte)
	+4	BSIZE	Buffer Size / 16 (0-F = 64-1024 bytes)
	+5	EVT0	
	+6	EVT1	Eleven separate Event Counters, see section 2.1.1 for details
	....		
	+F	EVT10	

As the WD2840 transitions to Network State, it reads and uses the first five bytes of the control block. The remaining eleven bytes of event counters are accessed by the WD2840 only when each specific event condition occurs.

Either the Receive (NXTR) or Transmit (NXTT) chain entries in the control block may initially be zero; in such a case the WD2840 expects the chain to be extended by the host's changing the zero link field in the control block. Thereafter any such zero link would be in a buffer.

The WD2840 uses constant size buffers; their length is set by the value in location BSIZE. The buffer size is indicated by a 4-bit count in the least significant 4 bits of the BSIZE byte in the WD2840 control block. The buffer sizes available are multiples of 64; (BSIZE + 1) 64 is the buffer size used by the WD2840. Thus a BSIZE range of 0-15 corresponds to actual buffer sizes of 64 through 1024 bytes. This buffer length is inclusive of control bytes and buffer link pointers.

The WD2840 includes a chained-block feature which allows the user more efficient use of memory, particularly in situations where the maximum packet size is much larger than the average packet size. One or up to 16 buffers may make up a frame but a buffer may not contain more than one frame.

Byte counters are associated with each frame (at the memory interface, not actually transmitted within the frame) so that frames on the network need not be integer multiples of buffers. The byte counters include all buffer management overhead. Therefore, a frame consisting of 100 transmitted data bytes, occupying two 64-byte buffers, would have a byte count of 108 (six bytes per frame + 2 bytes per buffer boundry).

Since the WD2840 receive and transmit buffer chains are linked lists (see section 2.1.2 and 2.1.3) and are "followed" by the WD2840 but managed by the host;

it is expected that the host will maintain both a FIRST and a LAST address for each chain. On transition into Network State, the chain origin information in the WD2840 control block is the same as FIRST. In fact, since the WD2840 does not change these control block entries, they can be maintained directly as FIRST by the host. An explicit LAST could be placed in an extended control block section.

The WD2840 "follows" the linked buffer chains by maintaining a NEXT address internally for each chain. This NEXT address can be in one of two states: 1) it can be the address of the next buffer in the chain, or 2) at the chain end (zero link), it can be the address of the buffer containing the zero link. The WD2840 uses a status bit for each chain, NXTR0 (receive) and NXTT0 (transmit), to differentiate the two states. When set they indicate the WD2840 chain NEXT address is in state 1 above; when clear they indicate state 2 above. This is an important distinction since it indicates whether the last buffer posted in a chain can be removed by the host (because the WD2840 has advanced to the buffer beyond) or must be left until the chain can be extended so the WD2840 can advance.

The host software monitors the progress of the NEXT pointer, and updates FIRST and LAST as it adds (and removes) buffers to (from) the chains as required. The WD2840 provides Interrupt Events (see IR0) and NXTR0, NXTT0 status bits to indicate when it advances along the two chains and exactly what state its NEXT address registers are in. The operation of these chains will be explained by example in later sections.

"Deadly Embrace" Prevention

A "Deadly Embrace" can occur when two processors reach a state where each is waiting for the other. In this case, the two processors are the user's CPU and the micro-controller inside the WD2840. Therefore, to prevent the "deadly embrace," the following rule is obeyed by the WD2840 and should also be obeyed by the user's CPU. This rule applies to the WD2840 memory registers and to the I/O registers. The Event Counters are an exception to this rule.

Rule:
If a bit is set by the CPU, it will not be set by the WD2840, and vice versa. If a bit is cleared by the WD2840, it will not be cleared by the CPU, and vice versa.

As an example, the NEWNA (CR10) control bit is only set by the host and is only cleared by the WD2840.

Dual DMA

The WD2840 may, for efficiency, interleave frame data fetch/store operations with fetches and stores of pointers and flags in memory. In all cases, operation sequencing is such as to prevent deadlocks and ambiguities between the WD2840 and software.

2.1.1 EVENT COUNTERS

Several non-fatal logical events are tabulated by the WD2840 and made visible to the host via memory based event counters (see WD2840 control block organization for specific locations). The WD2840 will increment each counter at the occurance of the specified event. Note that the WD2840 will not increment past 255. The host has the responsibility of initializing each counter.

COUNTER	DESCRIPTION
EVT0	"Set scan mode" frame received from the network. The NA register was redefined to MA + 1 at the time.
EVT1	Transmission error first attempt, second try successful. Can only occur for frames requiring an acknowledgement. It indicates no response was received for the first transmission; however, the second transmission was either ACK'ed or NAK'ed.
EVT2	Transmission error. Attempt aborted due to either transmitter underrun or frame length exceeding 16 buffers.
EVT3	Timer TD (network dead) expired.
EVT4	Access Control Frame Reception Error. A one or two byte supervisory frame (ACK/NAK, Token Pass, Scan Mode) has been received in error. This may be due to an FCS error, frame abort, or carrier loss detection.
EVT5	Data Frame Reception Error. An incoming data frame was incorrectly received due to an FCS error, frame abort, carrier loss detection, or receiving a data frame when expecting an ACK/NAK frame.
EVT6	NAK sent. Can occur for any of the following reasons: 1. Insufficient buffers in chain 2. Receiver not enabled (RXEN clear) 3. Receiver overrun 4. Frame length exceeded 16 buffers
EVT7	Invalid frame received. Caused by the detection of certain abnormal network conditions such as receiving an ACK/NAK frame when not expecting one, receiving a Scan mode frame when expecting an ACK/NAK frame, or receiving an invalid supervisory frame.
EVT8	Duplicate token detected. This counter will be incremented when the WD2840 determines that more than one token exists in the logical ring. This happens if a token pass is received when the WD2840 already has the token, or a data frame is received when the WD2840 is waiting for an acknowledgement frame.
EVT9	Not used.
EVT10	Duplicate node address. This counter will be incremented when a data frame being DMA'd into memory has a source address (SA) equal to the WD2840 node address (MA). This counter when used with COPY mode (CR02) is one way for detecting other nodes with the same node number (MA).

2.1.2 TRANSMIT MEMORY INTERFACE

When the token is received, data transmission is enabled (TXEN - CR06 and TXDEN - CR07 both set), and if the access hold-off counter has reached its limit, the WD2840 will determine whether any data frames are pending in the transmit chain. If so, it will transmit the first data frame in the chain. Otherwise the token will be passed. A given data frame will be the last frame transmitted for this token if any of several conditions occur:

1. ISOL (CR00) is set indicating the host has requested a transition to Isolate State.

2. TXDEN (CR07) is clear indicating the host has changed data frame transmission rights.

3. The frame FSB indicates this frame should be the last transmitted for this token.

4. The running frame counter has reached its limit (TXLT).

5. No further frames are pending in the transmit chain.

If any of the first four reasons above are true a token pass will occur. If the last frame does not require an acknowledgement, the WD2840 will piggyback the token pass if that is permitted (CR16). If the token cannot be piggybacked or if the last frame transmitted is the last frame pending (condition #5 above), an explicit token pass will occur. A piggyback token will not occur for the last pending frame because, for the general multiple buffer case, it is not known to be the last pending frame until after the transmission is complete.

The WD2840 will read and evaluate the address of the next frame at two specific points in time:

1. At the end of the prior frame, even if the prior frame is the last to be transmitted for this token.

2. When the token is received and data frame transmission is permitted.

If a non-zero frame address is found at time 1 above, it is kept and used without being re-read at time 2 above. However, if no pending frame is found at time 1, this is noted with the NXTT0 flag clear and the chain re-inspected on each occurrence of time 2 above.

As frame transmission commences, the WD2840 reads the address of the next buffer, the frame control byte, (FCB) and the frame length. It then starts reading bytes from the buffer and sending them until the frame length count or the end of the buffer is reached. The new buffer is read and data transmitted as before. (See Figure 2.1)

The frame length provided in the LENGTH field must include all overhead bytes (LINK, FSB, FCB, LENGTH) in all buffers used for the frame. For example LENGTH = 8 implies DA, SA but no data bytes. If buffer size is 64 then LENGTH = 67 implies DA, SA, and 57 data bytes (one data byte in an overflow buffer. As a result of this convention, certain LENGTH values are not valid (e.g., 65, 66 in the second example).

When the frame length is finally reached, the WD2840 pauses if an acknowledgement has been requested. The frame status byte (FSB) is updated when the frame is completed; its posting indicates frame completion and gives information about the success or failure of the frame transmission. At frame completion, the WD2840 attempts to advance along the transmission chain to identify the next frame regardless of whether it will be transmitted with this token or later.

The host may add frames to the end of the transmit chain at any time by changing the zero link in the last buffer. Also buffers of all posted frames up to but NOT including the last buffer of the most recently posted, may be arbitrarily removed from the chain. The last posted frame (more specifically, the last buffer of the last frame) may only be removed and reused if NXTT0 is set. This indicates that the WD2840 has advanced its NEXT address to the next frame but that its transmission has not been completed (in fact, perhaps not even started).

NOTE:
The WD2840 checks only the most significant byte of the link field for zero link detection. This has the following implications:

1. When writing into a zero link field, the host must write the LSB of the new link field first, followed by the corresponding MSB.

2. All buffers must have a starting address greater than or equal to Hex '0100'.

Transmit Frame Status and Control Bytes

Each frame has two bytes reserved, one for host control information needed by the WD2840, the other for status information posted by the WD2840 at frame transmission completion. The frame control byte (FCB) is only read by the WD2840, never changed; the frame status byte (FSB), is written (posted) by the WD2840 with no regard for its prior contents. On completion, the FSB value will always be non-zero; it is important that the host zero the FSB byte in order to be able to recognize a posted frame.

NOTE:
Specifically note in Figure 2.1 that the first buffer of each frame has a different structure than any overflow buffers for that frame. In particular, each frame has only one set of FSB, FCB, and LENGTH fields regardless of the number of buffers required by the frame.

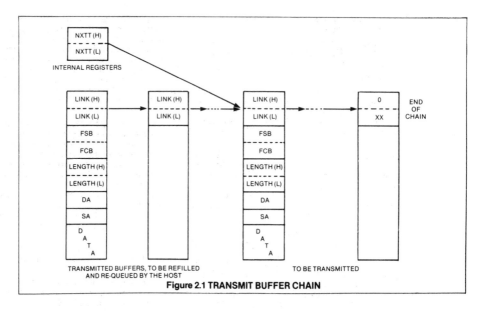

INTERNAL REGISTERS

TRANSMITTED BUFFERS, TO BE REFILLED
AND RE-QUEUED BY THE HOST

TO BE TRANSMITTED

Figure 2.1 TRANSMIT BUFFER CHAIN

2.1.3 Receive Memory Interface

After the third byte of an incoming data frame is detected, the WD2840 will begin to place frame data into memory if several conditions are satisfied:

1. Receiver Enabled (RXEN-CR05 set).
2. There is an available buffer in the receive buffer chain.
3. The frame is addressed to this node specifically, it is a broadcast frame, or COPY mode has been selected by the host.

As the frame continues, it may completely fill its buffer. If this happens the WD2840 reads and inspects the link field of the current buffer. If this link is zero, an error occurs and the receive chain is reset to reuse from the first buffer used by the dropped frame. However, if another buffer is available, the incoming frame is continued beginning in the third byte of that buffer. This continues until one of several things happen:

1. Receiver overrun. The WD2840 has a four byte FIFO to buffer incoming frame data; however, if the host DMA responds too slowly a receiver overrun will occur. If this happens an event counter is incremented, the frame is dropped, and the receiver buffer chain is reset to reuse buffers of the dropped frame.

2. Current buffer capacity exhausted. If 16 buffers have been used for the current frame, an event occurs with the frame being dropped and the chain reset. Otherwise the WD2840 attempts to advance to the next buffer in the receiver buffer chain. The frame data will be continued in this subsequent buffer. If the end of the receiver buffer chain is reached an event counter is incremented, the frame is dropped, and the chain reset.

3. Frame ends. If the FCS is not corrected an event counter is incremented, the frame is dropped, and the chain is reset. If corrected however, the frame length is placed in the LENGTH field and the Frame Status Byte (FSB) is posted "done, no error."

If the frame is addressed to this node and indicates an acknowledgement is required (TC = 255), whether or not an error occurs, the WD2840 responds with an ACK/NAK supervisory frame indicating either success or failure. In case of receiver over-run, bad FCS, and SA = MA acknowledgement request will be ignored. (See section 1.4.3 for details)

It is the host's responsibility to ensure that buffers are available, initialized (FSB zero'ed), and attached to the end of the receive buffer chain.

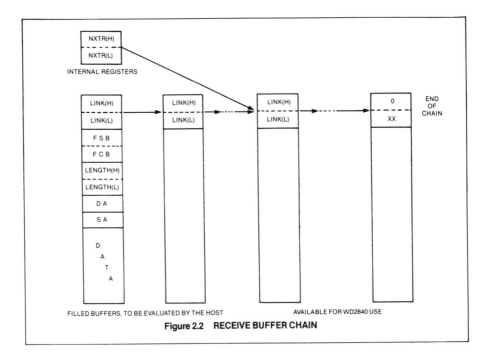

INTERNAL REGISTERS

END OF CHAIN

FILLED BUFFERS, TO BE EVALUATED BY THE HOST   AVAILABLE FOR WD2840 USE

Figure 2.2   RECEIVE BUFFER CHAIN

2.2 MODEM INTERFACE

The modem interface is the conventional half duplex NRZ type with separate data and clock (Figure 2.3). When the WD2840 desires to transmit, it asserts $\overline{RTS}$ and awaits $\overline{CTS}$. $\overline{RTS}$ is generally used to enable the modem transmitter. After a system dependent preamble is generated, the modem asserts $\overline{CTS}$ which allows the WD2840 to begin the actual transmission of the frame. (Note: $\overline{CTS}$ may be asserted permanently if the transmission system does not need to generate a preamble).

The $\overline{SQ}$ input is used on receive to indicate a valid carrier. If this term is negated anytime during a receive message, the WD2840 will presume the message is in error and treat it as an abort. This signal is used to augment message integrity beyond that of the CRC by allowing a modem to detect and report low level faults (such as out-of-frequency carrier or missing clock).

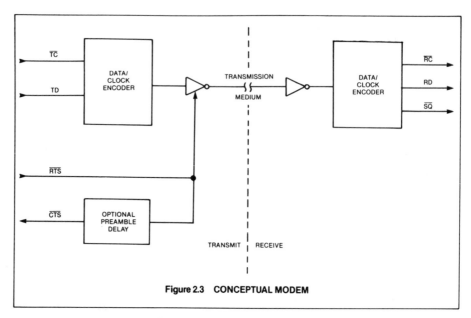

Figure 2.3   CONCEPTUAL MODEM

3.0 NETWORK PROTOCOL

To enable operation on a broadcast medium without the need for a central controller performing device polling, the WD2840 implements a media access protocol. The particular access protocol designed into the WD2840 prevents self-induced transmission collisions and ensures a fair and guaranteed distribution of transmission time among attached controllers.

This design-out of collisions allows the WD2840 a greatly expanded selection of transmission media, since no physical characteristics of a particular medium are relied upon for proper network operation. Another benefit of this lack of collisions is the visibility of network faults. If a collision is detected, it is treated consistently in a error recovery mode by the WD2840 and is also unambiguously visible to service personnel as a fault.

Secondly, the WD2840 can ensure that a transmitted message was correctly received and buffered by requiring acknowledgement of its receipt. This is sometimes called "acknowledging datagrams" where the sender awaits a predefined period after a frame is sent for a reply from its destination. With this method, no sequence counters nor multi-frame retransmission buffering is required. The scheme is efficient since local network applications such as the WD2840 address do not encounter extremely long transmission delays (such as satellite links) as in conventional data networks (such as X.25).

Both functions are parameterized, allowing tuning and optimization by the user to his unique application. These parameters may be adjusted in real time by the user's software, allowing a dynamic network, responsive to constantly changing requirements.

The two functions, access control and data transmission, function simultaneously though independently. Thus they are described separately as subprotocols for clarity.

3.1 Data Transmission

The data transmission cycle is entered after the token has been received and data transmission rights validated (see section 3.2 "access method"). The WD2840 determines if there is a frame to be sent and, if not, simply sends the token to the next station.

If something is queued for transmit, the WD2840 DMA's it from memory and sends it. After the complete frame has been sent, the WACK (Wait for ACK) bit is tested in the TFSB (Transmit Frame Status Byte). If set, the WD2840 waits for, and expects, an acknowledgement from the frames recipient. A timer (TA) is started. In the normal case, the ACK is received before TA expires which causes the WD2840 to send the next frame queued, repeating this procedure. Thus, the WD2840 sends multiple frames to various destinations until the transmit queue is emptied or a programmed limit (register TXLT) is exceeded.

In the event TA expires, the frame is re-transmitted once. (Note: it is the responsibility of higher level protocol operating in the host to protect against the possibility of duplicate frame reception.) If TA expires again, usually indicating the destination node is off-line, the FSB is updated to reflect the unsuccessful transmission, interrupt bit ITA is set, and the frame is skipped.

A frame is also skipped and tagged if the destination station sends a NAK, indicating it cannot presently process the frame.

TRANSMISSION OF ABORT

An ABORT is transmitted by the WD2840 to terminate a frame in such a manner that the receiving station will ignore the frame. An ABORT is sent when there is a Transmitter Under-Run. The abort sequence is a zero, followed by seven ones, after which RTS is set false.

3.2 ACCESS METHOD

The WD2840 network access method is based on the use of tokens, the specific granting of transmission rights passed from station to station. At any given time, exactly one station has the right to transmit (this right is called the token) and is obligated to pass it on when finished with it.

This can be clarified by referring to Figure 3.1. We assume in this figure that the network has already been initialized (meaning that the linkages in the access ring have already been established) and the token is held at this instant by station 4 (the station whose MA register = 4).

When station 4 is ready to pass his access right on, he sends a message to the station number called out in his internal register NA, in this case 11. The message, and thus the token, are received by station 11 who can now transmit its message(s). When station 11 is ready to pass the token, it sends a message to station 19, as directed by its internal register NA and the cycle continues, in a circular fashion, from station 4 to 11 to 19 to 54 to 4 . . .

Notice that the station numbers need not be contiguous. This relatively arbitrary station numbering (in the example) poses no inefficiency to the access method. The value of this is the ability to add and remove stations (re-configure) to the network without re-arranging everyone elses addresses. (See section 3.2.2 for an example.)

In this way, the token is passed from one station to the next in a logical ring.

3.2.1 ACCESS INITIALIZATION/ ERROR RECOVERY

When the WD2840 is commanded into Network State, the Next Address Request (NAR) register and the NEWNA (CR10) flag must be used to define the Next Address (NA) register. When it is necessary to pass the token, it is passed to the current node number in register NA. If station NA is not on-line, determined by its lack of response, station NA + 1 is tried. This process continues until a station is found

which does respond. The responding station number is written into register NA so that this scanning procedure need not be repeated on subsequent access cycles.

NOTE: 1. Node numbers 0 and 255 are reserved and cannot be used. Consequently scanning occurs circularly in the range 1-254.

2. During Scan mode token passing each node is only tried once.

Anytime a station cannot successfully pass a token within two attempts, register NA is updated to NA + 1, and a new "next" station is searched for. The result is the removal of non-responding station(s) from the access ring. An interrupt (INS) is generated indicating a network exception caused a change to NA.

The above description covers network recovery from station failure and purposeful removal of stations during on-line network operation. Setting stations in the scan mode can also be accomplished by sending control frames (a Scan frame redefines NA = MA + 1) over the network. The control frame may be directed to a single station, or all stations simultaneously (using the broadcast address). It is this scanning for new stations that permits on line addition to the access ring.

NOTE:
The policy of the SCAN frame is redefined by the user software as required by the application. For example: in a process control environment where stations are not often added while the network is in use, this procedure would be initiated rarely if at all.

3.2.2 REMOVING A STATION

There are two ways a station can be removed from the access ring: non-response due to station failure and non-response due to host commanded transition to the Isolate State. Both are treated identically from a network point of view.

Referring to Figure 3.1, assume that station 19 is removed from the network (either physically or logically). In this example, station 11 would detect a network fault when trying to pass the token to 19 (time TA would expire since station 19 will not respond). Station 11 detects this and finds the next station in the access ring by using the "scan" function (similar to initialization). The next attempt at passing the token would be to station 20, register NA + 1.

By starting the token ring recovery procedure at the intended station plus one (station 20) rather than MA + 1 (station 12) as is done in initialization, recovery delays are minimized (since fewer stations are tested for presence, 8 less in this example).

The next station found would be number 54 in the example which station 11 writes into his register NA (now "patching out" dead station 19). The next time station 11 is finished with the token, it directly sends it to 54, making the sequence now 11 to 54 to 4 to 11 to 54 . . .

3.2.3 INTERACTION OF THE SUB-PROTOCOLS

After a station is given the token, it will send an information frame, a token frame, or a combination of both. It is this combination frame, referred to as a "piggy back" token, that causes the sub-protocols to interact slightly.

In the normal case (no time-out), the SOURCE may transmit a combination frame to the DATASINK when his access period is over. All stations on the network observe this; after the reception of the current frame is complete, the one whose MA register matches the token address in the frame (TC) knows it has the token.

In the case of a combination frame, the SENDer resets his timer TA on transmission complete and waits for the NA station to transmit something valid, to verify his reception of the piggy back token. If the timer expires, the sender sends an explicit token (the data from the combination frame is assumed to have been accepted) and enters the normal token sub-protocol.

The user is prevented from sending a combination frame and requesting an acknowledgement at the same time to prevent possible network state confusions under time-out conditions.

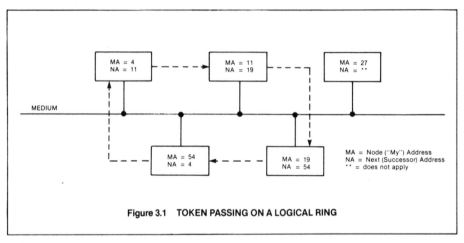

Figure 3.1   TOKEN PASSING ON A LOGICAL RING

3.3 FRAME FORMAT

The frame format the WD2840 uses to transmit all data and control frames is similar to the industry standard HDLC. A 16 bit CRC is implemented and standard zero insertion (CRC16-CCITT) is used for framing. This framing method allows the use of standard network monitoring and diagnostic equipment such as data scopes and logic analyzers.

Additional address fields and control points are defined as required to support the protocol.

Normal Frame Format:

F - TC - DA - SA - I - FCS - F

F	= Flag, binary pattern 01111110
TC	= Token Control (8 bit)
DA	= Destination Address (8 bit)
SA	= Source Address (8 bit)
I	= Information Field (0 to 2048 bytes or 16 buffers, whichever is less).
FCS	= Frame Check Sequence (16 bit)

Access Control Format:

F - DA - AC - FCS - F

F	= Flag, binary pattern 01111110
DA	= Destination Address (8 bit)
AC	= Access Control Field (8 bit)
FCS	= Frame Check Sequence (16 bit)

Token Pass Format:

F - TC - FCS - F

F	= Flag, binary pattern 01111110
TC	= Token Control (8 bit)
FCS	= Frame Check Sequence (16 bit)

C

16-Bit Microprocessor: MC68000

The Motorola MC68000 microprocessor is a very qualified representative of modern 16-bit machines. It is built with the use of advanced high-density short-channel metal-oxide semiconductor (HMOS) VLSI technology. It has sixteen 32-bit registers, large memory space, supervisor, user, and debug modes of operation and a seven-level prioritized, vectored interrupt system that effectively supports modern applications in complex, multiuser, and multiprocessor systems.

C.1 INPUT AND OUTPUT SIGNALS

The MC68000 communicates with memories, coprocessors, and peripheral devices through its inputs and outputs, which are shown in Fig. C.1-1. It is powered by a single supply voltage, +5V; however, four pins are used for power supply: two pins for +5 V (Vcc) and two pins for ground (GND). MC68000 also requires one external clock signal (CLK) for timing all its internal operations. The clock should have a fixed frequency of 4, 6, 8, or 12.5 MHz, depending on the processor version. Most of the lines are either inputs or outputs. The data lines and -HALT and -RESET lines are bidirectional. The 23-bit, unidirectional, three-state address bus can address up to 8 megawords (16 Mbytes) of data. The least significant bit of the address A0 is not used in the address bus, and therefore address lines determine only even addresses (words). A byte within a word is additionally specified by upper and lower data strobes (-UDS and -LDS).

The 16-bit data bus is bidirectional and three-state and is used to transfer data

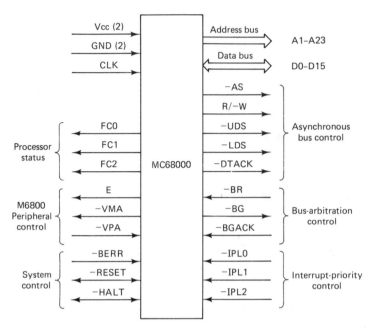

Figure C-1.1 Input and Output Signals of the MC68000. (Note: -XXX means that signal XXX is asserted (active) when in a low state.)

into or from the processor in words (D0-D15) or bytes (D0-D7)/(D8-D15) (see Fig. C.1-2).

The asynchronous bus-control lines are used to control data transfers to and from memories and all peripheral devices apart from 6800 family devices, which require synchronous transfers. Address strobe (-AS) is generated by the microprocessor to confirm that there is a valid address on the address bus. The read/write signal (R/-W) determines the direction of data transfer. Upper and lower data strobes are used to determine the word or byte data transfer. Data-transfer acknowledge (-DTACK) is used by memory or a peripheral device to inform the microprocessor that data transfer has been completed. This signal is essential because of the asynchronous character of data transfers. It allows the cooperation of the microprocessor with memories and peripher-

MC68000 memory structure

$1000	AA	BB	$1001
$1002	CC	DD	$1002

Byte $1000 = $AA
Word $1000 = $AABB
Long word $1000 = $AABBCCDD
Byte $1001 = $BB
Word $1002 = $CCDD

Figure C-1.2 MC68000—memory structure. (Note: Words and long words can begin at even addresses only.)

als of different speeds. Asynchronous bus operations during read and write cycles can be presented as follows:

microprocessor	memory/peripheral
. . . .	. . . .

microprocessor	memory/peripheral
set address lines;	wait until address-myaddress;
set -UDS, -LDS strobes;	wait until -AS = 0;
if read cycle then	·
set R/-W = 1	·
else	·
set R/-W = 0;	
reset -AS to 0;	if R/-W = 1 then
wait until -DTACK = 0;	set data on data lines
·	else
·	read data from data lines;
·	generate -DTACK = 0 pulse;
if read cycle then	
read data from data lines;	
end cycle.	end cycle.

The corresponding block diagram is shown in Fig. C.2.

The M6800 peripheral family control lines provide necessary synchronization for data transfers between synchronous M6800 devices and asynchronous MC68000 processor. The enable (E) signal is generated by MC68000, and its period is equal to 10 basic clock periods of MC68000. The valid peripheral address signal (-VPA) informs the microprocessor that M6800 peripheral has been addressed and is ready for data transfer synchronous with enable signal. The valid memory address signal (-VMA) informs a M6800 peripheral that there is a valid address on the address lines, and the processor is synchronized with enable signal.

Three interrupt-control input lines are used by the interrupting peripheral to inform the processor about its encoded priority level. Level 7 (all three lines at state low) is the highest priority, whereas level 0 indicates no interrupt request.

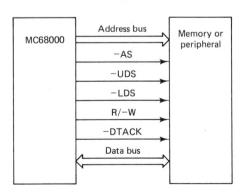

Figure **C-2** MC68000—memory asynchronous interface.

Three outgoing processor-status lines inform peripheral devices or other processors in multiprocessor systems about the current mode and cycle type of the MC68000.

The bus-arbitration lines are used in multiprocessor systems or in systems where some other device may be a bus master (for example DMA controller). Bus request input (-BR) informs the processor that some other device wants to become a bus master. The microprocessor informs the requesting device that it may take over the control of the bus through the bus grant output (-BG). The bus grant acknowledge input informs the MC68000 that another bus master has assumed control of the bus. Simplified operations (without details) during bus arbitration cycle are as follows:

MC68000	other bus master
. . . .	. . . .
process ultil -BR = 0;	assert -BR (0);
assert -BG (0);	wait until -BG = 0;
.	wait until end of cycle;
wait until -BGACK = 0;	assert -BGACK (0);
negate -BG;	negate -BR;
.	operate as bus master;
wait until -BGACK = 1;	negate -BGACK.
resume processing.	

The corresponding block diagram is shown in Fig. C.3.

There are three system-control I/O signals that are used to inform the processor about bus error, reset the processor or halt its operation. The bus-error input (-BERR) is driven by an external bus-error-detecting device, which may detect illegal access (for example, an attempt to write into the supervisor program area of memory), a lack of the -DTACK response from asynchronous device, or other bus errors. The bidirectional -RESET and -HALT lines are used to externally reset or halt the

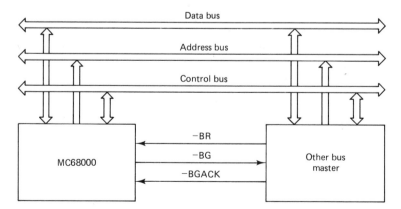

Figure C-3 Bus-arbitration interface.

processor. These lines are also used to inform external devices that the processor has been reset or halted by software or as a result of a double bus error.

C.2 PROGRAMMING MODEL AND INSTRUCTION FORMATS

The MC68000 microprocessor is a general register machine with a set of 16 registers divided into 8 data registers, D0–D7, and 8 address registers, A0–A7. Apart from these registers, the processor has a program counter (PC), supervisor stack pointer (A7'), and a status register (SR). The A7 register has a double role and is also used as a user-stack pointer. The SR register is 16 bits long; all other registers are 32 bits long. The programming model of MC68000 is shown in Fig. C.4.

The MC68000 instructions operate on byte, word, and long-word data sizes. Data and address registers are divided accordingly, as shown by lines in Fig. C.4. Thus data registers may be used to manipulate data in bytes (bits 0 through 7), words (0–15) and long words (0–31), whereas address registers may be used to hold addresses in a form of a word (0–15) or a long word (0–31). The PC is 32 bits long. However, only the 24 low-order bits (0–23) are actually used in MC68000 due to address-bus limitation to 23 lines (plus -UDS and -LDS strobes). The SR is divided into halves. The 8 low-order bits (0–7) form a condition-code register (CCR) containing all available condition flags: carry (C), zero (Z), sign (N), overflow (V), and auxiliary overflow (X). The high-order bits of SR (8–15) form a supervisor-status byte containing 5 status bits: trace (T), supervisor state (S) and interrupt mask bits (I0, I1, I2).

The MC68000 can operate on five basic data types: bits, BCD digits (4 bits), bytes (8 bits), words (16 bits), and long words (32 bits). There are two general types of instructions: data oriented, which result in a change of some data operand, and program-control oriented, which result in a change of program flow—for example, which affect the contents of the PC. In general, each instruction consists of an operation code field and an operand field:

| opcode | operand | Notation : OPC oper |

The opcode field determines the operation of an instruction whereas the operand field determines the operand(s), if any, of the instruction with the use of available addressing modes. With reference to the instruction format, the MC68000 instructions can be divided into following groups:

Double-operand instructions   : OPC src,dst   (e.g., MOVE)

Single-operand instructions   : OPC dst   (NEG)

Program-control instructions   : OPC addr   (JMP)

Implied addressing instructions   : OPC   (RTS)

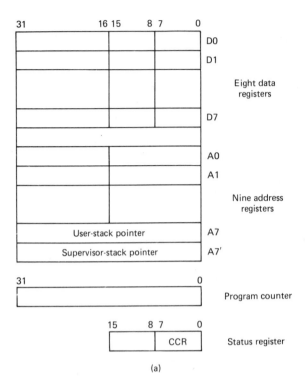

(a)

MC68000 status register

T = Trace mode
S = Supervisor mode
I0, I1, I2 = Interrupt mask
X = Extend
N = Negative
Z = Zero
V = Overflow
C = Carry
Unused bits are at 0.

(b)

FIGURE C-4 Programming model of the MC68000.

The difference between a single-operand data instruction and a program-control instruction is that in the former, the operand field contains an effective address of data operand on which the instruction operates, whereas in the latter, the operand field contains the address of an operand that is used to compute a new value of the PC.

Instructions of the MC68000 occupy from one to five words in memory, depending on the number of operands and the addressing modes used to determine their effective addresses. Double-operand instructions occupy one to five words, single-operand instructions, one to three words, program-control instructions, one to three words, and implied addressing instructions, only one word. The length of the instruction, the operation to be performed, and the operand size and addressing are specified by the first word, called the *operation word*. The remaining words, if any, further specify the operand(s).

C.3 ADDRESSING MODES

The MC68000 provides a programmer with a choice of 14 addressing modes, which may be used to specify the effective address of an operand. However, only one instruction, MOVE, may use all possible addressing modes to specify effective addresses of its both operands. Some instructions—for instance, RTS—may use only one of the addressing modes. Double-operand instructions may use the same or different addressing modes for each of their operands. Addressing modes of MC68000 (Table C.1) can be divided into six basic types:

- Register direct (1, 2)
- Absolute (3, 4),
- Immediate (5, 6),
- Register indirect (7–11),
- PC relative (12, 13)
- Implied (14)

The generation column in Table C.1. shows how the effective address (EA) of an operand is determined in a given addressing mode.

The data register and address register direct-addressing modes specify that the operand is located in one of the data registers (D0–D7) or in one of the address registers (A0–A7), respectively. Specification of the register in which the operand is located is contained within the operational word of the instruction.

In the absolute addressing modes, the instruction specifies the absolute address of the operand located in memory. There are two absolute addressing modes in the MC68000 processor. In absolute short-addressing, only the lower 16 bits of the operand's address are defined by the instruction. This address is sign-extended by the processor to form a full 24-bit address. Therefore, the absolute short-addressing mode can be used only to reference the operands in either the bottom 32K or in the top 32K of the total 16-Mbyte addressing space. In the absolute long-addressing mode, the instruction specifies the full 24-bit address of an operand. Absolute short- and absolute long-addressing modes use one and two words, respectively, to specify the address of an operand.

TABLE C.1 ADDRESSING MODES

No.	Mode	Generation of the effective address	Notation example
1	Data register direct	EA = Dn	CLR D1
2	Add. register direct	EA = An	CLR A0
3	Absolute short	EA = (next word)	CLR $1000
4	Absolute long	EA = (next two words)	CLR $10000
5	Immediate	EA = (next word(s))	ADDI #$1000,D1
6	Quick immediate	DATA specified by bits 9–11 of operation word	ADDQ #$7,D1
7	Address register indirect	EA = (An)	CLR (A0)
8	Address register indirect with postinctrement	EA = (An); An ← (An) + N	CLR (A0)+
9	Address register indirect with predecrement	An ← (An)-N; EA = (An)	CLR -(A0)
10	Address register indirect with displacement	EA = (An) + disp16	CLR $12(A0)
11	Address register indexed indirect with displacement	EA = (An) + (Rm) + disp8	CLR $F(A0, D1.W)
12	Relative with displacement	EA = (PC) + disp16	JMP $100(PC)
13	Relative with index and displacement	EA = (PC) + (Rn) + disp8	JMP $5(PC,A0.W)
14	Implied	EA = SR, USP, SP, PC	RTS

In the immediate addressing mode, an operand is specified by the instruction in value and is contained, depending on its size, in one or two words following the operational word. Some instructions can use the quick immediate addressing mode in which the operand's value is limited to the range zero to seven and is specified within the operational word of the instruction.

In the address register indirect-addressing mode, the instruction specifies an address register, and the contents of this register are taken by the processor as the absolute address of an operand located in memory. Only address registers can be used for indirect modes. Register specification is contained in the operational word.

The address register indirect with postincrement and the address register indirect with predecrement addressing modes are different from the plain address register indirect-addressing mode in that the execution of the instruction using one of these two modes affects not only the operand but also the contents of the address register used to locate the operand in memory. *Postincrement* implies that the contents of the address register are incremented after the instruction has accessed the operand. *Predecrement* implies that the contents of the address register are decremented first and then the operand is accessed. The contents of the address register are incremented or decremented by one, two, or four, depending on the size of an operand.

In the address register indirect with displacement addressing mode, the absolute address of an operand in memory is computed by the processor as a sum of the contents of the address register specified by the operational word and the sign-extended 16-bit displacement specified by one extension word of the instruction. The contents of the address register are not affected by instruction execution.

In the address register indexed indirect with displacement addressing, the absolute value of the address of an operand located in memory is computed by the processor as the sum of the contents of the address register, the index register, and the sign-extended 8-bit displacement. Either a data or an address register may be used as an index register. The address and index registers are specified in the operational word. The 8-bit displacement is specified in the lower byte of an extension word.

In the PC relative with displacement-addressing mode, the absolute address of the operand in memory is determined by the sum of the contents of the PC and the value of the sign-extended 16-bit displacement specified in an extension word. Note that the contents of the PC, when used for this computation, is always equal to the absolute address of the extension word (not the operational word of the instruction).

In the PC relative with index and displacement addressing, the absolute address of the operand in memory is obtained by adding the contents of PC, the contents of index register, and the sign-extended value of the 8-bit displacement. Either data or address register may be used as an index register. The 8-bit displacement is specified by the lower byte of an extension word. Again, the PC, when used for this computation, points to the extension word.

In the implied addressing, the operand is pointed to by the op-code of the instruction; for example, RTS instruction implies that the program counter will be loaded with the return address saved on the stack and pointed to by the contents of stack pointer, that is, address register A7 or A7'.

C.4 INSTRUCTION SET OVERVIEW

The set of instructions available for MC68000 programmer can be divided into the following groups:

- Data movement
- Arithmetic
- Logical

* Shift and rotate
* Bit manipulation
* Program control
* System control

Most of the instructions that affect data operands can operate on bytes, words, and long words. The size of the operand is always denoted by the suffix following the opcode of the instruction. Byte-long operands are denoted by .B suffix; .W and .L suffices denote word and long-word operands, correspondingly. The default size of the operand (in case no suffix is used) is word. The instructions that affect an address operand can operate on words and long words only. The MC68000 instructions are summarized in Tables C.2 through C.9. The syntax of the instruction determines the mnemonic code of the instruction and types of its operands (if any). The operations of the instructions are presented in the ''operation'' column of each table.

The arithmetic instructions allow for basic operations of add (ADD), subtract (SUB), multiply (MUL), and divide (DIV) as well as for the compare (CMP), clear (CLR), and negate (NEG) operations. The add and subtract instructions can use all sizes of data operands and word or long-word address operands. Compare instructions can use all sizes of operands located in data or address registers or in memory. The clear and negate instructions may use all sizes of operands located in data registers or in memory. The multiply and divide instructions operate on signed or unsigned operands. The multiply instructions perform the word-by-word multiplication and produce a long-word product. The divide instructions use a long-word dividend and a word divisor to produce a word quotient and a word remainder. For multiprecision or mixed-size computations, a programmer can use extended instructions such as add with extend (ADDX), subtract with extend (SUBX), negate with extend (NEGX), or sign extend (EXT). Add, subtract, and negate instructions can also operate in the binary coded decimal (BCD) arithmetic mode (ABCD, SBCD, NBCD). The test (TST) instruction compares an operand with zero and affects condition flags. The test and set instruction is designed specifically for synchronization purposes in the multiprocessor systems. The arithmetic instructions are summarized in Table C.2.

Data-transfer operations are supported primarily by the MOVE instruction and its variations. The MOVE instructions can transfer byte, word, and long-word operands from register to register, from register to memory, from memory to register or from memory to memory. If either the source or the destination of the operand is an address register, then only word or long-word operands can be used. A programmer can also use special data move instructions: move peripheral data (MOVEP), move multiple registers (MOVEM), move quick data (MOVEQ), swap data-register halves (SWAP), and exchange registers (EXG). The use of subroutines is efficiently supported by the link stack (LINK) and unlink stack (UNLK) instructions, together with the load effective address (LEA) and push effective address (PEA) instructions. The data-transfer instructions are presented in Table C.3.

TABLE C.2 ARITHMETIC INSTRUCTIONS

Syntax	Size	Operation	Description
ADD src, dst	B, W, L	dst ← src + dst	Add
SUB src, dst	B, W, L	dst ← dst − src	Subtract
NEG dst	B, W, L	dst ← 0 − dst	Negate
ADDX src, dst	B, W, L	dst ← src + dst + X	Add with extend
SUBX src, dst	B, W, L	dst ← dst − src − X	Subtract with extend
NEGX dst	B, W, L	dst ← 0 − dst − X	Negate with extend
ABCD src, dst	B	dst ← src10 + dst 10 + X	Add decimal with extend
SBCD src, dst	B	dst ← dst 10 − src 10 − X	Subtract decimal with extend
NBCD dst	B	dst ← 0 − dst 10 − X	Negate decimal with extend
MULS src, dst	Sig. W	dst ← src * dst	Signed multiply
MULU src, dst	W	dst ← src * dst	Unsigned multiply
DIVS src, dst	Sig. W	dst ← dst / src	Signed divide
DIVU src, dst	W	dst ← dst / src	Unsigned divide
EXT dst	W, L	dst[15:8] ← dst[7] or dst[31:16] ← dst[15]	Sign extend
CLR dst	B, W, L	dst ← 0	Clear operand
CMP src, dst	B, W, L	N, Z, V, C flags set acc. to dst − src	Compare
TST dst	B, W, L	V ← 0, C ← 0, N, Z flags set acc. to dst value	Test
TAS dst	B	V ← 0, C ←), N, Z flags set acc. to dst value; dst[7] ← 1	Test and set

The logical instructions AND, OR, EOR, and NOT can operate on all sizes of operands located in data registers or in memory. The source operand for these instructions can also be specified by value by using immediate addressing mode. The logical instructions are summarized in Table C.4.

The shift and rotate instructions can operate in both directions. All sizes of operands located in data or address registers can be shifted or rotated by a number of bits specified in the operational word of the instruction (1–8) or in a data register (0–63). Operands located in memory can be only of word size and can be shifted or rotated by 1 bit only. Table C.5 presents the syntax and operations of the shift and rotate instructions.

TABLE C.3 DATA-MOVEMENT INSTRUCTIONS

Syntax	Size	Operation	Description
MOVE src, dst	B, W, L	dst ← src	Move operand
MOVEP src, dst	W, L	dst ← src	Move peripheral data
MOVEM src, dst	W, L	dst ← src	Move multiple registers
MOVEQ data, dst	L	dst ← data	Move quick
SWAP Dn	L	Dn [31:16] ↔ Dn [15:0]	Swap data register halves
EXG Rn, Rm	L	Rn ↔ Rm	Exchange registers
LEA src, An	L	An ← src	Load effective address
PEA src	L	− (SP) ← src	Push effective address
LINK An, disp	Unsized	− (SP) ← An ; An ← SP; Sp ← SP + disp	Link stack
UNLK An	Unsized	SP ← AN ; An ← (SP) +	Unlink

TABLE C.4 LOGIC INSTRUCTIONS

Syntax	Size	Operation	Description
AND src, dst	B, W, L	dst ← src ˆ dst	Logical AND
OR src, dst	B, W, L	dst ← src v dst	Logical OR
EOR src, dst	B, W, L	dst ← src + dst	Logical exclusive OR
NOT dst	B, W, L	dst ← ~ dst	One's complement

    The set of bit manipulation instructions contains bit test and clear (BCLR), bit test and set (BSET), bit test and change (BCHG), and bit test (BTST) instructions. These instructions can test and modify single bits in either byte operands located in memory or long-word operands located in data registers. The bit number can be specified either by an immediate data or in the data register. The bit-manipulating instructions are summarized in Table C.6.

    Program-flow control can be accomplished using the instructions which allow unconditional and conditional branches, subroutine calls, and returns. The unconditional branches are supported by branch always (BRA) and jump (JMP) instructions. Branch instructions use relative addressing and are suitable for relocatable program applications. Conditional program branching and loop control can be achieved using the branch conditionally (Bcc) and test condition and decrement and branch (DBcc)

TABLE C.5 SHIFT AND ROTATE INSTRUCTIONS

Syntax	Size	Operation	Description
ASL count, dst ASL dst	B, W, L W		Arithmetic shift left
ASR count, dst ASR dst	B, W, L W		Arithmetic shift right
LSL count, dst LSL dst	B, W, L W		Logical shift left
LSR count, dst LSR dst	B, W, L W		Logical shift right
ROL count, dst ROL dst	B, W, L W		Rotate left without extend
ROR count, dst ROR dst	B, W, L W		Rotate right without extend
ROXL count, dst ROXL dst	B, W, L W		Rotate left with extend
ROXR count, dst ROXR dst	B, W, L W		Rotate right with extend

TABLE C.6 BIT-MANIPULATION INSTRUCTIONS

Syntax	Size	Operation	Description
BCLR bnmb, dst	B, L	Z ← ~dst[bnmb]; dst[bnmb] ← 0	Bit test and clear
BSET bnmb, dst	B, L	Z ← ~dst[bnmb]; dst[bnmb] ← 1	Bit test and set
BCHG bnmb, dst	B, L	Z ← ~dst[bnmb]; dst[nmb] ← ~dst[bnmb]	Bit test and change
BTST bnmb, dst	B, L	Z ← ~dst[bnmb]	Bit test

instructions. The set byte conditionally (Scc) instruction supports the use of Boolean variables coded in bytes so that $FF represents true and $00 represents false value. Use of subroutines is facilitated by jump to subroutine (JSR), branch to subroutine (BSR), return from subroutine (RTS), and return from subroutine and restore condition codes (RTR) instructions. Conditional instructions use the following condition encoding:

CC	carry clear	LS	low or same
CS	carry set	LT	less than
EQ	equal	MI	minus
F	never true	NE	not equal
GE	greater or	PL	plus
GT	greater than	T	always true
HI	high	VC	no overflow
LE	less or equal	VS	overflow

The program control instructions are summarized in Table C.7.

System-control instructions allow for privilege-state changes, status-register modifications, and user-stack pointer modifications and provide the means to reset external devices or stop program execution. Some of these instructions can be executed in the *supervisor* state only and are called the *privileged instructions*. An attempt to execute one of the privileged instructions while the processor is in the *user* state causes the privilege-violation exception. System-control instructions are summarized in Tables C.8 and C.9. Table C.9 lists the privileged instructions. Privilege state can be changed by unconditional or conditional trap (TRAP, TRAPV, CHK) instructions, return from exception (RTE) instructions, or by the instructions modifying the S flag in the SR. Condition code flags—Z, X, V, N—can be modified by logical or data-move instructions using the condition code register (CCR) as a destination operand. Other flags in the status register, S, T, I0, I1, I2, can be modified by logical or data-move instructions using the whole SR as a destination operand. External devices can be reset by the RESET instruction, which does not affect any processor registers. Program execution can be stopped by the STOP instruction.

TABLE C.7 PROGRAM-CONTROL INSTRUCTIONS

Syntax	Size	Operation	Description
JMP addr	—	PC ← addr	Jump
BRA disp	B, W	PC ← PC + disp	Branch always
JSR addr	—	−(SP) ← PC; PC ← addr	Jump to subroutine
BSR disp	B, W	−(SP) ← PC; PC ← PC + disp	Branch to subroutine
RTS	—	PC ← (SP) +	Return from subroutine
RTR	—	CCR ← (SP) + PC ← (SP) +	Return from subroutine and restore CCR
Bcc disp	B, W	If condition true then PC ← PC + disp	Branch conditionally

DBcc Dn, disp	W	If condition false then
		 Dn ← Dn − 1
		 if Dn <> −1 then
		 PC ← PC + disp
		 else PC ← PC + 2
			Test condition,
			 decrement data
			 register, and branch

Scc dst	B	If condition true then dst ← 1s else dst ← 0s	Set conditionally

TABLE C.8 SYSTEM-CONTROL INSTRUCTIONS

Syntax	Size	Operation	Description
TRAP vector	—	−(SSP) ← PC; −(SSP) ← SR; PC ← vector	Trap
TRAPV	—	If V set then TRAP	Trap on overflow
CHK src, Dn	W	If Dn < 0 or Dn > src then TRAP	Check register against bounds
ANDI data, CCR	B	CCR ← data ˆ CCR	AND immediate to CCR
ORI data, CCR	B	CCR ← data v CCR	OR immediate to CCR
EORI data, CCR	B	CCR ← data + CCR	EOR immediate to CCR
MOVE src, CCR	W, (B)	CCR ← src[7:0]	Move to CCR
MOVE CCR, dst	W	dst ← CCR	Move from CCR

TABLE C.9 PRIVILEGED INSTRUCTIONS (TRAP IF NOT IN SUPERVISOR STATE)

Syntax	Size	Operation	Description
RESET	—	Assert RESET line	Reset external devices
STOP data	—	SR ← data; stop	Stop
RTE	—	SR ← (SP) + ; PC ← (SP) +	Return from exception
ANDI data, SR	W	SR ← data ˆ SR	AND immediate to SR
ORI data, SR	W	SR ← data v SR	OR immediate to SR
EORI data, SR	W	SR ← data + SR	EOR immediate to SR
MOVE src, SR	W	SR ← src	Move to SR
MOVE An, USP or MOVE USP, An	L	An ← USP; USP ← An	Move to/from user-stack pointer

D

MC68000 — Exception Processing

The MC68000 microprocessor operates in one of two states of privilege: the *supervisor* state, which has higher privilege, or the *user* state, which has lower privilege. Internally, the *privilege* state determines which instructions are legal (all instructions are legal in *supervisor* state) and which of the stack pointers (*supervisor* or *user*) is to be used. Externally, the information about the *privilege* state of the processor is used by memory-management devices to translate addresses and detect illegal memory references. Privilege states provide a mechanism for program and data protection. For example, with the processor in the *user* state, the program cannot execute instructions restricted for the *supervisor* state or make references to the memory area reserved for the operating system, which runs in *supervisor* state.

The processor may change its state because of some external events or because of executing a state-changing instruction. The change from the higher-priority (*supervisor*) state to the lower-priority (*user*) state occurs only as a result of executing one of the following privileged instructions: return from exception (RTE), move to status register (MOVE to SR), AND immediate to status register (ANDI to SR), or exclusive OR immediate to status register (EORI to SR). It means that the operating system software has full control of the transition from operating system to the user program.

The transition from the *user* state to the *supervisor* state may be forced only as a result of exception processing. Exception processing may be generated internally as a result of an exception-generating instruction (for example, TRAP), as a result of executing an illegal or nonexistent instruction (for example, RTE in the *user* state), or as a result of address error (odd address for a word-size operand). Externally, exception processing can be forced by an interrupt, bus error, or reset. Refer to Fig. D.1.

S: *supervisor* state   **Figure D-1** State diagram.
U: *user* state

Generally speaking, MC68000 exceptions behave as software or hardware interrupts and are processed like vectored interrupts, that is, for each exception, a vector (new value of the PC) is stored in a specified memory location. Each exception is associated with a unique vector number (0–255). The processor obtains a vector by reading the long word (4 bytes) from the address obtained by multiplying the vector number by 4. Altogether, 512 words (1024 bytes) of memory are reserved for exception vectors. The vector for RESET requires 4 words (it uses vector numbers 0 and 1); all other vectors occupy 2 words each. The assignment of exception vector numbers and addresses is shown in the Table D.1.

There are three operational states of the MC68000: *normal processing* (when instructions are being executed), *exception-processing* (i.e., the sequence of context saving and obtaining new PC values), and *halted* (when no memory references are made by processor until reset). Transitions between the operational states are shown in Fig. D.2. The exception-processing sequence consists of the following four steps:

- Copy status register and change state to *supervisor*.
- Determine the vector number.
- Use the supervisor stack pointer (A7') to save the PC and the copy of status register on supervisor stack.
- Fetch the new PC from the vector determined in Step 2.

TABLE D.1 EXCEPTION VECTOR ASSIGNMENT

Vector Number(s)	Dec	Address Hex	Space	Assignment
0	0	000	SP	Reset: Initial SSP[2]
	4	004	SP	Reset: Initial PC[2]
2	8	008	SD	Bus Error
3	12	00C	SD	Address Error
4	16	010	SD	Illegal Instruction
5	20	014	SD	Zero Divide
6	24	018	SD	CHK Instruction

TABLE D.1 EXCEPTION VECTOR ASSIGNMENT (cont'd.)

Vector Number(s)	Dec	Address Hex	Space	Assignment
7	28	01C	SD	TRAPV Instruction
8	32	020	SD	Privilege Violation
9	36	024	SD	Trace
10	40	028	SD	Line 1010 Emulator
11	44	02C	SD	Line 1111 Emulator
12[1]	48	030	SD	(Unassigned, Reserved)
13[1]	52	034	SD	(Unassigned, Reserved)
14[1]	56	038	SD	(Unassigned, Reserved)
15	60	03C	SD	Uninitialized Interrupt Vector
16-23[1]	64	040	SD	(Unassigned, Reserved)
	95	05F		—
24	96	060	SD	Spurious Interrupt[3]
25	100	064	SD	Level 1 Interrupt Autovector
26	104	068	SD	Level 2 Interrupt Autovector
27	108	06C	SD	Level 3 Interrupt Autovector
28	112	070	SD	Level 4 Interrupt Autovector
29	116	074	SD	Level 5 Interrupt Autovector
30	120	078	SD	Level 6 Interrupt Autovector
31	124	07C	SD	Level 7 Interrupt Autovector
32-47	128	080	SD	TRAP Instruction Vectors[4]
	191	0BF		
48-63[1]	192	0C0	SD	(Unassigned, Reserved)
	255	0FF		—
64-255	256	100	SD	User Interrupt Vectors
	1023	3FF		—

NOTES

1 Vector numbers 12, 13, 14, 16 through 23, and 48 through 63 are reserved for future enhancements by Motorola. No user peripheral devices should be assigned these numbers.

2 Reset vector (0) requires four words, unlike the other vectors which only require two words, and is located in the supervisor program space.

3 The spurious interrupt vector is taken when there is a bus error indication during interrupt processing. Refer to Paragraph 5.5.2.

4 TRAP n uses vector number 32 + n.

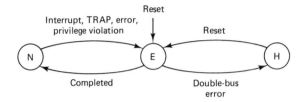

E: *exception-processing* state
N: *normal processing* state
H: *halted* state

Figure D-2 Transitions between operational states.

Internally, there might be only one situation requiring exception processing at a time, for example, the TRAP instruction or privilege violation. External events, like external reset, bus error, or interrupt request may happen at random, and, for example, bus error may occur at the same instant of time as some interrupt request or an interrupt request may occur when a TRAP instruction is being executed. As a result, the processor may have to resolve the problem of which exception should be processed first. The MC68000 exceptions are divided into three groups: group 0, having the highest priority, and group 2 having the lowest priority. Table D.2 lists the exception groups and defines their processing. Note that illegal instruction and privilege violation are detected before the beginning of instruction execution cycle.

The group 0 exceptions are reset, bus error, and address error. Within group 0, reset has the highest priority and address error has the lowest priority. These exceptions force the processor to abort currently executed instruction, and exception processing starts within two clock cycles. The group 1 exceptions include trace, interrupt request, illegal instruction, and privilege violation. Within group 1, highest priority is assigned to trace. Interrupt request has priority lower than trace but higher than illegal instruction or privilege violation. There is no priority distinction between illegal instruction or privilege violation, since they are mutually exclusive. The group 1 exceptions permit completion of the currently executed instruction, and exception processing begins before next instruction. The lowest-priority group, group 2, includes TRAP, TRAPV,

TABLE D.2

Group	Exception	Processing
0	Reset Bus error Address error	Current instruction aborted; exception processing begins after two clock cycles.
1	Trace Interrupt Illegal instruction Privilege violation	Current instruction completed; exception processing begins before next instruction.
2	TRAP, TRAPV, CHK, Zero divide	Exception processing starts as a result of an instruction.

and CHK instructions and divide-by-zero error. All these exceptions result from normal execution of an instruction and so there is no priority relation within this group.

The MC68000 is equipped with the seven-level prioritized-interrupt system. Interrupts are processed as group 1 exceptions, that is, all interrupts are vectored and have lower priority than group 0 or trace exceptions. Interrupt-priority levels are numbered from 1 to 7, with level 7 being the highest priority. Level 0 corresponds to the lack of an interrupt request. The processor obtains the information about the priority level of an interrupt by reading the IPL0-IPL2 input lines (refer to Section D.1). The status register contains a 3-bit mask that indicates the current processor priority (I0–I2 flags), and interrupts are inhibited for all priority levels less than or equal to processor's priority.

Interrupt requests arriving at the processor do not force immediate exception processing but are made pending. Pending interrupts are detected by the processor between instruction executions. If the priority of the pending interrupt is found to be lower than or equal to the current mask, the processor starts the next instruction and the interrupt-exception processing is postponed. When the priority of the pending interrupt is found to be greater than the current mask, the exception processing begins. In addition to general exception-processing steps, the processor priority level (interupt mask) is set to the level of an interrupt being served and the processor reads the vector number from the interrupting device. If external logic requests an automatic vectoring (e.g., the interrupting device cannot provide the interrupt vector number), the processor internally generates a vector number corresponding to the interrupt priority level (autovector). If external logic indicates a bus error during interrupt-acknowledge cycle, the processor regards the interrupt as spurious and the internally generated vector number points to the spurious interrupt vector.

Level 7 interrupts cannot be prohibited by the interrupt-priority mask and therefore are nonmaskable. An interrupt is generated each time the interrupt-request level changes from some lower level to level 7.

E

Educational Computer Board (ECB)

The single-board computer MEX68KECB based on an MC68000 microprocessor and manufactured by Motorola is designed specifically to provide cost-efficient equipment for the introduction to MC68000-based systems. ECB implements only a subset of available MC68000 features; however, it can help a student learn how to program an MC68000-based system with serial and parallel interfaces for time-dependent applications.

The functional block diagram of ECB is shown in Fig. E.1. From the hardware point of view, the major building blocks are as follows:

- The 16-bit, 4 MHz, MC68000 microprocessor
- 16K-byte (8K-word) ROM/EPROM memory with TUTOR firmware
- 32K-byte (16K-word) dynamic RAM memory
- Two RS-232C-compatible serial-communication ports
- 16-bit parallel port
- 24-bit programmable timer

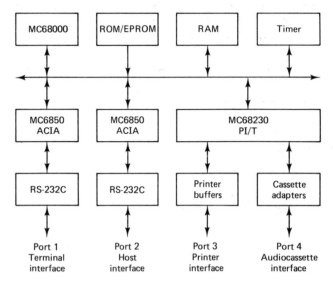

FIGURE E-1 Functional block-diagram of ECB.

F

Tutor Commands

The TUTOR firmware is a resident package stored in 16Kb of ROM memory on the ECB board and is designed to support user program editing and debugging functions. Some Tutor functions allow for ECB reconfiguration and i/o data-transfer control. A group of Tutor routines may also be used by user programs. All Tutor routines are executed in the supervisor mode. The general algorithm of Tutor's operation follows. The return from user program to the Tutor is achieved by exception processing: either by reset or by special TRAP 14 function. The basic algorithm of Tutor's operation is shown in Fig. F.1. The commands may be entered via the terminal keyboard after Tutor's prompt, that is, the text TUTOR 1.X > has been displayed. There is a wide variety of commands, which can be divided into three general groups: editing, debugging and execution, and I/O control. The editing commands allow the user to modify or display the contents of ECB's RAM memory with or without the use of line assembler-disassembler option. If the line assembler is not used, the contents of the memory are displayed or modified in a form of hexadecimal numbers. The software-accessible registers of programmable peripheral devices (serial and parallel ports and timer) can also be accessed using editing commands.

The line assembler-disassembler allows the user to load assembly-language programs from the keyboard by entering them one line at a time. The source code is not stored in memory; rather, the line entered is assembled and the object code is stored in RAM memory. When the memory contents are displayed with the disassembly option, the assembly-language formatted line is displayed on the screen. The Tutor's assembler is a subset of Motorola's resident assembler for the MC68000. Standard line format, instruction op-codes, and data types are used. However, Tutor's assembler does not allow for the use of labels and line numbers, and it allows only one directive, the

```
repeat
  initialize;
  repeat
    display prompt; (* TUTOR 1.X >  , X is a version number *)
    wait for new line from terminal;
    if command calling for user program execution then
       enter user state and jump to user program start
    elseif executable command then
       execute command
    else
       display command error message
  until reset
until power down.
```

Figure F-1   Basic algorithm of Tutor's operations.

define constant word (DC.W) directive. Still, it is a powerful tool for editing user programs and is sufficiently convenient for programming examples and problems given in network laboratory experiments and projects.

The editing group of commands includes the following:

MM		Memory modify
MM	;DI	MM/Memory modify with assembler-disassembler option
MD		Memory display
MD	;DI	Memory display with assembler-disassembler option,
BF		Fill block of memory
BM		Move block of memory
BS		Search block of memory

BR	Set breakpoint
NOBR	Delete breakpoint
GO	Start user program
TR	Trace (single-step) user program
DF	Display formatted contents of processor registers
.rn	Display or modify single register; rn = register name:
	Address registers, A0, . ., A7
	Data registers, D0, . . ., D7
	Program counter, PC
	Status register, SR
	System stack pointer, SS
	User stack pointer, US

PA	Printer attach
TM	Transparent mode
DU	Dump memory to port
LO	Load memory from port
VE	Verify memory loaded from port

For details of commands formats and operation as well as for the commands not listed here, refer to ECB user's manual.

TUTOR-supplied functions (routines) can be invoked by the use of the TRAP 14 instruction in user programs provided the function has been selected by storing its number in the lowest byte of the D7 register before TRAP 14 is executed. The user programs can call several versions of character-string input and output or code-conversion functions. Function 229 (decimal) restarts the TUTOR from the user program.

G

Serial Interface: MC6850 (ACIA)

The ACIA is a programmable device that performs buffering, formatting, and control functions, allowing for easy interfacing between the parallel microprocessor bus and serial asynchronous data-communications path. On the microprocessor side, the Motorala MC6850 ACIA operates with synchronous parallel data transfers and is compatible with the MC6800 and MC68000 families of microprocessors. The operation of the MC6850 can be programmed by the processor, that is, the processor can select various data formats, parity generation or check, data-transfer rate, and transmit-receive control modes, including interrupt enable-disable options. The ACIA is used in microcomputer systems for serial I/O ports, which, via the signal-level adapters, can be used for direct interface to RS232C devices such as video terminals or modems. Apart from parallel-serial conversion and byte formatting, the ACIA can also activate and detect the readiness of an RS232C device for data transfers. The I/O signals of the MC6850 ACIA are presented in Fig. G.1.

On the processor side there are eight bidirectional data lines, D0–D7, read/write strobe (R/W), enable strobe (E), used for data-transfer synchronization, register-select line (RS) (usually the least-significant address bit), for internal register addressing, chip select lines, CS0–CS2, used to activate the ACIA, and interrupt request line (IRQ). On the terminal side, a TxD line is used for serial data output, and an RxD line is used for serial data input. There are three control lines here: clear to send (CTS), data-carrier detect (DCD), and request to send (RTS). RTS is used by MC6850 to inform the peripheral that it is willing to transmit. If ready, the peripheral responds by asserting the CTS line. For all data-transfer purposes over the modem, the DCD line informs the MC6850 whether the modem-to-modem connection is operational and active. One of the possible byte frames that can be programmed for the MC6850 is

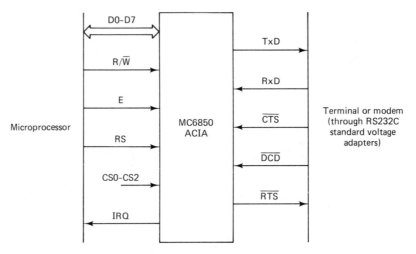

Figure G-1   Inputs and outputs of the ACIA.

shown in Fig. G.2. Note that the idle-line state on the TxD or RxD line is the logical 1 (high) state.

| Idle line | Start bit | 8 information bits | 2 stop bits |

Figure G-2   A byte frame for serial asynchronous transmission.

The programming and operation of the MC6850 is facilitated by internal 8-bit registers: control register, status register, transmit-data register, and receive-data register. The set of internal registers and corresponding information-flow paths are shown in Fig. G.3.

Note that the output and input shift registers are not accessible by software. The microprocessor can write only to the transmit-data register or to control register. The receive-data register and status register can only be read. The selection of register for read/write data transfers is accomplished by the RS line. The RS line in 8-bit microcomputer systems is driven by the least significant address bit, and the set of ACIA's registers occupies two consecutive bytes in the addressing space. In MC68000 applications, due to the 16-bit data path, it would be two consecutive even or two consecutive odd addresses, depending on which half of the data bus is used for MC6850. When a byte is to be serially transmitted, the microprocessor writes it into the transmit-data register. If the output-shift register is empty (previous transmission completed) and external conditions permit (CTS = 0 and DCD = 0), the byte is moved in parallel to the output-shift register, start, stop, and parity bits are added, and the byte frame (start, data, parity, and stop bits) is shifted out, one bit at a time, over the TxD line with the preselected speed. While the shifting is being performed, a new byte may be written into the transmit-data register.

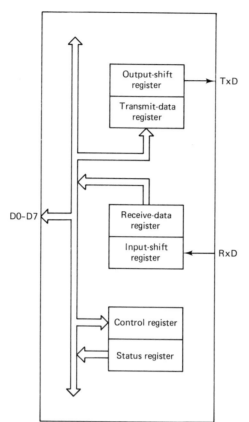

FIGURE G-3   Main information flow paths within the ACIA.

The receiving part operates as follows. In the idle-line state, first transition on the RxD line from 1 to 0 marks the beginning of the start bit. The length (duration time) of the start bit is tested, and if it happens to be a *false-start bit* (line noise), it is disregarded. If the start bit is correct, the RxD line is probed at the middle-of-a-bit moments, which are determined from the receive-clock signals. The data is then shifted into the receive-shift register. The parity and frame format are tested and status bits are set accordingly (see the paragraph on status-register description that follows). After all the data bits have been shifted in and if the receive-data register is empty (previously arrived byte has been read), the newly arrived byte is moved in parallel to the receive-data register. If the receive-data register does not become empty until the moment when another byte starts coming in over the RxD line, the last accepted byte in the shift register is lost and a byte overwrite condition occurs. This condition is reflected in the status register. The incoming data is asynchronous, and neither the processor nor the ACIA can slow it down. The bytes have to be read by the processor from the receive-data register one at a time and fast enough, that is, at least every $N \times t$ seconds (where N is a number of bits in a frame and t is a bit slot time in seconds).

The data-transfer rate, frame formats, and parity can be programmed by writing appropriate data into the control register. The initialization of the ACIA, that is, clearing of all status bits, can also be achieved by writing the master reset code into the control register. The meaning of control-register bits follows.

Bits b0 and b1 are used for the selection of the data transfer rate and master reset. The data-transfer rate selected applies both to the transmit and receive parts of the ACIA. For master reset, both bits have to be set to 1. The data-transfer rate is selected by choosing one of three available clock divide ratios: by 1, by 16, and by 64.

b1	b0	Function
0	0	÷ 1
0	1	÷ 16
1	0	÷ 64
1	1	Master reset

Bits b2, b3, and b4 are used for selecting data-frame format. A frame can have 8 or 7 data bits, positive, negative, or no parity bit, and 1 or 2 stop bits. Selected format applies to both transmit and receive parts.

b4	b3	b2	Function
0	0	0	7 bits + even parity + 2 stop bits
0	0	1	7 bits + odd parity + 2 stop bits
0	1	0	7 bits + even parity + 1 stop bit
0	1	1	7 bits + odd parity + 1 stop bit
1	0	0	8 bits + 2 stop bits
1	0	1	8 bits + 1 stop bit
1	1	0	8 bits + even parity + 1 stop bit
1	1	1	8 bits + odd parity + 1 stop bit

Bits b5 and b6 are used to control the operation of transmitter part of the MC6850. The interrupt request on byte transmit completion can be enabled or disabled. The RTS line can be set or reset, and, finally, the TxD line can be set to the *break-level* state, that is, to logical 0 as opposed to normal *idle-line* state, logical 1.

b6	b5	Function
0	0	RTS = low, transmit irq disabled
0	1	RTS = low, transmit irq enabled
1	0	RTS = high, transmit irq disabled
1	1	RTS = low, TxD at break level, transmit irq disabled

The most significant bit (b7) is used to enable or disable the interrupt generated when the receive-data register becomes full, a byte-overrun condition occurs, or the data-carrier detect line changes from logical 0 to 1. Bit b7 set to 1 enables and b7 reset to 0 disables this interrupt request.

The cause-effect relationship illustrating the meaning of all 8 bits of the status register is as follows:

A new byte received over RxD	$\rightarrow$ b0 := 1
A byte read from receive data register	$\rightarrow$ b0 := 0
A byte sent out over TxD	$\rightarrow$ b1 := 1
A new byte written into transmit data register	$\rightarrow$ b1 := 0
DCD line = 0	$\rightarrow$ b2 := 1
DCD line = 1	$\rightarrow$ b2 := 0
CTS line = 0	$\rightarrow$ b3 := 1
CTS line = 1	$\rightarrow$ b3 := 0
A byte received with frame error	$\rightarrow$ b4 := 1
A byte received without frame error	$\rightarrow$ b4 := 0
A byte overrun condition occurred	$\rightarrow$ b5 := 1
No byte overwrite condition	$\rightarrow$ b5 := 0
Byte received with parity error	$\rightarrow$ b6 := 1
Byte received without parity error	$\rightarrow$ b6 := 0
Interrupt generating condition occured	$\rightarrow$ b7 := 1
Byte read from receive data register or Byte written into transmit data register	$\rightarrow$ b7 := 0

In addition, all status bits b0–b7 are cleared by a master reset operation.

H

Parallel Interface and Timer: MC68230 (PI/T)

The main functions of a programmable parallel interface adapter include data buffering, data flow direction selection, external handshaking and interrupt generation. A programmable timer is used to generate interrupts in prescribed instants of time. Quite often the timer, which essentially is built as a counter of clock pulses, can be used alternatively as a counter of external events represented by digital pulses. The MC68230 programmable parallel interface/timer (PI/T) contains both the 3-port parallel interface and 24-bit timer. Each parallel interface line can be individually programmed to be either inputs or outputs, and they can also operate as three independent 8-bit parallel ports. Several operating modes are available, and external handshaking lines are provided for data-exchange synchronization between the MC68230 and external parallel devices such as printers. The I/O bits can also be used separately to control or sense individual external elements such as light-emitting diodes (LEDs), relays, or switches. Ports A and B are 8-bit I/O ports. Port C can also be programmed to be an 8-bit port; however, some of the pins used by port C are multifunction pins that may be also used for timer or DMA request operations. If this is the case, port C may be limited to just two I/O lines. The timer part of the MC68230 can be used to generate interrupts after a programmable period of time, generate repetitive interrupts with the programmable frequency, or count external impulses. The timer I/O consists of three signals: clock input, interrupt request, and interrupt acknowledge. The I/O signals of MC68230 are presented in Fig. H.1.

The data exchange on the processor side is asynchronous, and there is no need for an E signal, which is used by MC6850. Instead, data exchange over an 8-bit data bus is controlled by chip select (CS), read/write (R/W) and data-transfer acknowledge (DTACK) lines. The registers inside the MC68230 are addressed by five register-select

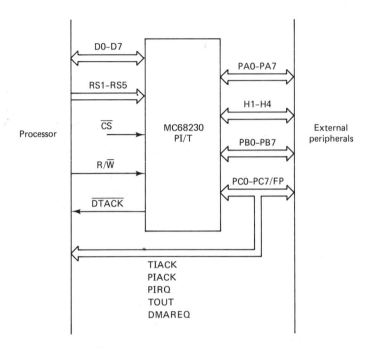

Figure H-1   MC68230: inputs and outputs.

lines (RS1,..,RS5). For interrupt and DMA-request purposes, five lines from port C may be used (if necessary) to perform the functions of peripheral interrupt request (PIRQ), peripheral interrupt acknowledge (PIACK), timer-interrupt request (called timeout TOUT), timer-interrupt acknowledge (TIACK), and DMA request (DMAREQ). All these lines are active low, which means, for instance, that the interrupt request is signaled to the processor by a low voltage (logical 0) signal level on the corresponding line.

On the external peripheral side, two buffered bidirectional parallel ports, PA and PB, are supported by four handshaking lines, H1–H4, for the purpose of data-transfer synchronization. H1 and H2 serve port A, whereas H3 and H4 serve port B. Bits b0 and b1 of port C are used for I/O, and bits b3 through b7 may be used alternatively for I/O or interrupt and DMA purposes. Bit b2 may be used for I/O or for external timer input (TIN) for timer clocking or impulse-counting purposes.

There are 22 software-accessible registers within the MC68230 PI/T. They can be divided generally into the port and timer parts. The port part consists of general port control and status group and PA, PB, and PC groups (see Fig. H.2.). The general group includes the port general-control register (PGCR), port service-request register (PSRR), port interrupt-vector register (PIVR) and port status register (PSR). PA and PB groups are identical and include port A (B) data register, PADR (PBDR), port A (B) data-direction register, PADDR (PBDDR), port A (B) alternate register, PAAR (PBAR), and port A (B) control register, PACR (PBCR). Port C group includes port C data register (PCDR) ad port C data-direction register (PCDR).

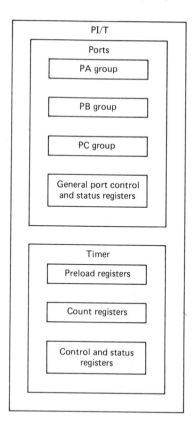

FIGURE H-2 MC68230—internal register groups.

The PGCR register is used to control functions that are common to ports A and B, that is, operation-mode selection and the meaning and operation of handshaking lines H1–H4. The PSRR register is used to define whether the multifunction pins of port C are to be used for I/O or for port-interrupt and direct-memory access requests and acknowledgment. Also, the priority system for the interrupts generated by handshaking lines can be selected through PSRR register. The timer interrupt, which also takes some of PC bits, is programmed by the timer-control register. The PIVR register is used to define the vector number for port interrupt, which will be read by the processor during the interrupt-acknowledge cycle. Only bits b2–b7 of the PIVR may be programmed. Two least significant bits are filled automatically by MC68230 on handshake interrupt according to the priority system selected in PSRR register. The PSR reflects the level and interrupt status of handshaking lines. If an interrupt-generating transition has occurred on a handshaking line, the corresponding status bit is set to 1, and as long as it remains set, the port requests interrupt service. The interrupt-status bit (and, therefore, the interrupt-request bit) can be cleared by writing logical 1 to the corresponding bit in PSR.

Port A (B)(C) data registers are used as parallel, 8-bit bidirectional data buffers. Port A (B) alternate registers allow direct read operations to obtain current status of unbuffered port A (B) i/o lines. Port A (B)(C) data-direction registers control data direction at each pin separately: Logical 0 indicates input and logical 1 indicates output on the corresponding bit of port-data register. Port A (B) control registers allow selection of port submodes of operation as well as define the operation and service technique for the relevant handshaking lines.

The timer part of the MC68230 consists of a timer-control register (TCR), a timer-interrupt vector register (TIVR), a timer-status register (TSR), three timer-preload registers (TPRH, TPRM, and TPRL), and three timer-count registers (TCRH, TCRM, and TCRL). The TCR register is used to enable or disable the timer, select the prescaling clock-division ratio, enable or disable timer interrupts, and select the timer-operational mode (reload or roll over on zero count). Enabling or disabling timer interrupts is associated with programming two of port C bits for TOUT and TIACK or I/O functions. The TIVR register allows the programming of a timer-interrupt vector number. Since there is only one reason for an interrupt from the timer (count = 0), a full 8-bit vector number can be programmed in PIVR. The TSR register contains only 1 active bit (least significant) that reflects the zero detect and, therefore, the timer-interrupt status. This bit is set on first zero-count detection and can be cleared by writing $01 to TSR.

I

Assembly-Language Programs for Chapter 5 Experiments

The assembly programs are written for laboratory network nodes based on ECB single board microcomputers equipped with network nodes as described in Chapter 4.

```
****************************************************************
* global declarations:
****************************************************************
*
* The following code defines all constants and variables used in
* assembly language routines given in this appendix for laboratory
* experiments 1 to 10. The names of constants and variables defined
* here are written in lower case letters throughout the assembly
* language code.
*
****************************************************************
* constants:
****************************************************************
*
* ASCII codes for nonprintable characters:
*
cr      EQU     $0D     * carriage return
lf      EQU     $0A     * line feed
space   EQU     $20     * space
pre     EQU     $00     * preamble byte
eot     EQU     $04     * end of text byte
*
* CPU status control word:
*
eni     EQU     $0000   * enable CPU interrupts and enter user
*                       * mode
*
* addresses of the top of user and supervisor stacks
*
ustack  EQU     $F00    * the top of user stack
sstack  EQU     $C00    * the top of supervisor stack
*
* communications port (terminal and network) programming
* constants - control bytes:
*
rst     EQU     $03     * reset port
di      EQU     $15     * disable all port interrupts
eri     EQU     $95     * enable receive interrupts
eti     EQU     $35     * enable transmit interrupts
tst     EQU     $7C     * error test mask
*
* terminal port programming constants - addresses:
*
tpsc    EQU     $10040  * terminal port status and control registers
tprt    EQU     $10042  * terminal port data registers
tpva    EQU     $74     * interrupt vector address for terminal port
*                         (autovector for level 5 interrupt)
*
* network port programming constants - addresses:
*
```

```
npsc    EQU     $10041  * network port status and control registers
nprt    EQU     $10043  * network port data registers
npva    EQU     $78     * interrupt vector address for network port
*                         (autovector for level 6 interrupt)
*
* timer programming constants - addresses and control bytes:
*
tcr     EQU     $10021  * timer control register
cprh    EQU     $10027  * counter preload register - high byte
cprm    EQU     $10029  * counter preload register - middle byte
cprl    EQU     $1002B  * counter preload register - low byte
tivr    EQU     $10023  * timer interrupt vector register
tvnmb   EQU     $40     * timer vector number
tva     EQU     $100    * interrupt vector address (4 * $40)
tstop   EQU     $A0     * timer stop control byte
tstart  EQU     $A1     * timer start control byte
*
*
* timer programming constants - delay values:
*
wft     EQU     $04     * wait for token time
wfr     EQU     $01     * wait for response time
stu     EQU     $08     * sleep time unit
bdelay  EQU     1000    * approx. 1/120 sec. delay in lab.9
n       EQU     100     * used in START8 routine in lab.8
*
* collision detector programming constants - addresses and
* control bytes (note that collision detection logic uses
* parallel port on the ECB microcomputer):
*
pgcr    EQU     $10001  * port general control register
psrr    EQU     $10003  * port service request register
pbcr    EQU     $1000F  * port B control register
psr     EQU     $1001B  * port status register
pivr    EQU     $1000B  * port interrupt vector register
pvnmb   EQU     $42     * port vector number
pva     EQU     $108    * port vector address (4 * $42)
pmode   EQU     $20     * port mode control byte
bmode   EQU     $82     * port B mode control byte
initi   EQU     $18     * initialize interrupt pins control byte
clri    EQU     $04     * clear collision interrupt control byte
*
* message buffers, starting addresses:
*
rborg   EQU     $1000   * start of the receive buffer
tborg   EQU     $1100   * start of the transmit buffer
tborg1  EQU     tborg+1 * second byte in the transmit buffer (DID)
tforg   EQU     $1200   * start of the token frame
tforg1  EQU     tforg+1 * second byte of the token frame (NID)
tforg2  EQU     tforg+2 * third byte of the token frame
tfend   EQU     tforg+3 * end address of the token frame
*
```

```
* text strings:
* (Note: the names of text strings will be used in assembly
*        routines as beginning addresses of the strings).
*
inpmid  DC.B     'input MID ',0
inpnid  DC.B     'input NID ',0
inptok  DC.B     'input token ',0
coltxt  DC.B     'collision ',0
tlost   DC.B     'token lost ',0
newnid  DC.B     'new NID = ',0
nonodes DC.B     'no other nodes on the network ',0
*
* node identifier (network address) limits:
*
minid   EQU      $31      * lowest node ID
maxid   EQU      $39      * highest node ID
*
****************************************************************
* variables:
****************************************************************
*
* node identifiers (network addresses):
*
mid     EQU      $900     * this node's identifier (my id)
did     EQU      $901     * destination node id
nid     EQU      tforgl   * next node id (used in token frames only)
*
* one-byte buffer for data received from the network bus:
*
dbyte   EQU      $902     * data byte
tbyte   EQU      $903     * terminal byte
nbyte   EQU      $904     * network byte
*
* send and display request flags:
*
sp      EQU      $910     * request to send packet
dp      EQU      $911     * request to display packet
sf      EQU      $912     * request to send frame
df      EQU      $913     * request to display frame
dnn     EQU      $914     * request to display the nonodes message
dnid    EQU      $915     * request to display the newnid message
dtl     EQU      $916     * request to display the tlost message
*
* application layer state encoding flags:
*
byi     EQU      $920     * busy inputing
byd     EQU      $921     * busy displaying
*
* network layer state encoding flags and variables:
*
byr     EQU      $922     * busy receiving
bys     EQU      $923     * busy sending
```

```
state    EQU      $924     * network layer state
rstate   EQU      $925     * network layer receive sub-state
tl       EQU      $925     * token lost
tr       EQU      $926     * token received
*
* buffer status flags:
*
rbf      EQU      $930     * receive buffer full
tbf      EQU      $931     * transmit buffer full
*
* buffer pointers:
*
rbnxt    EQU      $940     * receive buffer next byte pointer
rbend    EQU      rbnxt+4  * receive buffer end pointer
tbnxt    EQU      $950     * transmit buffer next byte pointer
tbend    EQU      tbnxt+4  * transmit buffer end pointer
frnxt    EQU      $960     * frame next byte pointer
frend    EQU      frnxt+4  * frame end pointer
txtptr   EQU      $970     * text string pointer
*
********************************************************************
* Assembly language routines for experiment 1
********************************************************************
*
* Assembly language program for the transmitter node:
*
* The Main routine:
*
MAINTR1 MOVE.L   #ustack,A0    * initialize user stack pointer
        MOVE.L   A0,USP        *
        MOVE.L   #sstack,A7    * initialize supervisor stack pointer
        MOVE.L   #TISR1,tpva   * initialize Tport interrupt vector
        MOVE.B   #eri,tpsc     * enable receive interrupts at Tport
        MOVE.B   #di,npsc      * disable all interrupts at Nport
        MOVE.W   #eni,SR       * enable external interrupts and
                               * enter user mode
                               * repeat
IDLET1  BRA      IDLET1        *    idle
                               * until reset.
*
* The Terminal port interrupt service routine:
*
TISR1   MOVE.L   D1,-(A7)      * save register D1 on stack
        MOVE.B   tprt,dbyte    * dbyte := Tport
        MOVE.B   tpsc,D1       * if status OK then
        AND.B    #tst,D1       *
        BNE      TIS1EX        *
        BSR      SEND1         *    Send_byte
        BSR      DSPTX1        *    Display_byte
                               * endif
TIS1EX  MOVE.L   (A7)+,D1      * restore register D1
        RTE                    * return
```

```
*
* The Send_byte routine:
*
SEND1   BTST.B  #1,npsc         * wait until Nport ready for output
        BEQ     SEND1           *
        MOVE.B  dbyte,nprt      * Nport := dbyte
        RTS                     * return
*
* The Display_byte routine:
*
DSPTX1  BTST.B  #1,tpsc         * wait until Tport ready for output
        BEQ     DSPTX1          *
        MOVE.B  dbyte,tprt      * Tport := dbyte
        RTS                     * return
*
*
* Assembly language program for the receiver node:
*
* The Main routine:
*
MAINRX1 MOVE.L  #ustack,A0      * initialize user stack pointer
        MOVE.L  A0,USP          *
        MOVE.L  #sstack,A7      * initialize supervisor stack pointer
        MOVE.L  #NISR1,npva     * initialize Nport interrupt vector
        MOVE.B  #eri,npsc       * enable receive interrupts at Nport
        MOVE.B  #di,tpsc        * disable all interrupts at Tport
        MOVE.W  #eni,SR         * enable external interrupts and
                                * enter user mode
                                * repeat
IDLER1  BRA     IDLER1          *   idle
                                * until reset.
*
* The Network port interrupt service routine:
*
NISR1   MOVE.L  D1,-(A7)        * save register D1 on stack
        MOVE.B  nprt,dbyte      * dbyte := Nport
        MOVE.B  npsc,D1         * if status OK then
        AND.B   #tst,D1         *
        BNE     NISR1EX         *
        BSR     DSPRX1          *   Display_byte
                                * endif
NISR1EX MOVE.L  (A7)+,D1        * restore register D1
        RTE                     * return
*
* The Display_byte routine:
*
DSPRX1  BTST.B  #1,tpsc         * wait until Tport ready for output
        BEQ     DSPRX1          *
        MOVE.B  dbyte,tprt      * Tport := dbyte
        RTS                     * return
*
****************************************************************
```

```
*   Assembly language routines for experiment 2
********************************************************************
*
* The Assembly language program for the transmitter node:
*
* The Main routine:
*
MAINTX2 MOVE.L   #ustack,A0      * initialize user stack pointer
        MOVE.L   A0,USP          *
        MOVE.L   #sstack,A7      * initialize supervisor stack pointer
        CLR.B    sf              * SF := 0
        CLR.B    bys             * BYS := 0
        MOVE.L   #tborg1,tbnxt   * tbnxt := tborg+1
        MOVE.L   #tborg,A0       *
        MOVE.B   #pre,(A0)       * tborg^ := PRE
        MOVE.L   #NISRTX2,npva   * init. vector for Nport interrupt
        MOVE.L   #TISRTX2,tpva   * init. vector for Tport interrupt
        MOVE.B   #rst,npsc       * reset Nport
        MOVE.B   #di,npsc        * disable all interrupts at Nport
        MOVE.B   #eri,tpsc       * enable receive interrupts at Tport
        MOVE.W   #eni,SR         * enable external interrupts and
                                 * enter user mode
                                 * repeat
REPTX2  CMPI.B   #1,SF           * if SF = 1 and
        BNE      REPTX2          *
        CMPI.B   #0,bys          *    BYS = 0 then
        BNE      REPTX2          *
        BSR      STSEN2          *       Start_send_frame
                                 * endif
        BRA      REPTX2          * until reset.
*
* The Start_send_frame routine:
*
STSEN2  MOVE.L   #tborg,tbnxt    * tbnxt := tborg
        CLR.B    sf              * SF := 0
        MOVE.B   #1,bys          * BYS := 1
        MOVE.B   #eti,npsc       * enable transmit interrupts at Nport
        RTS                      * return
*
* The Terminal port interrupt service routine:
*
TISRTX2 MOVEM.L  D1/A0,-(A7)     * save registers D1/A0 on stack
        MOVE.B   tprt,tbyte      * tbyte := Tport
        MOVE.B   tpsc,D1         * if status OK then
        ANDI.B   #tst,D1         *
        BNE      TIS2EX          *
        CMPI.B   #0,bys          *    if BYS = 0 and
        BNE      TIS2EX          *
        CMPI.B   #0,sf           *       SF = 0 then
        BNE      TIS2EX          *
        MOVE.L   tbnxt,A0        *
        MOVE.B   tbyte,(A0)+     *          tbnxt^ := tbyte
```

```
          MOVE.L   A0,tbnxt        *        tbnxt := tbnxt+1
          BSR      ECHOTX2         *        Echo_byte
          CMPI.B   #cr,tbyte       *        if tbyte = CR then
          BNE      TIS2EX          *
          MOVE.B   #lf,tbyte       *           tbyte := LF
          BSR      ECHOTX2         *           Echo_byte
          MOVE.B   tbyte,(A0)+     *           tbnxt^ := tbyte
          MOVE.B   #eot,(A0)+      *           tbnxt+1^ := EOT
          MOVE.L   A0,tbend        *           tbend := tbnxt
          MOVE.L   #tborg,tbnxt    *           tbnxt := tborg
          MOVE.B   #1,sf           *           SF := 1
                                   *        endif
                                   *     endif
                                   *  endif
TIS2EX    MOVEM.L  (A7)+,D1/A0     * restore registers D1/A0
          RTE                      * return
*
* The Echo_byte routine:
*
ECHOTX2   BTST     #1,tpsc         * wait until Tport ready for output
          BEQ      ECHOTX2         *
          MOVE.B   tbyte,tprt      * Tport := tbyte
          RTS                      * return
*
* The Network port interrupt service routine:
*
NISRTX2   MOVE.L   A0,-(A7)        * save register A0 on stack
          MOVE.L   tbnxt,A0        *
          CMP.L    tbend,A0        * if bufnxt = bufend then
          BNE      NIST21          *
          CLR.B    bys             *    BYS := 0
          MOVE.B   #di,npsc        *    disable interrupts at Nport
          MOVE.L   #tborg1,tbnxt   *    tbnxt := tborg+1
          BRA      NITX2EX         *
                                   * else
NIST21    MOVE.B   (A0)+,nport     *    Nport := tbnxt^
          MOVE.L   A0,tbnxt        *    tbnxt := tbnxt+1
*                                  * endif
NITX2EX   MOVE.L   (A7)+,A0        * restore register A0
          RTE                      * return.
*
*
* The Assembly language program for the receiver node:
*
* The Main routine:
*
MAINRX2   MOVE.L   #ustack,A0      * init. user stack pointer
          MOVE.L   A0,USP          *
          MOVE.L   #sstack,A7      * init. supervisor stack pointer
          CLR.B    df              * DF := 0
          CLR.B    byd             * BYD := 0
          CLR.B    byr             * BYR := 0
```

```
              MOVE.L   #rborg,rbnxt      * rbnxt := rborg
              MOVE.L   #NISRRX2,npva     * init. vector for Nport interrupt
              MOVE.L   #TISRRX2,tpva     * init. vector for Tport interrupt
              MOVE.B   #rst,npsc         * reset network port
              MOVE.B   #eri,npsc         * enable receive interrupts at Nport
              MOVE.B   #di,npsc          * disable all interrupts at Tport
              MOVE.W   #eni,SR           * enable external interrupts and
                                         * enter user mode
                                         * repeat
REPTRX2       CMPI.B   #1,df             * if DF = 1 and
              BNE      REPTRX2           *
              CMPI.B   #0,byd            *    BYD = 0 then
              BNE      REPTRX2           *
              BSR      STDSP2            *       Start_disp_frame
                                         * endif
              BRA      REPTRX2           * until reset.
*
* The Start_disp_frame routine:
*
STDSP2        MOVE.L   #rborg,rbnxt      * rbnxt := rborg
              CLR.B    df                * DF := 0
              MOVE.B   #1,byd            * BYD := 1
              MOVE.B   #eti,tpsc         * enable transmit interrupts at Tport
              RTS                        * return
*
* The Network interrupt service routine:
*
NISRRX2       MOVEM.L  D1/A0,-(A7)       * save registers D1/A0 on stack
              MOVE.B   nprt,nbyte        * nbyte := Nport
              MOVE.B   npsc,D1           * if status OK then
              ANDI.B   #tst,D1           *
              BNE      NISR2EX           *
              CMPI.B   #0,byd            *    if BYD = 0 and
              BNE      NISR2EX           *
              CMPI.B   #0,df             *       DF = 0 then
              BNE      NISR2EX           *
              CMPI.B   #0,byr            *          if BYR = 0 and
              BNE      NISRX21           *
              CMPI.B   #pre,nbyte        *             nbyte = PRE then
              BNE      NISRX21           *
              MOVE.B   #1,byr            *             BYR := 1
              BRA      NISR2EX           *
NISRX21       CMPI.B   #1,byr            *          elseif BYR = 1 then
              BNE      NISR2EX           *
              CMPI.B   #eot,nbyte        *             if nbyte = EOT then
              BNE      NISRX22           *
              MOVE.B   #1,df             *                DF := 1
              MOVE.L   rbnxt,rbend       *                rbend := rbnxt
              MOVE.L   #rborg,rbnxt      *                rbnxt := rborg
              BRA      NISR2EX           *
                                         *             else
NISRX22       MOVE.L   rbnxt,A0          *
```

```
        MOVE.B   nbyte,(A0)+      *              rbnxt^ := nbyte
        MOVE.L   A0,rbnxt         *              rbnxt := rbnxt+1
                                  *            endif
                                  *          endif
                                  *        endif
                                  *      endif
                                  *    endif
NISR2EX MOVEM.L  (A7)+,D1/A0      * restore registers D1/A0 on stack
        RTE                       * return.
*
* The Terminal port interrupt service routine:
*
TISRRX2 MOVE.L   A0,-(A7)         * save register A0 on stack
        MOVE.L   rbnxt,A0         *
        CMP.L    rbend,A0         * if rbnxt = rbend then
        BNE      TISRX21          *
        CLR.B    byd              *    BYD := 0
        MOVE.B   #di,tpsc         *    disable interrupts at Tport
        MOVE.L   #rborg,rbnxt     *    rbnxt := rborg
        BRA      TISR2EX          *
                                  * else
TISRX21 MOVE.B   (A0)+,tprt       *    Tport := rbnxt^
        MOVE.L   A0,rbnxt         *    rbnxt := rbnxt+1
                                  * endif
TISR2EX MOVE.L   (A7)+,A0         * restore register A0
        RTE                       * return.
*
********************************************************************
*  Assembly language routines for experiment 3
********************************************************************
*
* The Main routine:
*
MAIN3   MOVEA.L  #ustack,A0       * init. user stack
        MOVEA.L  A0,USP           *
        MOVEA.L  #sstack,A7       * init. system stack
        BSR      CLRFL3           * Clear_flags
        BSR      INIT3            * Initialize
        MOVE.W   #eni,SR          * Enable interrupts and enter
                                  * user mode
                                  * repeat
REPT3   BSR      SCHD3            *    Schedule
        BRA      REPT3            * until reset
*
* The Clear_flags routine:
*
CLRFL3  CLR.B    sp               * SP := 0
        CLR.B    dp               * DP := 0
        CLR.B    tbf              * TBF := 0
        CLR.B    rbf              * RBF := 0
        CLR.B    byd              * BYD := 0
        CLR.B    byi              * BYI := 0
        CLR.B    bys              * BYS := 0
```

```
              CLR.B    byr              * BYR := 0
              RTS                       * return
*
* The Initialize routine:
*
INIT3-   MOVE.L    #rborg,rbnxt         * rbnxt := rborg
         MOVE.L    #tborg1,tbnxt        * tbnxt := tborg+1
         MOVE.B    #pre,tborg           * tborg^ := PRE
         MOVE.L    #TISR3,tpva          * init. interrupt vector for Tport
         MOVE.L    #NPISR3,npva         * init. interrupt vector for Nport
         MOVE.B    #di,tpsc             * enable receive interrupt for Tport
         MOVE.B    #di,npsc             * enable receive interrupt for Nport
         RTS                            * return
*
* The Schedule routine:
*
SCHD3    CMPI.B    #1,sp                * if SP = 1 and
         BNE       SCHD31               *
         CMPI.B    #0,bys               * BYS = 0 then
         BNE       SCHD31               *
         BSR       STSEN3               *   Start_send
         BRA       SCH3EX               *
SCHD31   CMPI.B    #1,dp                * elseif DP = 1 and
         BNE       SCH3EX               *
         CMPI.B    #0,byd               * BYD = 0 and
         BNE       SCH3EX               *
         CMPI.B    #0,byi               * BYI = 0 then
         BNE       SCH3EX               *
         BSR       STDSP3               *   Start_display
                                        * endif
SCH3EX   RTS                            * return
*
* The Start_send routine:
*
STSEN3   MOVE.B    #1,bys               * BYS := 1
         CLR.B     sp                   * SP := 0
         MOVE.B    #eti,npsc            * enable transmit and disable receive
                                        * interrupts for Nport
         RTS                            * return
*
* The start display routine:
*
STDSP3   MOVE.B    #1,byd               * BYD := 1
         CLR.B     dp                   * DP := 0
         MOVE.B    #eti,tpsc            * enable transmit and disable receive
                                        * interrupts for Tport
         RTS                            * return
*
* The Terminal port interrupt service routine (Tisr):
*
TISR3    CMPI.B    #1,byd               * if BYD = 1 then
         BNE       TISR31               *
```

```
            BSR     OUTPT3          *    Output
            BRA     TIS3EX          *
                                    * else
TISR31  BSR     INPUT3          *    Input
                                    * endif
TIS3EX  RTE                     * return
*
* Application layer, The Input routine:
*
INPUT3  MOVEM.L D0/A0,-(A7)      * save registers D0/A0 on stack
            MOVE.B  tprt,tbyte      * tbyte := Tport
            MOVE.B  tpsc,D0         * if Tport status OK then
            ANDI.B  #tst,D0         *
            BNE     INP3EX          *
            CMPI.B  #0,tbf          *    if TBF = 0 then
            BNE     INP3EX          *
            CMPI.B  #0,byi          *       if BYI = 0 then
            BNE     INP31           *
            MOVE.B  #1,byi          *          BYI := 1
                                    *       endif
INP31   BSR     ECHOB3          *       Echo_byte
            MOVE.L  tbnxt,A0        *
            MOVE.B  tbyte,(A0)+     *       tbnxt^ := tbyte
            MOVE.L  A0,tbnxt        *       tbnxt := tbnxt+1
            CMPI.B  #cr,tbyte       *       if tbyte = CR then
            BNE     INP3EX          *
            MOVE.B  #lf,tbyte       *          tbyte := LF
            BSR     ECHOB3          *          Echo_byte
            MOVE.B  tbyte,(A0)+     *          tbnxt^ := tbyte
            MOVE.B  #eot,(A0)+      *          tbnxt^ := EOT
            MOVE.L  A0,tbnxt        *          tbnxt := tbnxt+1
            MOVE.B  #1,sp           *          SP := 1
            MOVE.B  #1,tbf          *          TBF := 1
            CLR.B   byi             *          BYI := 0
            MOVE.L  tbnxt,tbend     *          tbend := tbnxt
            MOVE.L  #tborg,tbnxt    *          tbnxt := tborg
                                    *       endif
                                    *    endif
                                    * endif
INP3EX  MOVEM.L (A7)+,D0/A0      * restore registers D0/A0
            RTS                     * return
*
* Application layer, The Echo_byte routine:
*
ECHOB3  BTST.B  #1,tpsc         * wait until Tport ready for output
            BEQ     ECHOB3          *
            MOVE.B  tbyte,tprt      * Tport := tbyte
            RTS                     * return
*
* Application layer, The Output routine:
*
OUTPT3  MOVE.L  A0,-(A7)        *
```

```
        MOVE.L   rbend,A0          *
        CMP.L    A0,rbnxt          * if rbnxt = rbend then
        BNE      OUT31             *
        CLR.B    byd               *   BYD := 0
        CLR.B    rbf               *   RBF := 0
        MOVE.L   #rborg,rbnxt      *   rbnxt := rborg
        MOVE.B   #eri,tpsc         *   disable transmit and enable
                                   *      receive interrupts at Tport
        BRA      OUT3EX            * else
OUT31   MOVE.L   tbnxt,A0          *
        MOVE.B   (A0)+,tprt        *   Tport := rbnxt^
        MOVE.L   A0,tbnxt          *   rbnxt := rbnxt + 1
OUT3EX  MOVE.L   (A7)+,A0          * endif
        RTS                        * return
*
* Network port interrupt service routine:
*
NPISR3  CMPI.B   #1,bys            * if BYS = 1 then
        BNE      NPIS31            *
        BSR      TRANS3            *   Transmit
        BRA      NPI3EX            * else
NPIS31  BSR      RECV3             *   Receive
                                   * endif
NPI3EX  RTE                        * return
*
* Network layer, The Receive routine:
*
RECV3   MOVE.L   A0,-(A7)          * save register A0 on stack
        MOVE.B   nprt,nbyte        * nbyte := Nport
        MOVE.B   tpsc,D0           * if Nport status OK then
        ANDI.B   #tst,D0           *
        BNE      REC3EX            *
        CMPI.B   #0,rbf            *   if RBF = 0 then
        BNE      REC3EX            *
        CMPI.B   #0,byr            *     if BYR = 0
        BNE      RECV31            *
        CMPI.B   #pre,nbyte        *     and nbyte = PRE then
        BNE      RECV31            *
        MOVE.B   #1,byr            *       BYR := 1
        BRA      REC3EX            *
RECV31  CMPI.B   #1,byr            *     else if BYR = 1 then
        BNE      REC3EX            *
        CMPI.B   #eot,nbyte        *       if nbyte = EOT then
        BNE      RECV32            *
        MOVE.B   #1,dp             *         DP := 1
        MOVE.B   #1,rbf            *         RBF := 1
        CLR.B    byr               *         BYR := 0
        MOVE.L   rbnxt,rbend       *         rbend := rbnxt
        MOVE.L   #rborg,rbnxt      *         rbnxt := rborg
        BRA      REC3EX            *       else
RECV32  MOVE.L   rbnxt,A0          *
        MOVE.B   nbyte,(A0)+       *         rbnxt^ := nbyte
```

```
            MOVE.L  A0,rbnxt         *           rbnxt := rbnxt + 1
                                     *         endif
                                     *       endif
                                     *     endif
                                     * endif
REC3EX      MOVE.L  (A7)+,A0         * restore register A0
            RTS                      * return
*
* Network layer, The Transmit routine:
*
TRANS3      MOVE.L  A0,-(A7)         * save register A0 on stack
            MOVE.L  tbend,A0         *
            CMP.L   tbnxt,A0         * if tbnxt = tbend then
            BNE     TRAN31           *
            CLR.B   bys              *   BYS := 0
            CLR.B   tbf              *   TBF := 0
            MOVE.L  #tborg1,tbnxt    *   tbnxt := tborg+1
            BSR     ENRCV3           *   Enable_receive
            BRA     TRA3EX           * else
TRAN31      MOVE.L  tbnxt,A0         *
            MOVE.B  (A0)+,nprt       *   Nport := tbnxt^
            MOVE.L  A0,tbnxt         *   tbnxt := tbnxt + 1
                                     * endif
TRA3EX      MOVE.L  (A7)+,A0         * restore register A0
            RTS                      * return
*
* Network layer, The Enable_receive routine:
*
ENRCV3      BTST.B  #0,npsc          * wait until Nport receives new byte
            BEQ     ENRCV3           *
            MOVE.B  nprt,nbyte       * nbyte := Nport
ENR31       BTST.B  #0,npsc          * wait until Nport receives new byte
            BEQ     ENR31            *
            MOVE.B  nprt,nbyte       * nbyte := Nport
ENR32       BTST.B  #0,nprt          * wait until Nport receives new byte
            BEQ     ENR32            *
            MOVE.B  nprt,nbyte       * nbyte := Nport
            MOVE.B  #eri,npsc        * enable receive and disable transmit
                                     * interrupts at Nport
            RTS                      * return
*
*****************************************************************
*  Assembly language routines for experiment 4
*****************************************************************
*
* The Main routine:
*
MAIN4       MOVEA.L #ustack,A0       * init. user stack
            MOVEA.L A0,USP           *
            MOVEA.L #sstack,A7       * init. system stack
            BSR     INMID4           * Input_MID
            BSR     INIT3            * Initialize (3)
```

```
            MOVE.W   #eni,SR          * enable CPU interrupts and
                                      * enter user mode
                                      * repeat
REPT4   BSR      SCHD3                *   Schedule (3)
        BRA      REPT4                * until reset
*
* The Input_MID routine:
*
INMID4  MOVE.L   #inpmid,txtptr   * txtptr := inpmid
        BSR      DSP4             * Display
        BSR      INBYT4           * Input_byte
        MOVE.B   tbyte,mid        * MID := tbyte
        BSR      ENDSP4           * End_display
        RTS                       * return
*
* The Display routine:
*
DSP4    MOVE.L   A0,-(A7)         * save register A0 on stack
        MOVE.L   txtptr,A0        *
DSP41   CMPI.B   #0,(A0)          * while txtptr^ <> 0 do
        BEQ      DSP4EX           *
DSP42   BTST.B   #1,tpsc          *    wait until Tport ready for output
        BEQ      DSP42            *
        MOVE.B   (A0)+,tprt       *    Tport := txtptr^
        MOVE.L   A0,txtptr        *    txtptr := txtptr+1
        BRA      DSP41            *
                                  * enddo
DSP4EX  MOVE.L   (A7)+,A0         * restore register A0
        RTS                       * return
*
* The Input_byte routine:
*
INBYT4  BTST.B   #0,tpsc          * wait until Tport receives new byte
        BEQ      INPB4            *
        MOVE.B   tprt,tbyte       * tbyte := Tport
        RTS                       * return
*
* The End_display routine:
*
ENDSP4  BTST.B   #1,tpsc          * wait until Tport ready for output
        BEQ      ENDSP4           *
        MOVE.B   tbyte,tprt       * Tport := tbyte
ENDS41  BTST.B   #1,tpsc          * wait until Tport ready for output
        BEQ      ENDS41           *
        MOVE.B   #cr,tprt         * Tport := CR
ENDS42  BTST.B   #1,tpsc          * wait until Tport ready for output
        BEQ      ENDS42           *
        MOVE.B   #lf,tprt         * Tport := LF
        RTS                       * return
*
* The Input routine:
*
```

```
INPUT4   MOVEM.L  D0/A0,-(A7)     * save registers D0/A0 on stack
         MOVE.B   tprt,tbyte      * tbyte := Tport
         MOVE.B   tpsc,D0         * if Tport status OK then
         ANDI.B   #tst,D0         *
         BNE      INP4EX          *
         CMPI.B   #0,tbf          *    if TBF = 0 then
         BNE      INP4EX          *
         CMPI.B   #0,byi          *      if BYI = 0 then
         BNE      INP41           *
         MOVE.B   #1,byi          *        BYI := 1
         BSR      ECHOB3          *        Echo_byte (3)
         MOVE.L   #tbnxt,A0       *
         MOVE.B   tbyte,(A0)+     *        tbnxt^ := tbyte
                                  *        tbnxt := tbnxt+1
         MOVE.B   mid,tbyte       *        tbyte := MID
         MOVE.B   tbyte,(A0)+     *        tbnxt^ := tbyte
         MOVE.L   A0,tbnxt        *        tbnxt := tbnxt+1
                                  *      endif
INP41    BSR      ECHOB3          *      Echo_byte (3)
         MOVE.L   tbnxt,A0        *
         MOVE.B   tbyte,(A0)+     *      tbnxt^ := tbyte
         MOVE.L   A0,tbnxt        *      tbnxt := tbnxt+1
         CMPI.B   #cr,tbyte       *      if tbyte = CR then
         BNE      INP4EX          *
         MOVE.B   #lf,tbyte       *        tbyte := LF
         BSR      ECHOB3          *        Echo_byte (3)
         MOVE.B   tbyte,(A0)+     *        tbnxt^ := tbyte
                                  *        tbnxt := tbnxt+1
         MOVE.B   #eot,(A0)+      *        tbnxt^ := EOT
         MOVE.L   A0,tbnxt        *        tbnxt := tbnxt+1
         MOVE.B   #1,sp           *        SP := 1
         MOVE.B   #1,tbf          *        tbf := 1
         CLR.B    byi             *        BYI := 0
         MOVE.L   tbnxt,tbend     *        tbend := tbnxt
         MOVE.L   #tborg,tbnxt    *        tbnxt := tborg
                                  *      endif
                                  *    endif
                                  * endif
INP4EX   MOVEM.L  (A7)+,D0/A0     * restore registers D0/A0
         RTS                      * return
*
* The Receive routine:
*
RECV4    MOVE.L   D0,-(A7)        * save register D0 on stack
         MOVE.B   nprt,nbyte      * nbyte := Nport
         MOVE.B   npsc,D0         * if Nport status OK then
         ANDI.B   #tst,D0         *
         BNE      REC4EX          *
         CMPI.B   #pre,nbyte      *    if nbyte = PRE then
         BNE      RECV41          *
         BSR      PRERC4          *      PRE_received
         BRA      REC4EX          *
```

```
RECV41   CMPI.B   #1,rstate        *   elseif rstate = 1 then
         BNE      RECV42           *
         BSR      DIDRC4           *      DID_received
         BRA      REC4EX           *
RECV42   CMPI.B   #2,rstate        *   elseif rstate = 2 then
         BNE      RECV43           *
         BSR      ACEPT4           *      Accept
         BRA      REC4EX           *
                                   *   else
RECV43   CLR.B    rstate           *      rstate := 0
                                   *   endif
                                   * endif
REC4EX   MOVE.L   (A7)+,D0         * restore register D0
         RTS                       * return
*
* The PRE_received routine:
*
PRERC4   CMPI.B   #0,rstate        * if rstate <> 0 and
         BEQ      PRE4EX           *
         CMPI.B   #0,rbf           * RBF = 0 then
         BNE      PRE4EX           *
         MOVE.L   #rborg,rbnxt     *   rbnxt := rborg
                                   * endif
PRE4EX   MOVE.B   #1,rstate        * rstate := 1
         RTS                       * return
*
* The DID_received routine :
*
DIDRC4   CMP.B    mid,nbyte        * if nbyte = MID and
         BNE      DID41            *
         CMPI.B   #0,rbf           * RBF = 0 then
         BNE      DID41            *
         MOVE.B   #2,rstate        *   rstate := 2
         BRA      DID4EX           *
                                   * else
DID41    CLR.B    rstate           *   rstate := 0
                                   * endif
DID4EX   RTS                       * return
*
* The Accept routine:
*
ACEPT4   MOVE.L   A0,-(A7)         * save register A0 on stack
         CMPI.B   #eot,nbyte       * if nbyte = EOT then
         BNE      ACPT41           *
         MOVE.B   #1,dp            *   DP := 1
         MOVE.B   #1,rbf           *   RBF := 1
         CLR.B    rstate           *   rstate := 0
         MOVE.L   rbnxt,rbend      *   rbend := rbnxt
         MOVE.L   #rborg,rbnxt     *   rbnxt := rborg
         BRA      ACP4EX           *
                                   * else
ACPT41   MOVE.L   rbnxt,A0         *
```

```
           MOVE.B   nbyte,(A0)+        *    rbnxt^ := nbyte
           MOVE.L   A0,rbnxt           *    rbnxt := rbnxt+1
                                       *  endif
ACP4EX     MOVE.L   (A7)+,A0           *  restore register A0
           RTS                         *  return
*
********************************************************************
*  Assembly language routines for experiment 5
********************************************************************
*
* The Main routine:
*
MAIN5      MOVEA.L  #ustack,A0         *  init. user stack
           MOVEA.L  A0,USP             *
           MOVEA.L  #sstack,A7         *  init system stack
           BSR      INMID4             *  Input_MID (4)
           BSR      INIT4              *  Initialize (4)
           MOVE.W   #eni,SR            *  enable interrupts and
                                       *  enter user mode
                                       *  repeat
REPT5      BSR      SCHD3              *    Schedule (3)
           BRA      REPT5              *  until reset
                                       *
*
* The Start_send routine:
*
STSEN5     MOVEM.L  D0-D1,-(A7)        *  save registers D0-D1 on stack
           CLR.B    nby               *  NBY := 0
                                       *
           MOVE.B   #2,D1              *  wait 2 byte times
STS1       MOVE.L   #bdelay,D0         *
STS2       SUBI.L   #1,D0              *
           BNE      STS2               *
           SUBI.B   #1,D1              *
           BNE      STS1               *
                                       *
           CMPI.B   #0,nby             *  if NBY = 0 then
           BNE      STS5EX             *
           MOVE.B   #1,bys             *    BYS := 1
           CLR.B    sp                 *    SP := 0
           MOVE.B   #eti,npsc          *    enable transmit/ disable receive
                                       *    interrupts at Nport
                                       *  endif
           MOVEM.L  (A7)+,D0-D1        *  restore registers D0-D1
STS5EX     RTS                         *  return
*
* The Receive routine:
*
RECV5      MOVE.L   D0,-(A7)           *  save register D0 on stack
           MOVE.B   nprt,nbyte         *  nbyte := Nport
           MOVE.B   #1,nby             *  NBY := 1
           MOVE.B   npsc,D0            *
```

```
            ANDI.B   #tst,D0          * if Nport status OK then
            BNE      REC5EX           *
            CMPI.B   #pre,nbyte       *   if nbyte = PRE then
            BNE      REC51            *
            BSR      PRERC4           *     PRE_received (4)
            BRA      REC5EX           *
REC51       CMPI.B   #1,rstate        *   elseif rstate = 1 then
            BNE      REC52            *
            BSR      DIDRC4           *     DID_received (4)
            BRA      REC5EX           *
REC52       CMPI.B   #2,rstate        *   elseif rstate = 2 then
            BNE      REC53            *
            BSR      ACEPT4           *     Accept (4)
            BRA      REC5EX           *
                                     *   else
REC53       CLR.B    rstate           *     rstate := 0
                                     *   endif
                                     * endif
REC5EX      MOVE.L   (A7)+,D0         * restore register D0
            RTS                       * return
*
*******************************************************************
*  Assembly language routines for experiment 6
*******************************************************************
*
* The Main routine:
*
MAIN6       MOVEA.L  #ustack,A0       * init. user stack
            MOVEA.L  A0,USP           *
            MOVEA.L  #sstack,A7       * init. system stack
            BSR      INMID4           * Input_MID (4)
            BSR      INNID6           * Input_NID
            BSR      CLRFL6           * Clear_flags
            BSR      INTOK6           * Input_token
            BSR      INIT6            * Initialize
            MOVE.W   #eni,SR          * enable CPU interrupts
            CMPI.B   #1,tr            * if TR = 1 then
            BNE      REPT6            *
            MOVE.B   #1,bst           *   BST := 1
            MOVE.B   #eti,npsc        *   enable transmit & disable receive
                                     *   interrupts at Nport
                                     * endif
                                     * repeat
REPT6       BSR      SCHD6            *   Schedule
            CMPI.B   #1,tl            *
            BNE      REPT6            * until TL = 1
            BSR      DSPTL6           * Display_token_lost
END6        BRA      END6             * end
*
* The Input_NID routine:
*
INNID6      MOVE.L   #inpnid,txtptr   * txtptr := inpnid
```

```
        BSR     DSP4            * Display (4)
        BSR     INBYT4          * Input_byte (4)
        MOVE.B  tbyte,nid       * NID := tbyte
        BSR  .  ENDSP4          * End_display (4)
        RTS                     * return
*
* The Clear_flags routine:
*
CLRFL6  CLR.B   tr              * TR := 0
        CLR.B   tl              * TL := 0
        CLR.B   sp              * SP := 0
        CLR.B   dp              * DP := 0
        CLR.B   bys             * BYS := 0
        CLR.B   byr             * BYR := 0
        CLR.B   bst             * BST := 0
        CLR.B   byi             * BYI := 0
        CLR.B   byd             * BYD := 0
        RTS                     * return
*
* The Initialize routine:
*
INIT6   MOVE.L  A0,-(A7)        * save register A0 on stack
        MOVE.L  #tforg,A0       *
        MOVE.B  #pre,(A0)+      * tforg^ := PRE
        MOVE.B  nid,(A0)+       * tforg+1^ := NID
        MOVE.B  #eot,(A0)+      * tforg+2^ := EOT
        MOVE.L  #tforg,tfnxt    * tfnxt := tforg
        MOVE.L  #tborg,A0       *
        MOVE.B  #pre,(A0)       * tborg^ := PRE
        MOVE.L  #tborg1,tbnxt   * tbnxt := tborg+1
        MOVE.L  #rborg,rbnxt    * rbnxt := rborg
        MOVE.B  #tvnmb,tivr     * init. vector for timer interrupt
        MOVE.L  #TMISR6,tva     *
        MOVE.L  #TISR3,tpva     * init. vector for Tport interrupt
                                * TISR3 defined in exp.3
        MOVE.L  #NISR6,npva     * init. vector for Nport interrupt
        MOVE.B  #di,tpsc        * select mode for Tport
        MOVE.B  #rst,npsc       * clear Nport
        MOVE.B  #di,npsc        * select mode for Nport
        MOVE.L  (A7)+,A0        * restore register A0
        RTS                     * return
*
* The Input_token routine:
*
INTOK6  MOVE.L  #inptok,txtptr  * txtptr := inptok
        BSR     DSP4            * Display (4)
        BSR     INBYT4          * Input_byte (4)
        BSR     ENDSP4          * End_display (4)
        CMPI.B  #$59,tbyte      * if tbyte = "Y" then
        BNE     INT6EX          *
        MOVE.B  #1,tr           *    TR := 1
                                * endif
```

```
INT6EX  RTS                     * return
*
* The Schedule routine:
*
SCHD6   CMPI.B  #1,dp           * if DP = 1 and
        BNE     SCH6EX          *
        CMPI.B  #0,byd          *    BYD = 0 and
        BNE     SCH6EX          *
        CMPI.B  #0,byi          *    BYI = 0 then
        BNE     SCH6EX          *
        BSR     STDSP3          *    Start_display (3)
                                * endif
SCH6EX  RTS                     * return
*
* The Display_token_lost routine:
*
DSPTL6  MOVE.L  #tlost,txtptr   * txtptr := tlost
        BSR     DSP4            * Display (4)
        BSR     ENDSP4          * End_display (4)
        RTS                     * return
*
* The Network_interrupt_service routine:
*
NISR6   CMPI.B  #1,bys          * if BYS = 1 then
        BNE     NISR61          *
        BSR     SEND6           *    Send
        BRA     NIS6EX          *
NISR61  CMPI.B  #1,bst          * elseif BST = 1 then
        BNE     NISR62          *
        BSR     SETOK6          *    Send_token
        BRA     NIS6EX          *
                                * else
NISR62  BSR     RECV6           *    Receive
                                * endif
NIS6EX  RTE                     * return
*
* The Send routine:
*
SEND6   MOVE.L  A0,-(A7)        * save register A0 on stack
        MOVE.L  #tbend,A0       *
        CMP.L   A0,tbnxt        * if tbnxt = tbend then
        BNE     SEND61          *
        CLR.B   bys             *    BYS := 0
        CLR.B   tbf             *    TBF := 0
        MOVE.L  #tborg1,tbnxt   *    tbnxt := tborg+1
        MOVE.B  #1,bst          *    BST := 1
        BRA     SEN6EX          *
                                * else
SEND61  MOVE.L  tbnxt,A0        *
        MOVE.B  (A0)+,nprt      *    Nport := tbnxt^
        MOVE.L  A0,tbnxt        *    tbnxt := tbnxt+1
                                * endif
```

```
SEN6EX  MOVE.L   (A7)+,A0        * restore register A0
        RTS                      * return
*
* The Send_token routine:
*
SETOK6  MOVE.L   A0,-(A7)        * save register A0 on stack
        MOVE.L   #tfend,A0       *
        CMP.L    A0,tfnxt        * if tfnxt = tfend then
        BNE      STOK61          *
        CLR.B    bst             *    BST := 0
        MOVE.L   #tforg,tfnxt    *    tfnxt := tforg
        BSR      WFTOK6          *    Start_timer_to_wait_for_token
        BSR      ENREC3          *    Enable_receive (3)
        BRA      STK6EX          *
                                 * else
STOK61  MOVE.L   tfnxt,A0        *
        MOVE.B   (A0)+,nprt      *    Nport := tfnxt^
        MOVE.L   A0,tfnxt        *    tfnxt := tfnxt+1
                                 * endif
STK6EX  MOVE.L   (A7)+,A0        * restore register A0
        RTS                      * return
*
* The Receive routine:
*
RECV6   MOVE.L   D0,-(A7)        * save register D0 on stack
        MOVE.B   nprt,nbyte      * nbyte := Nport
        MOVE.B   npsc,D0         *
        ANDI.B   #tst,D0         * if Nport status OK then
        BNE      REC6EX          *
        CMPI.B   #pre,nbyte      *    if nbyte = PRE then
        BNE      RECV61          *
        BSR      PRERC6          *       PRE_received
        BRA      REC6EX          *
RECV61  CMPI.B   #1,rstate       *    elseif rstate = 1 then
        BNE      RECV62          *
        BSR      DIDRC6          *       DID_received
        BRA      REC6EX          *
RECV62  CMPI.B   #2,rstate       *    elseif rstate = 2 then
        BNE      RECV63          *
        BSR      TOKRC6          *       Token_received
        BRA      REC6EX          *
RECV63  CMPI.B   #3,rstate       *    elseif rstate = 3 then
        BNE      REC6EX          *
        BSR      ACEPT4          *       Accept (4)
                                 *    endif
                                 * endif
REC6EX  MOVE.L   (A7)+,D0        * restore register D0
        RTS                      * return
*
* The PRE_received routine:
*
PRERC6  MOVE.B   #1,rstate       * rstate := 1
```

```
            RTS                     * return
*
* The DID_received routine:
*
DIDRC6  CMPI.B  mid,nbyte       * if nbyte = MID then
        BNE     DIDR61          *
        MOVE.B  #2,rstate       *   rstate := 2
        BRA     DID6EX          *
                                * else
DIDR61  CLR.B   rstate          *   rstate := 0
                                * endif
DID6EX  RTS                     * return
*
* The Token_received routine:
*
TOKRC6  MOVE.L  A0,-(A7)        * save register A0 on stack
        CMPI.B  #eot,nbyte      * if nbyte = EOT then
        BNE     TOK61           *
        CLR.B   rstate          *   rstate := 0
        MOVE.B  #tstop,tcr      *   stop timer
        BSR     STRTX6          *   Start_transmit
        BRA     TOK6EX          *
                                * else
TOK61   CMPI.B  #0,rbf          *   if RBF = 0 then
        BNE     TOK62           *
        MOVE.L  rbnxt,A0        *
        MOVE.B  nbyte,(A0)+     *     rbnxt^ := nbyte
        MOVE.L  A0,rbnxt        *     rbnxt := rbnxt+1
        MOVE.B  #3,rstate       *     rstate := 3
        BRA     TOK6EX          *
                                *   else
TOK62   CLR.B   rstate          *     rstate := 0
                                *   endif
                                * endif
TOK6EX  MOVE.L  (A7)+,A0        * restore register A0
        RTS                     * return
*
* The Start_transmit routine:
*
STRTX6  CMPI.B  #1,sp           * if SP = 1 then
        BNE     STX61           *
        CLR.B   sp              *   SP := 0
        MOVE.B  #1,bys          *   BYS := 1
        BRA     STX6EX          *
                                * else
STX61   MOVE.B  #1,bst          *   BST := 1
                                * endif
STX6EX  RTS                     * return
*
* The Start_timer_to_wait_for_token routine:
*
WFTOK6  MOVE.B  #tstop,tcr      * stop timer
```

```
           MOVE.B   #wft,cprh      * load preload registers with WFT
           MOVE.B   #0,cprm        *
           MOVE.B   #0,cprl        *
           MOVE.B   #tstart,tcr    * start timer
           RTS                     * return
*
* The timer interrupt service routine (Timer_isr):
*
TMISR6     MOVE.B   #1,tl          *
           MOVE.B   #tstop,tcr     * stop timer and clear timer interrupt
           RTE                     * return
*
******************************************************************
*   Assembly language routines for experiment 7
******************************************************************
*
* The Main routine:
*
MAIN7      MOVEA.L  #ustack,A0     * init. user stack
           MOVEA.L  A0,USP         *
           MOVEA.L  #sstack,A7     * init. system stack
           BSR      INMID4         * Input_MID (4)
           BSR      CLRFL3         * Clear_flags (3)
           BSR      INIT7          * Initialize
           MOVE.W   #eni,SR        * enable interrupts and
                                   * enter user mode
                                   * repeat
REPT7      BSR      SCHD3          *   schedule (3)
           BRA      REPT7          * until reset
*
* The Initialization routine:
*
INIT7      MOVE.L   A0,-(A7)       * save register A0 on stack
           MOVE.L   #rborg,rbnxt   * rbnxt := rborg
           MOVE.L   #tborg1,tbnxt  * tbnxt := tborg+1
           MOVE.L   #tborg,A0      *
           MOVE.B   #pre,(A0)      * tborg^ := PRE
           MOVE.L   #NISR3,npva    * init. Nport interrupt vector
                                   * NPISR defined in exp.3
           MOVE.L   #TISR3,tpva    * init. Tport interrupt vector
                                   * TISR defined in exp.3
           MOVE.B   #di,npsc       * init. Nport
           MOVE.B   #pvnmb,pivr    * init. interrupt vector for
           MOVE.L   #COLIS7,pva    * collision detector
           MOVE.B   #pmode,pgcr    * init. collision detector
           MOVE.B   #initi,psrr    *
           MOVE.B   #clri,psr      *
           MOVE.B   #bmode,pbcr    *
           MOVE.L   (A7)+,A0       * restore register A0
           RTS                     * return
*
* The Collision interrupt routine (Col_isr):
```

```
*
COLIS7   MOVE.B   #di,npsc        * disable Nport interrupt
         MOVE.B   #clri,psr       * clear collision interrupt
         MOVE.L   #coltxt,txtptr  * txtptr := coltxt
         BSR      DSP4            * Display (4)
         BSR      ENDSP4          * End_display (4)
         CMPI.B   #1,bys          * if BYS = 1 then
         BNE      COL71           *
         CLR.B    bys             *      BYS := 0
         CLR.B    tbf             *      TBF := 0
         MOVE.L   #tborg1,tbnxt   *      tbnxt := tborg+1
         BRA      COL72           *
COL71    CMPI.B   #2,rbnxt        * elseif rbnxt = 2 then
         BNE      COL72           *
         MOVE.L   #rborg,rbnxt    *      rbnxt := rborg
         CLR.B    rstate          *      rstate := 0
                                  * endif
COL72    MOVE.B   #rst,npsc       * clear Nport
         MOVE.B   #eri,npsc       * enable receive interrupt
                                  * at Nport
         RTE                      * return
*
*********************************************************************
*  Assembly language routines for experiment 8
*********************************************************************
*
* The Main routine:
*
MAIN8    MOVE.L   #ustack,A0      * init. user stack
         MOVE.L   A0,USP          *
         MOVE.L   #sstack,A7      * init. system stack
         BSR      INMID4          * Input_MID (4)
         BSR      CLRFL8          * Clear_flags
         BSR      INIT8           * Initialize
         BSR      START8          * Start
         MOVE.W   #eni,SR         * enable interrupts and
                                  * enter user mode
                                  * repeat
REPT8    BSR      SCHD8           *   Schedule
         BRA      REPT8           * until reset
*
* The Schedule routine:
*
SCHD8    CMPI.B   #1,dnid         * if DNID = 1 then
         BNE      SCH81           *
         CLR.B    dnid            *   DNID := 0
         BSR      DSNID8          *   Display_NID
         BRA      SCH8EX          *
SCH81    CMPI.B   #1,dtl          * elseif DTL = 1 then
         BNE      SCH82           *
         CLR.B    DTL             *   DTL := 0
         BSR      DSPTL8          *   Display_Tlost
```

```
          BRA     SCH8EX          *
SCH82     CMPI.B  #1,dnn          * elseif DNN = 1 then
          BNE     SCH8EX          *
          CLR.B   dnn             *   DNN := 0
          BSR     DSPNN8          *   Display_Nonodes
                                  * endif
SCH8EX    RTS                     * return
*
* The Clear_flags routine:
*
CLRFL8    CLR.B   dnid            * DNID := 0
          CLR.B   byd             * BYD  := 0
          CLR.B   tbf             * TBF  := 0
          CLR.B   sp              * SP   := 0
          CLR.B   dtl             * DTL  := 0
          CLR.B   byi             * BYI  := 0
          CLR.B   rbf             * RBF  := 0
          CLR.B   dp              * DP   := 0
          CLR.B   dnn             * DNN  := 0
          RTS                     * return
*
* The Initialize routine:
*
INIT8     MOVE.L  A0,-(A7)        * save register A0 on stack
          CLR.B   state           * state := 0
          CLR.B   rstate          * rstate := 0
          MOVE.L  #tforg,A0       *
          MOVE.B  #pre,(A0)+      * tforg^ := PRE
          MOVE.L  #tforg,frnxt    * frnxt := tforg
          MOVE.L  #tfend,frend    * frend := tfend
          MOVE.B  mid,(A0)        * tforg+1^ := MID
          MOVE.B  #tvnmb,tivr     * init. timer interrupt vector
          MOVE.L  #TMISR8,tva     *
          MOVE.L  #NISR8,npva     * init. Nport interrupt vector
          MOVE.B  #di,npsc        * init. Nport
          MOVE.L  (A7)+,A0        * restore register A0
          RTS                     * return
*
* The Start routine:
*
START8    MOVE.L  D0,-(A7)        * save register D0 on stack
          MOVE.W  #n,D0           * for k := 1 to N do
STA80     BTST.B  #1,npsc         *   wait until
          BEQ     STA80           *   Nport ready for output
          MOVE.B  #pre,nprt       *   Nport := PRE
          DBEQ.W  D0,STA80        * enddo
          BSR     ENREC3          * Enable_receive (3)
          BSR     STSLP8          * Start_timer_to_sleep
          MOVE.L  (A7)+,D0        * restore register D0
          RTS                     * return
*
* The Start_timer_to_sleep routine:
```

```
*
STSLP8   MOVEM.L  D0-D1,-(A7)      * save registers D0-D1 on stack
         MOVE.B   #tstop,tcr       * stop timer
         MOVE.L   #stu,D0          * load timer preload registers
         MOVE.B   mid,D1           *
         AND.L    #$F,D1           *
         MULU.L   D1,D0            * with MID x T0
         MOVE.B   D0,cprl          * low byte
         ROR.L    #8,D0            *
         MOVE.B   D0,cprm          * middle byte
         ROR.L    #8,D0            *
         MOVE.B   D0,cprh          * high byte
         MOVE.B   #tstart,tcr      * start timer
         MOVEM.L  (A7)+,D0-D1      * restore registers D0-D1
         RTS                       * return
*
* The Display_NID routine:
*
DSNID8   MOVE.L   #newnid,txtptr   * txtptr := newnid
         BSR      DSP4             * Display (4)
         MOVE.B   #space,tbyte     * tbyte := SP
         BSR      ENDSP4           * End_display (4)
         RTS                       * return
*
* The Display_token_lost routine:
*
DSPTL8   MOVE.L   #tlost,txtptr    * txtptr := tlost
         BSR      DSP4             * Display (4)
         MOVE.B   #space,tbyte     * tbyte := SP
         BSR      ENDSP4           * End_display (4)
         RTS                       * return
*
* The Display_nonodes routine:
*
DSPNN8   MOVE.L   #nonodes,txtptr  * txtptr := nonodes
         BSR      DSP4             * Display (4)
         MOVE.B   #space,tbyte     * tbyte := SP
         BSR      DSEND4           * End_display (4)
         RTS                       * return
*
* The Timer_interrupt routine:
*
TMISR8   MOVE.B   #tstop,tcr       * stop timer
         CMPI.B   #3,state         * if state = 3
         BE       TIM80            *
         CMPI.B   #0,State         * or if state = 0 then
         BNE      TIM81            *
TIM80    MOVE.B   #1,state         *    state := 1
         BSR      POLL8            *    Poll
         BRA      TIM8EX           *
TIM81    CMPI.B   #4,state         * elseif state = 4 then
         BNE      TIM8EX           *
```

```
            CLR.B   state           *   state := 0
            MOVE.B  #1,dtl          *   DTL := 1
            BSR     STSLP8          *   Start_timer_to_sleep
            MOVE.B  mid,nid         *   NID := MID
                                    * endif
TIM8EX  RTE                         * return
*
* The Poll routine:
*
POLL8   ADDI.B  #1,nid              * NID := NID+1
            CMPI.B  #maxid,nid      * if NID > MAXID then
            BLE     POLL81          *
            MOVE.B  #minid,nid      *    NID := MINID
                                    * endif
POLL81  CMPI.B  mid,nid             * if NID = MID then
            BNE     POLL82          *
            MOVE.B  #1,dnn          *    DNN := 1
            MOVE.B  #2,state        *    state := 2
            BRA     POL8EX          *
                                    * else
POLL82  MOVE.L  #tforg,frnxt        *    frnxt := tforg
            MOVE.L  #tfend,frend    *    frend := tfend
            MOVE.B  #eti,npsc       *    enable transmit /disable
                                    *    receive interrupt
                                    * endif
POL8EX  RTS                         * return
*
* The Network_port_interrupt routine:
*
NISR8   CMPI.B  #0,state            * if state = 0
            BE      NISR80          *
            CMPI.B  #3,state        * or state = 3
            BE      NISR80          *
            CMPI.B  #4,state        * or state = 4 then
            BNE     NISR81          *
NISR80  BSR     RECEV8              *    Receive
            BRA     NIS8EX          *
NISR81  CMPI.B  #2,state            * elseif state = 2 then
            BNE     NISR82          *
            CLR.B   state           *    state := 0
            BSR     STSLP8          *    Start_timer_to_sleep
            BRA     NIS8EX          *
                                    * else
NISR82  BSR     SEND8               *    Send
                                    * endif
NIS8EX  RTE                         * return
*
* The Receive routine:
*
RECV8   MOVE.L  D0,-(A7)            * save register D0 on stack
            MOVE.B  nprt,nbyte      * nbyte := Nport
            MOVE.B  npsc,D0         * read status from Nport
```

```
          ANDI.B    #tst,D0           * if status OK then
          BNE       REC8EX            *
          CMPI.B    #pre,nbyte        *   if nbyte = PRE then
          BNE       RECV81            *
          MOVE.B    #1,rstate         *     rstate := 1
          CMPI.B    #3,state          *     if state = 3 then
          BNE       RECV80            *
          MOVE.B    #4,state          *       state := 4
          MOVE.B    #1,dnid           *       DNID := 1
          BSR       WFTOK6            *       Start_timer_to_wait
                                      *        _for_token (6)
RECV80    BRA       REC8EX            *     endif
RECV81    CMPI.B    #1,rstate         *   elseif rstate = 1
          BNE       RECV82            *
          CMP.B     mid,nbyte         *   and nbyte = MID then
          BNE       RECV82            *
          MOVE.B    #2,rstate         *     rstate := 2
          BRA       REC8EX            *
RECV82    CMPI.B    #2,rstate         *   elseif rstate = 2
          BNE       RECV85            *
          CMPI.B    #eot,nbyte        *   and nbyte = EOT then
          BNE       RECV85            *
          CMPI.B    #0,state          *     if state = 0 then
          BNE       RECV83            *
          MOVE.B    #1,state          *       state := 1
          MOVE.B    mid,nid           *       NID := MID
          BSR       POLL8             *       Poll
          BRA       RECV84            *
RECV83    CMPI.B    #4,state          *     elseif state = 4 then
          BNE       RECV84            *
          MOVE.B    #5,state          *       state := 5
                                      *     endif
RECV84    MOVE.B    #tstop,tcr        *     stop timer
          MOVE.L    #tforg,frnxt      *     frnxt := tforg
          MOVE.L    #tfend,frend      *     frend := tfend
          CLR.B     rstate            *     rstate := 0
          MOVE,B    #eti,npsc         *     enable transmit /disable
                                      *     receive interrupts at Nport
          BRA       REC8EX            *
                                      *   else
RECV85    CLR.B     rstate            *     rstate := 0
                                      *   endif
                                      * endif
REC8EX    MOVE.L    (A7)+,D0          * restore register D0
          RTS                         * return
*
* The Send routine:
*
SEND8     MOVE.L    A0.-(A7)          * save register A0 on stack
          MOVE.L    frnxt,A0          *
          CMPI.L    #frend,A0         * if frnxt = frend then
          BNE       SEND83            *
```

```
          CMPI.B  #1,state         *    if state = 1 then
          BNE     SEND81           *
          MOVE.B  #3,state         *       state := 3
          BSR     WFRES8           *       Start_timer_to_wait_for_response
          BRA     SEND82           *
SEND81    CMPI.B  #5,state         *    elseif state = 5 then
          BNE     SEND82           *
          MOVE.B  #4,state         *       state := 4
          BSR     WFTOK6           *       Start_timer_to_wait_for_token(6)
                                   *    endif
SEND82    BSR     ENREC3           *    Enable_receive (3)
          BRA     SEN8EX           *
                                   * else
SEND83    MOVE.B  (A0)+,nport      *    Nport := frnxt^
          MOVE.L  A0,frnxt         *    frnxt := frnxt+1
                                   * endif
SEN8EX    MOVE.L  (A7)+,A0         * restore register A0
          RTS                      * return
*
* The

Start_timer_to_wait_for_response routine:
*
WFRES8    MOVE.B  #tstop,tcr       * stop timer
          MOVE.B  #twr,cprh        * load timer preload regs with TWR
          MOVE.B  #0,cprm          *
          MOVE.B  #0,cprl          *
          MOVE.B  #tstart,tcr      * start timer
          RTS                      * return
*
******************************************************************
*  Assembly language routines for experiment 9
******************************************************************
*
* The Col_isr routine:
*
COLIS9    MOVE.B  #clri,psr        * clear collision interrupt
          MOVE.B  #di,npsc         * disable Nport interrupts
          CMPI.B  #1,bys           * if BYS = 1 then
          BNE     COL91            *
          BSR     BCKOF9           *    Back_off
          MOVE.L  #tborg,tbnxt     *    tbnxt := tborg
          MOVE.B  #1,sp            *    SP := 1
          BRA     COL9EX           *
COL91     CMP.B   #2,rstate        * else if rstate = 2 then
          BNE     COL9EX           *
          MOVE.L  #rborg,rbnxt     *    rbnxt := rborg
          CLR.B   rstate           *    rstate := 0
                                   * endif
COL9EX    MOVE.B  #rst,npsc        * clear Nport
          MOVE.B  #eri,npsc        * enable receive interrupts
                                   * at Nport
```

```
          RTE                      * return
*
* The Back_off routine:
*
BCKOF9    MOVEM.L  D0-D1,-(A7)     * save registers D0-D1 on stack
          MOVE.L   #bdelay,D0      * init. delay counter
          MOVE.B   mid,D1          *
          AND.L    #$F,D1          *
          MULU.W   D1,D0           * multiply counter by MID
BKOF91    SUBI.L   #1,D0           * delay MID*(1/120 of sec.)
          BNE      BKOF91          *
          MOVE.L   (A7)+,D0-D1     * restore registers D0-D1
          RTS                      * return
*
*******************************************************************
*   Assembly language routines for experiment 10
*******************************************************************
*
* The Main routine:
*
MAIN10    MOVEA.L  #ustack,A0      * initialize user stack
          MOVEA.L  A0,USP          *
          MOVEA.L  #sstack,A7      * initialize system stack
          BSR      INMID4          * Input_MID (4)
          BSR      CLRFL10         * Clear_flags
          BSR      INIT10          * Initialize
          BSR      START8          * Start (8)
          MOVE.W   #eni,SR         * enable interrupts and enter
                                   * user mode
                                   * repeat
REPT10    BSR      SCHD10          *    Schedule
          BRA      REPT10          * until reset
*
* The Schedule routine:
*
SCHD10    CMPI.B   #0,byd          * if BYD = 0 AND
          BNE      SC10EX          *
          CMPI.B   #0,byi          *    BYI = 0 then
          BNE      SC10EX          *
          CMPI.B   #1,dnid         *    if DNID = 1 then
          BNE      SCH101          *
          CLR.B    dnid            *       DNID := 0
          BSR      DSNID8          *       Display_NID (8)
          BRA      SC10EX          *
SCH101    CMPI.B   #1,dtl          *    elseif DTL = 1 then
          BNE      SCH102          *
          CLR.B    dtl             *       DTL := 0
          BSR      DSPTL8          *       Display_Tlost (8)
          BRA      SC10EX          *
SCH102    CMPI.B   #1,dnn          *    elseif DNN = 1 then
          BNE      SCH103          *
          CLR.B    dnn             *       DNN := 0
```

```
         BSR     DSPNN8           *     Display_Nonodes (8)
         BRA     SC10EX           *
SCH103   CMPI.B  #1,dp            *   elseif DP = 1 then
         BNE     SC10EX           *
         CLR.B   dp               *     DP := 0
         MOVE.B  #1,byd           *     BYD := 1
         MOVE.B  #eti,npsc        *     enable transmit /
                                  *     disable recv. interrupt
                                  *   endif
                                  * endif
SC10EX   RTS                      * return
*
* The Clear_flags routine:
*
CLRFL10  CLR.B   dnid             * DNID := 0
         CLR.B   sp               * SP   := 0
         CLR.B   byd              * BYD  := 0
         CLR.B   tbf              * TBF  := 0
         CLR.B   dtl              * DTL  := 0
         CLR.B   dp               * DP   := 0
         CLR.B   byi              * BYI  := 0
         CLR.B   rbf              * RBF  := 0
         CLR.B   dnn              * DNN  := 0
         RTS                      * return
*
* The Initialize routine:
*
INIT10   MOVE.L  A0,-(A7)         * save register A0 on stack
         CLR.B   state            * state := 0
         CLR.B   rstate           * rstate := 0
         MOVE.L  #tforg,A0        *
         MOVE.B  #pre,(A0)+       * tforg^ := PRE
         MOVE.L  #tforg,frnxt     * frnxt := tforg
         MOVE.L  #tfend,frend     * frend := tfend
         MOVE.B  mid,(A0)         * tforg+1 := mid
         MOVE.B  #tvnmb,tivr      * init. timer interrupt vector
         MOVE.L  #TISR8,tpva      * TISR8 defined in exp.8
         MOVE.L  #NISR8,npva      * init. Nport interrupt vector
                                  * NISR8 defined in exp.8
         MOVE.B  #di,npsc         * init. Nport
         MOVE.L  (A7)+,A0         * restore register A0
         RTS                      * return
*
* The Receive routine:
*
RECV10   MOVE.L  D0,-(A7)         * save register D0 on stack
         MOVE.B  nprt,nbyte       * nbyte := Nport
         MOVE.B  npsc,D0          * read status from Nport
         ANDI.B  #tst,D0          * if Nport status OK then
         BNE     RE10EX           *
         CMPI.B  #pre,nbyte       *   if nbyte = PRE then
         BNE     REC101           *
```

```
          BSR     PRERC10          *      PRE_received
          BRA     RE10EX           *
REC101    CMPI.B  #1,rstate        * elseif rstate = 1 then
          BNE     REC102           *
          BSR     DIDRC10          *      DID_received
          BRA     RE10EX           *
REC102    CMPI.B  #2,rstate        * elseif rstate = 2 then
          BNE     REC106           *
          CMPI.B  #eot,nbyte       *      if nbyte = EOT then
          BNE     REC103           *
          BSR     TOKRC10          *        Token_received
          BRA     REC105           *
REC103    CMPI.B  #0,rbf           *      elseif RBF = 0 then
          BNE     REC104           *
          BSR     ACSID10          *        Accept_SID
          BRA     REC105           *
                                   *      else
REC104    CLR.B   rstate           *        rstate := 0
REC105    BRA     RE10EX           *      endif
REC106    CMPI.B  #3,rstate        * elseif rstate = 3 then
          BNE     REC109           *
          CMPI.B  #eot,nbyte       *      if nbyte = EOT then
          BNE     REC107           *
          BSR     PAKRC10          *        Packet_received
          BRA     REC108           *
                                   *      else
REC107    BSR     ACBYT10          *        Accept_byte
REC108    BRA     RE10EX           *      endif
                                   *   else
REC109    CLR.B   rstate           *      rstate := 0
                                   *   endif
                                   * endif
RE10EX    MOVE.L  (A7)+,D0         * restore register D0
          RTS                      * return
*
* The PRE_received routine:
*
PRERC10   MOVE.B  #1,rstate        * rstate := 1
          CMPI.B  #3,state         * if state = 3 then
          BNE     PRE10EX          *
          MOVE.B  #4,state         *   state := 4
          MOVE.B  #1,dnid          *   DNID := 1
          BSR     WFTOK6           *   Start_timer_to_wait_for_token (6)
                                   * endif
PRE10EX   RTS                      * return
*
* The DID_received routine:
*
DIDRC10   CMP.B   mid,nbyte        * if nbyte = MID then
          BNE     DID101           *
          MOVE.B  #2,rstate        *   rstate := 2
          BRA     DID10EX          *
```

```
                                      * else
DID101  CLR.B    rstate               *   rstate := 0
                                      * endif
DID10EX RTS                           * return
*
* The Token_received routine:
*
TOKRC10 CMPI.B   #0,state             * if state = 0 then
        BNE      TOK101               *
        MOVE.B   #1,state             *   state := 1
        MOVE.B   mid,nid              *   NID := MID
        BSR      POLL8                *   Poll (8)
        MOVE.L   #tforg,frnxt         *   frnxt := tforg
        MOVE.L   #tfend,frend         *   frend := tfend
        BRA      TOK103               *
TOK101  CMPI.B   #4,state             * elseif state = 4 then
        BNE      TOK103               *
        MOVE.B   #tstop,tcr           *   stop timer
        CMPI.B   #1,sp                *   if SP = 1 then
        BNE      TOK102               *
        CLR.B    sp                   *     SP := 0
        MOVE.B   #6,state             *     state := 6
        MOVE.L   #tborg,frnxt         *     frnxt := tborg
        MOVE.L   tbend,frend          *     frend := tbend
        BRA      TOK103               *
                                      *   else
TOK102  MOVE.B   #5,state             *     state := 5
        MOVE.L   #tforg,frnxt         *     frnxt := tforg
        MOVE.L   #tfend,frend         *     frend := tfend
                                      *   endif
                                      * endif
TOK103  CLR.B    rstate               * rstate := 0
        MOVE.B   #eti,npsc            * enable transmit / disable
                                      * receive interrupts at Nport
        RTS                           * return
*
* The Accept_SID routine:
*
ACSID10 MOVE.L   A0,-(A7)             * save register A0 on stack
        MOVE.B   #3,rstate            * rstate := 3
        MOVE.L   rbnxt,A0             *
        MOVE.B   nbyte,(A0)+          * rbnxt^ := nbyte
        MOVE.L   A0,rbnxt             * rbnxt := rbnxt+1
        MOVE.L   (A7)+,A0             * restore register A0
        RTS                           * return
*
* The Packet_received routine:
*
PAKRC10 MOVE.B   #1,dp                * DP := 1
        MOVE.B   #1,rbf               * RBF := 1
        MOVE.L   rbnxt,rbend          * rbend := rbnxt
        MOVE.L   #rborg,rbnxt         * rbnxt := rborg
```

```
                CLR.B   rstate          * rstate := 0
                RTS                     * return
        *
        * The Accept_byte routine:
        *
        ACBYT10 MOVE.L  A0,-(A7)        * save register A0 on stack
                MOVE.L  rbnxt,A0        *
                MOVE.B  nbyte,(A0)+     * rbnxt^ := nbyte
                MOVE.L  A0,rbnxt        * rbnxt := rbnxt+1
                MOVE.L  (A7)+,A0        * restore register A0
                RTS                     * return
        *
        * The Send routine:
        *
        SEND10  MOVE.L  A0,-(A7)        * save register A0 on stack
                MOVE.L  frnxt,A0        *
                CMP.L   #frend,A0       * if frnxt = frend then
                BNE     SEN103          *
                CMPI.B  #6,state        *   if state = 6 then
                BNE     SEN101          *
                MOVE.B  #5,state        *     state := 5
                CLR.B   tbf             *     TBF := 0
                MOVE.L  tfnxt,frnxt     *     frnxt := tfnxt
                MOVE.L  #tfend,frend    *     frend := tfend
                MOVE.B  #eti,npsc       *     enable transmit /disable receive
                                        *     interrupts at Nport
                BRA     SE10EX          *
        SEN101  CMPI.B  #1,state        *   elseif state = 1 then
                BNE     SEN102          *
                MOVE.B  #3,state        *     state := 3
                BSR     WFRES8          *     Start_timer_to_wait_for_response
                                        *     WFRES8 defined in exp.8
                BSR     ENREC3          *     Enable_receive (3)
                BRA     SE10EX          *
        SEN102  CMPI.B  #5,state        *   elseif state = 5 then
                BNE     SE10EX          *
                MOVE.B  #4,state        *     state := 4
                BSR     WFTOK3          *     Start_timer_to_wait_for_token
                                        *     WFTOK3 defined in exp.3
                BSR     ENREC3          *     Enable_receive (3)
                BRA     SE10EX          *   endif
                                        * else
        SEN103  MOVE.L  frnxt,A0        *
                MOVE.B  (A0)+,nprt      *   Nport := frnxt^
                MOVE.L  A0,frnxt        *   frnxt := frnxt+1
                                        * endif
        SE10EX  MOVE.L  (A7)+,A0        * restore register A0
                RTS                     * return
        *
```

J

LAN Experiments with IBM-PC

The LAN experiments from Chapters 5 and 6 can be easily implemented using a personal computer. The LAN interface board described here may be used with any IBM-PC/XT/AT or other compatible microcomputer. The experiments require a serial port with a bidirectional serial data line, a timer, and a collision detector. All three are implemented on the LAN interface board. It is also possible to use an original IBM serial communication port and to add the bidirectional cable adapter, timer, and collision detection circuit on another board using the design given in this appendix.

Use of a PC has the advantage of allowing the LAN protocols to be programmed in a higher-level language; for example, in C. An Instant-C programming environment with an incremental compiler is used here to illustrate the use of the LAN interface board for our experiments. The Instant-C provides editing and debugging tools that are ideal for classwork on problems of this complexity. Moreover, the Instant-C provides low-level functions specific for IBM-PC microcomputers, not normally available with C compilers. It also provides full support for interrupt handling on IBM-PCs, which is essential for our LAN protocol programming projects.

In this appendix, the Instant-C is used to illustrate programming of the LAN interface board. Also, full Instant-C programs are given for Lab 1 and Lab 3 experiments. The programming style and techniques given in these programs directly extend to all other experiments from Chapters 5 and 6.

J.1 THE LAN INTERFACE BOARD DESIGN

The LAN interface board is designed using the concept of an IBM-PC prototype board and occupies addresses 0x300 to 0x33F in the PC's I/O addressing space. Only addresses from the range 0x300 to 0x310 are actually used, leaving space for further development.

The LAN interface board consists of three parts: a serial port, a timer, and a collision detector. The serial port is built using an INS16450 Asynchronous Communication Element (ACE) similarly to the way it is used in an IBM serial adapter board. The main difference is that on the LAN bus side, a single bidirectional data line is used instead of separate input and output lines. The ACE requires a 1.8432 MHz oscillator to ensure proper clock frequencies for data transfers. The ACE on the LAN interface board can generate IRQ3 interrupts.

The timer is built using an Intel 8254 programmable device for time measurements necessary to implement LAN protocols. The timer can generate IRQ5 interrupts.

The collision detector is built using a concept identical to that described in Chapter 4. The actual design as shown here allows only four nodes to cooperate on a LAN segment with collision detection. More nodes can be used if the collision detection circuit is expanded. The output of the collision detector is used to generate IRQ7 interrupts.

The design of the LAN interface board is given on pages 269–272 (Fig. J.1). The PC's I/O bus interface connector (the edge connector on the board) is denoted as J1 on the diagrams. The LAN bus connector is denoted as J2. J3 is a jumper connector used to select one of four ''transmit copy'' lines for a given board for collision detection purposes. Only one jumper should be installed in J3 on each board, and no two boards can have the jumpers installed in the same positions. Otherwise, the collision detectors will not operate properly.

J.2 PROGRAMMING THE LAN INTERFACE BOARD

Programming of the ACE is defined in the ace.h and ace.c files given in Figs. J.2 and J.3. The reader can find the meaning of ACE registers and control and status byte values in either the IBM technical documentation or in the National Semiconductor catalog with INS16450 data sheets. The ace.h file defines addresses and special byte values for ACE-related functions.

Five such functions are defined in the ace.c file. The init_ace( ) function initializes the ACE operation at a 2400 bps data rate with 8-bit characters, single stop bit, and no parity control. It also leaves the ACE with all interrupts disabled. The set_ace_irqs( ) function sets the ACE interrupts according to the value of the cmd argument. As defined in the ace.h file, three values, ENBRI, ENBTI, and DISI, can be

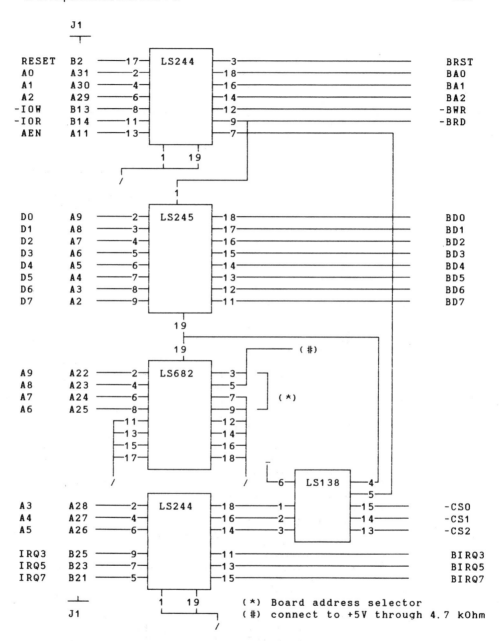

FIGURE J.1 The LAN interface board.

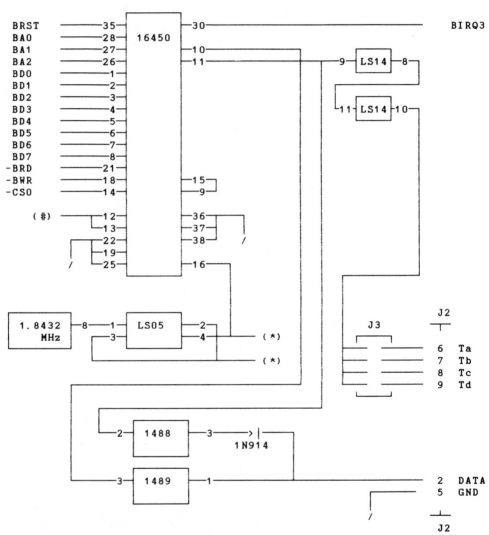

(*) connect to +5V through 750 Ohm resistor
(#) connect to +5V through 4.7 kOhm resistor

FIGURE J.1 (Continued.)

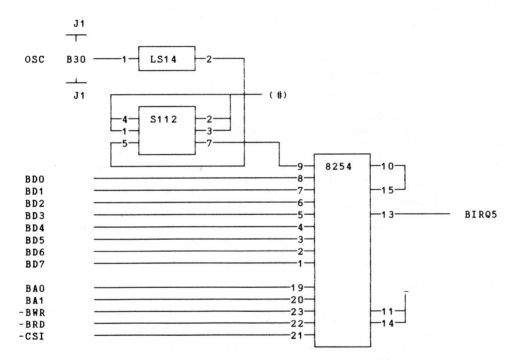

(#) connect to +5V through 4.7 kOhm resistor

FIGURE J.1 (Continued.)

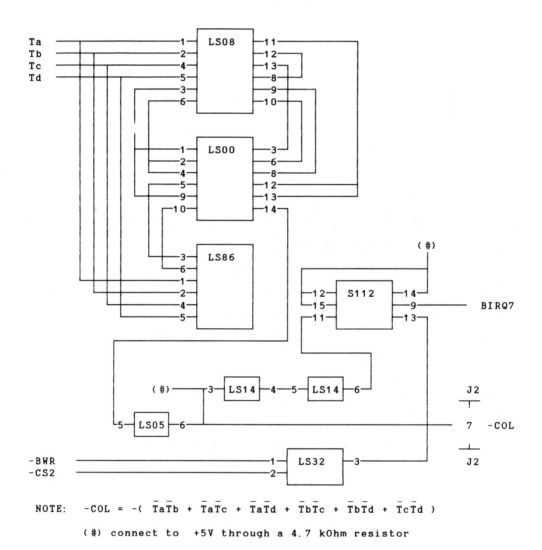

NOTE: $-COL = -(\overline{Ta}\overline{Tb} + \overline{Ta}\overline{Tc} + \overline{Ta}\overline{Td} + \overline{Tb}\overline{Tc} + \overline{Tb}\overline{Td} + \overline{Tc}\overline{Td})$

(#) connect to   +5V through a 4.7 kOhm resistor

FIGURE J.1   (Continued.)

```
/* ace.h the header file for ACE related functions */
/**************************************************/

#define      ACEBASE         0x300

#define      RBR             ACEBASE
#define      THR             ACEBASE

#define      IER             ACEBASE + 1
#define      IIR             ACEBASE + 2

#define      DLL             ACEBASE
#define      DLM             ACEBASE + 1

#define      LCR             ACEBASE + 3
#define      MCR             ACEBASE + 4
#define      LSR             ACEBASE + 5

#define      MODE            0x03
#define      DIVISOR         0x83

#define      RRDY            0x01
#define      TRDY            0x20

#define      ENBRI           0x01
#define      ENBTI           0x02
#define      DISI            0x00

#define      ENBIGEN         0x08

#define      BD24L           48
#define      BD24M           0

#define      ERROR           0x07
```

FIGURE J.2   The ACE header file.

```
/* ace.c - NS16450 (ACE) service file */
/*****************************************/

#include "ace.h"

int init_ace()
{
outportb( LCR,  DIVISOR);
outportb( DLL,  BD24L);
outportb( DLM,  BD24M);
outportb( LCR,  MODE);
outportb( IER,  DISI);
}

int set_ace_irqs(cmd)
char cmd;
{
outportb( MCR, ENBIGEN);
outportb( IER, cmd);
}

int getc_ace()
{
int data;
while((inportb(LSR) & RRDY) == 0);
data = inportb(RBR);
return(data);
}

int putc_ace(data)
char data;
{
while((inportb(LSR) & TRDY) == 0);
outportb(THR, data);
}

int error_ace()
{
int code;
if((inportb(LSR) & ERROR) == 0 ) code = 0;
else code = 1;
return(code);
}
```

FIGURE J.3 The ACE programming file.

used for the cmd argument. The ENBRI argument enables receive interrupts only. If the ENBTI argument is used, only the transmit interrupts are enabled. The DISI is used to disable all ACE interrupts. The getc_ace( ) and putc_ace( ) functions are used to input/output a data byte (character) from/to the ACE. Errors in bytes received by the ACE from the network can be tested using the error_ace( ) function. If there is an error, the error_ace( ) returns value 0, otherwise a 1 is returned.

Programming of the 8254 timer is defined in the 54.h and 54.c files given in Fig. J.4. The reader should refer to the Intel data catalog for the meaning of 8254 registers and control bytes. Two counters of the 8254 are cascaded on the LAN interface board to form a 32-bit counter. Actually, the two counters are used in different operating modes. Counter 0, the first in cascade, is used in the "rate generator" mode to provide

```
/* 54.h - the header file for 8254 related functions */
/**********************************************************/

#define      54BASE         0x308

#define      CNTCTRL        54BASE + 3
#define      COUNT0         54BASE
#define      COUNT1         54BASE + 1

#define      CNT0MODE       0x34      /* rate generator       */
#define      CNT1MODE       0x70      /* irq on terminal count */

#define      CNT0LO         49        /* to provide approx.   */
#define      CNT0HI         149       /* 1 millisecond period */


/* 54.c - the 8254 service file */
/********************************/

#include "54.h"

int start_cnt0()
{
    outportb( CNTCTRL, CNT0MODE);
    outportb( COUNT0,  CNT0LO);
    outportb( COUNT0,  CNT0HI);
}

int start_cnt1( low, high)
int low, high;
{
    outportb( CNTCTRL, CNT1MODE);
    outportb( COUNT1, low);
    outportb( COUNT1, high);
}

int stop_cnt1()
{
    outportb( CNTCTRL, CNT1MODE);
}
```

FIGURE J.4 The 8254 programming files.

a time reference signal with 1 millisecond period (1 KHz) for counter 1. Therefore, counter 1 can be easily used to measure time in milliseconds.

Three timer-programming functions are defined in the 54.c file. The start_cnt0( ) function is used to initiate operation of counter 0 as the rate generator. This function has to be used only once in a given program. The start_cnt1( ) function initiates time measurement by counter 1. The arguments for start_cnt1( ) specify the time in milliseconds as a low and high byte for a 16–bit down-counter. Counter 1 starts counting at the moment when the high byte is loaded. When the count value in counter 1 reaches 0, an IRQ5 interrupt is requested. The interrupt request is cleared when the stop_cnt1( ) function is executed. This function also stops the counting if it is executed before the interrupt request.

Programming of the collision detector is defined in the coldet.h and coldet.c files given in Fig. J.5. Only one function, the clr_col_irq( ) is used. The collision detector is always enabled and its interrupts are always delivered to the 8259 interrupt controller. Therefore, enabling and disabling of collision interrupts are actually done by the enabling or disabling of IRQ7 for the 8259, as described next. Whenever a collision situation occurs, the IRQ7 interrupt is requested. The interrupt-service routine must clear this interrupt by executing the clr_col_irqs( ) function.

All three interrupts generated by the LAN interface board are serviced through the interrupt-priority controller, the Intel 8259. Programming of this device is defined in the 59.h and 59.c files given in Fig. J.6. For an interrupt to be serviced by the CPU, an appropriate priority level must be enabled for the 8259. For example, interrupts generated by the ACE will not be serviced until the enable_int3( ) function is executed. The interrupt-service routines must clear the interrupt requests that caused their execution. An interrupt request from the 8259 will be cleared by executing the clr_ints( ) function. Nevertheless, the interrupt-service routines must also clear the original interrupt request. For example, a routine servicing ACE interrupts must clear both ACE and 8259 interrupts. ACE interrupts are cleared by executing the getc_ace( ) or putc_ace( ) functions, depending on the cause of the interrupt.

```
/* coldet. h - collision detector header file */
/**********************************************/

#define    COLDET    0x310


/* coldet. c - collision detector service file */
/**********************************************/

#include "coldet. h"

int clr_col_irq( )
{
    outportb( COLDET, 0);
}
```

FIGURE J.5 The collision-detector programming files.

```
/* 59.h - header file for 8259 interrupt priority controller  */
/*****************************************************************/

#define    BASE59     0x20
#define    IMR        BASE59 + 1

#define    IRQ3       0x0B
#define    IRQ5       0x0D
#define    IRQ7       0x0F

#define    ENB3       0xF7
#define    ENB5       0xDF
#define    ENB7       0x7F

#define    DIS3       0x08
#define    DIS5       0x20
#define    DIS7       0x80

#define    EOI        0x20


/*  59.c  -   8259 interrupt controller service file  */
/*********************************************************/

#include "59.h"

int enable_int3()
    {
    char mask;
    mask = inportb(IMR);
    mask &= ENB3;
    outportb(IMR, mask);
    }

int disable_int3()
    {
    char mask;
    mask = inportb(IMR);
    mask |= DIS3;
    outportb(IMR, mask);
    }

int enable_int5()
    {
    char mask;
    mask = inportb(IMR);
    mask &= ENB5;
    outportb(IMR, mask);
    }

int disable_int5()
    {

    char mask;
    mask = inportb(IMR);
    mask |= DIS5;
    outportb(IMR, mask);
    }
```

FIGURE J.6 The 8259 interrupt-priority controller programming files.

```
int enable_int7()
    {
    char mask;
    mask = inportb(IMR);
    mask &= ENB7;
    outportb(IMR, mask);
    }

int disable_int7()
    {
    char mask;
    mask = inportb(IMR);
    mask |= DIS7;
    outportb(IMR, mask);
    }

int clr_ints()
    {
    outportb(BASE59, EOI);
    }
```

FIGURE J.6   (Continued.)

J.3 EXAMPLE PROGRAMS

In the following, example programs for Lab 1 and Lab 3 experiments are given to illustrate how Chapter 5 experiments can be implemented using the LAN interface board and Instant-C programming tools. The programs require the "INTLIB.IC" file to be loaded to the Instant-C work space before program execution. Also, the programs use previously-defined service files for ACE and 8259 devices. Two more files, the lancon.h and lanvar.h, are used. These files, shown in Fig. J.7, define LAN protocol constants and variables. The lanmsg.h file given in Fig. J.7 defines operator messages. Only some of the constants and variables and none of the operator messages are actually used for Lab 1 and Lab 3 programs, but all can be useful for Labs 4 to 10.

J.3.1. Programs for Lab 1 Nodes

Programs for the receiver and transmitter nodes used in Lab 1 are given in Fig. J.8. The program for receiver nodes consists of the main( ), nisr( ), setup_irq3( ), restore_irq3( ),and kbdhit( )functions. The text of this program is given in the lab1r.c file. The algorithm is nearly identical to the one used for Lab 1 in Chapter 5. The main difference here is that the program terminates when the escape (ESC) character is received from the network. At this moment, the original interrupt vector for the IBM-PC is restored by the restore_irq3( ) function. This vector is initially modified by the setup_irq3( ) function to point to the nisr( ) routine.

The program for transmitter nodes is given in the lab1t.c file. The interrupt mechanism is not used to handle character input from the keyboard as it was in Chapter

```
/* lancon. h - lan protocol constants definition file */
/*********************************************************/

/* special characters */
#define PRE        0x00
#define EOT        0x04
#define CR         0x0D
#define LF         0x0A
#define SPACE      0x20
#define ESC        0x1B

/* lanvar. h - lan protocol variables definition file */
/*********************************************************/

char rbuf[100],            /* frame buffers          */
     tbuf[100], tframe[3];

char mid, did, nid;        /* node identifiers       */

char nbyte, tbyte;         /* port one-byte buffers  */

int sp, dp, sf, df,        /* service request flags  */
    dnn, dnid, dtl;

int byi, byd;              /* AL state encoding flags */

int byr, bys, tl, tr,      /* NL state encoding flags */
    state, rstate;         /* and variables          */

int rbf, tbf;              /* buffer status flags    */

char                       /* buffer pointers        */
     *tborg, *rborg, *tforg;
     *tbnxt, *rbnxt, *frnxt;
     *tbend, *rbend, *frend;


/* lanmsgs. h - lan messages definition file */
/*********************************************/

#define IMTXT      "Input MID \n"
#define INTXT      "Input NID \n"
#define ITTXT      "Input token \n"
#define COLTXT     "Collision \n"
#define TLOST      "Token lost \n"
#define NEWNID     "New NID = "
#define NONODES    "No other nodes on the network \n"
```

FIGURE J.7 LAN protocol definition files.

```
/* lab1r.c - program for the Lab 1 receiver node */
/***************************************************/

#include "LANCON.H"
#include "LANVAR.H"
#include "ACE.C"
#include "59.C"

#include "INTLIB.H"

struct _int_prologue *ip;
struct _int_vector save_irq3;

int main()
    {
    init_ace();
    set_ace_irqs(ENBRI);
    setup_irq3();
    clr_ints();
    enable_int3();

    nbyte = 0;
    while (nbyte != ESC)
        ;

    disable_int3();
    restore_irq3();
    }

void nisr()
    {
    nbyte = getc_ace();
    putch(nbyte);
    clr_ints();
    }

void setup_irq3()
    {
    interrupt_get(IRQ3, &save_irq3);    /* save default      */
                                        /* interrupt handler */
    ip = prologue_init(nisr, -1, 0, 2048);
    interrupt_install(IRQ4, ip);        /* install new       */
                                        /* interrupt handler */
    }

void restore_irq3()
    {
    interrupt_set(IRQ3, &save_irq3);
    }
```

FIGURE J.8 Programs for the receiver and transmitter nodes for Lab 1.

```
/* lab1t.c - program for the Lab 1 transmitter node */
/****************************************************/

#include "LANCON.H"
#include "LANVAR.H"
#include "ACE.C"

int main()
   {
   init_ace();

   nbyte = 0;
   while (nbyte != ESC)
      {
      if (kbdhit())
         {
         nbyte = getch();      /* get character from keyboard */
         putch(nbyte);         /* echo character to screen    */
         putc_ace(nbyte);      /* output character to Nport    */
         if (nbyte == CR)
            {
            putch(LF);
            putc_ace(LF);
            }
         }
      }
   }

int kbdhit()
   {
      return(bdos(11,0));
   }
```

FIGURE J.8   (Continued.)

5. Instead, a kbdhit( ) function is used to test whether a key has been pressed since the last character input. The same solution is used in a program for Lab 3 nodes. The transmitter program terminates when the ESC key is pressed.

J.3.2. A Program for Lab 3 Nodes

A program for Lab 3 nodes, which support bidirectional transfer of data frames, is given in the lab3.c file shown in Fig. J.9. The program consists of several functions which correspond directly to the application layer (AL) and network layer (NL) routines used for Lab 3 in Chapter 5. The use of ACE interrupts is supported by additional functions as in the Lab 1 programs discussed earlier. Again, the keyboard and display operations are performed without interrupts; the kbdhit( ), getch( ), and putch( ) functions are used instead. Characters entered from the keyboard are appended by the AL function input( ) to the transmit buffer (tbuf) and echoed to the screen. The data frame is sent from the tbuf to the network by the NL function transmit( ) when the carriage return (CR) key is pressed. While a data frame is being entered from the keyboard, another data frame may arrive from the network and be placed by the NL function

receive( ) into the receive buffer (rbuf). The frames that arrive from the network are
displayed on the screen by the AL function output( ). The program terminates whenever the escape (ESC) character is entered from the keyboard.

```
/* lab3.c - program for Lab 3 nodes */
/***********************************/

#include "LANCON.H"
#include "LANVAR.H"
#include "ACE.C"
#include "59.C"

#include "INTLIB.H"

struct _int_prologue *ip;
struct _int_vector save_irq3;

int main()
   {
   int done;

   clear_flags();
   initialize();

   done = 0;
   while (!done)
      {
      done = schedule();
      }
   restore();
   }

int clear_flags()
   {
   sp = dp = 0;
   tbf = rbf = 0;
   byd = byi = 0;
   bys = byr = 0;
   }

int initialize()
   {
   rborg = rbuf;
   rbnxt = rborg;

   tborg = tbuf;
   tbnxt = tborg + 1;
   *tborg = PRE;

   init_ace();
   set_ace_irqs(ENBRI);

   setup_irq3();
   clr_ints();
   enable_int3();
   }
```

FIGURE J.9   The program for Lab 3 nodes.

```
int schedule()
  {
  int retcode = 0;

  if ((sp == 1) & (byr == 0) & (bys == 0))
    start_send();
  else if ((dp == 1) & (byi == 0))
    output();
  else if (kbdhit())
    {
    tbyte = getch();
    if (tbyte == ESC)
      retcode = 1;
    else {
      input();
      retcode = 0;
      }
    }
  return (retcode);
  }

int restore()
  {
  disable_int3();
  restore_irq3();
  }

int start_send()
  {
  bys = 1;
  sp = 0;

  set_ace_irqs(ENBTI);
  }

int input()
  {
  if (tbf == 0)
    {
    if (byi == 0)
      byi = 1;
    putch(tbyte);
    *tbnxt++ = tbyte;
    if (tbyte == CR)
      {
      tbyte = LF;
      putch(tbyte);
      *tbnxt++ = tbyte;
      *tbnxt++ = EOT;
      sp = 1;
      tbf = 1;
      byi = 0;
      tbend = tbnxt;
      tbnxt = tborg;
      }
    }
  }
```

FIGURE J.9 (Continued.)

```
int output()
   {
   while (rbnxt < rbend)
      putchar(*rbnxt++);
   dp = 0;
   byd = 0;
   rbf = 0;
   rbnxt = rborg;
   }

void nisr()
   {
   if (bys == 1)
      transmit();
   else
      receive();
   clr_ints();
   }

int receive()
   {
   nbyte = getc_ace();
   if (!error_ace())
      {
      if (rbf == 0)
         {
         if ((byr == 0) & (nbyte == PRE))
            byr = 1;
         else
            if (byr == 1)
               {
               if (nbyte == EOT)
                  {
                  dp = 1;
                  rbf = 1;
                  byr = 0;
                  rbend = rbnxt;
                  rbnxt = rborg;
                  }
               else
                  *rbnxt++ = nbyte;
               }
         }
      }
   }
```

FIGURE J.9 (Continued.)

```
int transmit()
    {
    if (tbnxt == tbend)
        {
        bys = 0;
        tbf = 0;
        tbnxt = tborg + 1;
        enable_receive();
        }
    else
        putc_ace(*tbnxt++);
    }

int enable_receive()
    {
    char dump;

    dump = getc_ace();
    dump = getc_ace();
    dump = getc_ace();
    set_ace_irqs(ENBRI);
    }

void setup_irq3()
    {
    interrupt_get(IRQ3, &save_irq3);    /* save default        */
                                        /* interrupt handler   */
    ip = prologue_init(nisr, -1, 0, 2048);
    interrupt_install(IRQ3, ip);        /* install new         */
                                        /* interrupt handler   */
    }

void restore_irq3()
    {
    interrupt_set(IRQ3, &save_irq3);
    }

int kbdhit()
    {
        return(bdos(11,0));
    }
```

FIGURE J.9   (Continued.)

Index